ALL FOR THE
GREED OF GOLD

ALL FOR THE GREED OF GOLD

Will Woodin's Klondike Adventure

Edited by

Catherine Holder Spude

Washington State University Press
Pullman, Washington

WSU
PRESS

Washington State University Press
PO Box 645910
Pullman, Washington 99164-5910
Phone 800-354-7360
Fax: 509-335-8568
Email: wsupress@wsu.edu
Website: wsupress.wsu.edu

Library of Congress Cataloging-in-Publication Data

Names: Woodin, Will, 1874-1949. | Spude, Catherine Holder.
Title: All for the greed of gold : Will Woodin's Klondike adventure / edited
  by Catherine Holder Spude.
Description: Pullman, Washington : Washington State University Press, 2016. |
  Includes bibliographical references and index.
Identifiers: LCCN 2015044271 | ISBN 9780874223354 (alkaline paper)
Subjects: LCSH: Woodin, Will, 1874-1949. | Woodin, Will, 1874-1949--Diaries.
  | Pioneers--Yukon--Klondike River Valley--Biography. | Gold
  miners--Yukon--Klondike River Valley--Biography. | Working
  class--Yukon--Klondike River Valley--Biography. | Frontier and pioneer
  life--Yukon--Klondike River Valley. | Klondike River Valley (Yukon)--Gold
  discoveries--Sources. | Klondike River Valley (Yukon)--Biography. |
  Klondike River Valley (Yukon)--History--19th century--Sources.
Classification: LCC F1095.K5 W66 2016 | DDC 971.9/101092--dc23
LC record available at https://lccn.loc.gov/2015044271

On the cover: At Windy Arm, North West Territory, a boat with five men and two dogs on board is pulled along the shore, 1898. *Alaska State Library, John Kill Photograph Collection, P147-23*

CONTENTS

MAPS AND ILLUSTRATIONS

Foreword

Y GREAT-UNCLE, WILLIAM J. WOODIN, was born on January 18, 1874, in Gratiot County, Michigan, on land his paternal grandfather had homesteaded in the 1850s. His father, Jay Abram Woodin, worked these eighty acres of farmland by renting a horse to plow the field and hiring harvesters in the fall. In the winter, as the fields lay fallow, he worked in lumber camps to make enough money to support his rapidly growing family. They sold the farm and moved to Seattle in 1890, following the expanding lumber industry and the growth of the country westward.

I became the keeper of Will Woodin's papers along with detailed copies of genealogical materials that had been painstakingly compiled by Will's cousin and Jay's nephew, Wallace Isaac Woodin. My mother's mother was Nellie Woodin Thayer, a daughter of Jay Abram and sister of Will. My mother, Catherine Thayer Bixby, was a saver who kept everything, and she had accumulated a trove of old family photos, letters, and other memorabilia. She had also been a recipient of Wallace Woodin's genealogy.

Both of my parents were born and raised in Seattle, products of the westward expansion of the country. However, their future took them back to the East Coast, and my two sisters and I were born and raised in and around New York City. We grew up isolated from my parents' families. I never really met any of my mother's family until 1951 when I was fifteen years old. That summer we made a grand tour by automobile across the country to Seattle and down the West Coast. I was fascinated by the country and by the family. I had never known my great-grandparents or my grandparents; they were all gone before I was five. I was growing up with no roots, and suddenly, at a family gathering in Seattle, there were fifty or so people all related to me, and that was not all of them. My grandmother's three sisters were at the party, but her brother Will had died in 1949, two years before, and their three brothers were also gone.

The end result was that in 1970 my husband and I settled in the Puget Sound region, and our children grew up several hundred yards from the little farm where my parents were married. One of our daughters was subsequently married on the same spot.

In 1976, Will's widow, Jean Renton Woodin, passed away, and their son Jack asked my mother to come over and look through the house. In the basement were boxes of Will's papers. He had kept diaries all of his life, and he also must have hoped at some time to publish other writings, including his memoir of the Klondike. My mother, the great saver, took the boxes because it was obvious that they would be thrown away otherwise. When she died in 1986, the boxes were in her effects. I inherited my mother's propensity to save things, so I took the boxes and put them in my barn. From there, they ultimately went into my storage unit.

In the meantime, some of Will's writings had been left with his son Harold and passed on to another cousin, Carolyn Kramer. She and I both had an interest in the family history, and when she no longer felt able to do anything with her box of papers in about 1999, she passed them on to me. At that time she expressed her intention to donate the Klondike papers to the Klondike Gold Rush National Historical Park in Seattle. I will honor her wish to preserve them and ensure that they find an appropriate home.

Now it is 2014, the sands of time keep running through my hourglass, and although I am seventy-nine, I am still upright and functional. It is one hundred years since Will completed his memoir. Something had to be done. After my husband, Bill Dunn, died I edited and privately printed a memoir that he had written shortly before his death. With that experience behind me, I set about doing the same thing with Will's account. I consulted my girlhood college friend Ellie Schrader, a professional journalist and publisher, who just happened to have coffee several times a week with Catherine Spude. The rest, as they say, is history.

I can only hope that my great-uncle Will and my great-grandfather Jay Abram somehow know that Will's efforts have not been in vain, and at long last his vivid account of their Herculean labors over the trail to the Klondike is now being shared with the rest of the world.

Sandra Bixby Dunn
Great-niece to William J. Woodin (1874-1949)

PREFACE

WHEN SANDRA BIXBY DUNN asked me to take a look at a manuscript that her great uncle wrote about his trip to the Klondike in 1898, I was thrilled. I had done archaeological work in Skagway, Alaska, between 1978 and 1991, and extensive archival investigations on Skagway and the Klondike gold rush in the years since, so I had a familiarity with the trails of 1898. I hiked the Chilkoot Trail to Bennett Lake twice, in 1980 and 1985, both times in July. Each time I carried a fifty-pound pack and took five days and thought I was going to die. I could not imagine transferring a ton of supplies and taking more than four weeks to go the same distance. While I had read a number of memoirs, diaries, and sets of letters by people who had traveled to Dawson that year of the great gold rush, I welcomed the opportunity to see the trip again through another set of eyes.

As I read Will Woodin's memoir, which he wrote between 1910 and 1914, the entire time I had spent in Skagway and the Yukon came back to me. While I never had a chance to hike the White Pass Trail (it is still closed to visitors and my professional work for the National Park Service never required that I face the forest of devil's club that now infests the trail), I had ridden the White Pass and Yukon Route train over the pass to Bennett twice, and driven the long, lonely road from Skagway to Carcross and Lake Tagish, through to Whitehorse many times. I even made it all the way to Fairbanks through Dawson on the Dawson Highway twice in the early 1980s. I've taken a state ferry from Skagway to Seattle on the route that Will sailed in a steamship. I've even spent many weekends in a small cabin on the shore of Lake Tagish, and explored the ruins of the Tagish Mountie Post. I've been to most of the places Will wrote about. I almost cried when I read his description of the armada of boats leaving the lake in the golden light of late evening. I've seen that type of light shining on those very mountains and that lake. He made the gold rush come alive for me, more so than any other account that I've read.

Sandy wanted me to transcribe her great-uncle's hand-written memoir, a task I readily agreed to. When she mentioned that Will also kept a diary of his trip, I was ecstatic. One does not often get an opportunity to compare the reflections of a man in his late thirties with the fresh observations made when he was twenty-four years old. I was curious to see how he recorded the same events with the benefit of hindsight.

The diary was wonderful. He had left out so many aspects of the trip when he wrote about them more than a decade later. He ignored, for the most part, his loneliness, the harsh conditions of the trail, and his frustrations with other members of his party. For the memoir, he dealt with facts in order to explain to his readers (family and friends) the history and geography of the places he visited. In contrast, the notes he made in his diary were fresh, candid, and betray all of the enthusiasm of a young man on a great adventure.

So I told Sandy that I would love to transcribe Will's diary as well and integrate it with the memoir to include all of those observations that he originally did not think to include. His reasons were obviously to protect the identity of the people he discussed and to avoid any hurt to living friends and family. As these people are now long passed, his gentle and sensitive nature can be safely revealed to more fully illustrate the attitudes of the men who traveled to the Klondike in 1898.

Sandy had thought to privately publish Will's memoir and diary for friends and relatives. As an academic, I quickly realized that students of history and social relations would also be interested in his account. I could not help but compare what Will had written with the observations of others, people of different backgrounds and contexts. I wanted to understand the way he experienced the rush in the context of his social milieu. So I studied the people with whom he interacted and the events he described in order to place his account in the appropriate context. In the process, I discovered a critical difference between the people who were forming the emerging middle class of the early twentieth century and those who had been raised and nurtured in the merchant class of the nineteenth century. Will's account, therefore, has lasting lessons for all social historians.

I would like to thank Sandra Dunn for loaning me her genealogical material, letting me edit, integrate, and expand upon Will's work, and for her patience during the long, academic process involved in creating this book.

I was also helped by Karl Gurcke, historian at Klondike Gold Rush National Historical Park, in finding comparative materials. My husband, Bob Spude, who amassed many of the early archives for the park, guided me on the various other accounts to study. His library has been a treasure-house of comparative material. I also appreciate the assistance of Sandra Johnston at the Alaska State Historical Collections in Juneau. She was always willing to respond to any of my requests for information.

INTRODUCTION

O N MARCH 1, 1898, THE STEAMSHIP *Cleveland* left Seattle for the Alaskan ports of Skagway and Dyea. The 250 passengers aboard included twenty-four-year-old William Jay Woodin, embarking on the adventure of his life. When the S.S. *Excelsior* had arrived in San Francisco on July 14, 1897, more than six months before, miners from the Klondike brought a million dollars' worth of gold from the Far North. Within days, Will's father, Jay Abram Woodin, began planning the trip that would take him, his brother Hiram, his son, and three friends to Dawson. He made a reconnaissance visit to Skagway that fall, returned to Seattle, and used the winter to stock up on groceries, hardware, and other supplies to resell in the Klondike gold fields. Unlike most entrepreneurs who stampeded north that year, the Woodins understood that the best way to make their fortune lay not in the chance to find placer gold, but by supplying the needs of the miners. Despite their prosaic intentions, the men in the Woodin party became infected with gold fever and lived an adventure they would retell throughout their lives.

Will had long kept diaries in which he recorded not only the events of each day, but also his feelings and emotions. He continued this practice throughout his Klondike adventure. In 1910, he began to compile a narrative of the trip, a task that took him over four years to complete. During that time, he also penned a short story that recounted one of the more emotional events of the trip, the drowning of a man at the confluence of the Lewis (Yukon) and Big Salmon Rivers on June 10, 1898.

While Will may have hoped to publish both the memoir of the trip and the short story, neither intention was realized. After Will died in 1949, his papers eventually came to be owned by Sandra Bixby Dunn, his great niece. When she let me read the memoir and diaries, I was immediately struck with Will's candid observations, his keen eye for detail, and his commentary on the camaraderie of life on the trail. Will brought the trials, tribulations, and triumphs of the gold rush experience to life from the viewpoint of a common working man.

All for the Greed of Gold is an integration of Will Woodin's 1914 memoir, his diaries, and the short story he entitled "The Toll of the Yukon." It is a story that meshes a young man's fresh observations of daily life on the trail and mining camps with his later reflection of what that adventure meant to him and the people he encountered during the height of the Klondike gold rush. The resulting compilation constitutes a fresh look at the way partnerships were formed and broken—the way men coped with hardship, physical labor, illness, beauty, and grand adventure in the Far North. It further shows how a network of friendships and family connections extended throughout the country at the time, and how men used them to survive in the harsh wilderness.

The narrator of this story is William Jay Woodin, born on January 18, 1874, in rural Gratiot County, Michigan, just southwest of the small town of St. Louis. He was a proud descendent of pilgrim William Bassett, who arrived in Plymouth Colony in November 1621 aboard the *Fortune*, the second ship after the Mayflower to bring colonists to the port.[1] His parents moved the large family to Seattle, Washington, in 1890, when Will, the oldest of eight children, was sixteen years old. When he registered for the draft for World War I in 1918, he was recorded as medium of build and height, blue-eyed, and dark-haired.[2]

Will's father, Jay Abram Woodin, had been a farmer and lumberman in Michigan. Upon bringing his family to Seattle, Jay went to work as a carpenter for the Skookum Manufacturing Company, a lumber dealer owned by Elmer Eknortzel. By 1891, this company also hired Will as a cabinetmaker, and Will's brother, James, began work there as a box maker in 1893. Jay and his older sons continued to be employed by the company, the father rising to the rank of foreman in 1893, then general manager in 1895, at which time the business was renamed the Skookum Box Factory. By the time gold fever struck in 1897, Will had become a foreman there and Jay had struck off into his own general contracting business.[3]

Will was twenty-four years old when he left his mother, brothers, and sisters in March 1898 to follow his father, Jay, to the Klondike. He admits—more often in his diary than in his memoir—that he was of a "nervous" temperament. As one of the youngest of a party of middle-aged men, he gamely cooked, hauled packs, did what his father ordered him to do, and confined his complaints to his diary.

Will Woodin's memoir, combined with his diary entries about his journey to and from Dawson City in 1898, are extraordinary in the way they capture struggles of a class of men who were changing the face of America at the end of the nineteenth century. These men had left the farms and were engaging in trades and businesses of their own with a minimum of formal education. They worked for wages, saved money, invested in new businesses, and purchased property. They comprised the emerging middle class. Few other first-person narratives of this type exist. Most men of their class, when going to the Klondike, eschewed writing except for brief letters home. While the memoirs of miners and packers, much edited by better-educated sons, daughters, or grand-children, did get published, we often wonder how much they suffer from the cleansing effect of time or changing moralities. By contrasting Will Woodin's memoir with his diary, we can see what he believed was important to erase as inconsequential to the story (his lonesomeness, his heartsickness for his fiancé, the minor squabbles between the traveling companions) and what was important about the journey to pass on to his descendants (the adventure of the undertaking, the comradeship, and the beauty of the wilderness). The two accounts also offer a self-evident contrast between the attitude of a young man and his older, more mature reflections on the adventure of his youth.

Janet Floyd, professor of American Studies at King's College in London, observes that most of those who wrote about the Klondike gold rush focused on the journey there rather than the mining experience, because so few actually made it all the way. She, like Canadian writer Pierre Berton before her, commented that the Chilkoot Pass served as a metaphor for life itself; if a stampeder could overcome the most difficult part of the journey, he was a success.[4] Others have noted that few wrote about their journey over the White Pass Trail. In fact, one author stated the diaries and memoirs of those accounts were notable for their brevity because everyone that went over the White Pass used packers and did it in two or three days.[5] Will's diary and his detailed memoir, written only a few years later, belie this assertion. Many men went over the White Pass in the spring of 1898 under conditions just as harrowing as those on the Chilkoot Trail, and that and the rest of the journey to Dawson was as much a metaphor for the rest of their lives as anything encountered by the people who went over the better-known pass. Will's party's use of the Tutshi Trail instead of the cut-off to Bennett and his description of the hardships endured there provides Klondike historians and advocates a rich supplement not previously recorded. Will himself noted on April 22, when they first arrived at Windy Arm, "I have been unable to find, after a thorough research, but a meager mention of the Tut Schi Trail and Windy Arm, and nothing regarding the hundreds of Klondikers who used that trail and prepared for the river course at Windy Arm." As an editor who spent months pouring over other accounts of the Yukon route to the Klondike, I have to agree with Will. There are no published descriptions of this trail and the camp that rose up on the Windy Arm of Lake Tagish.

Will lamented the fact that no one in his party took along a camera (see record of the week of June 29–July 4, in Chapter 6). Sandra Dunn is in possession of a number of family photographs, but none, unfortunately, of the Woodins' trip to the Klondike. To illustrate Will's narrative, I have chosen a few photographs from archival collections in Alaska and Yukon Territory that were taken about the same time that he was in each location. For those interested in viewing other photographs taken along Will's course in the spring and summer of 1898, I refer you to the published collection of photographs by E. A. Hegg.[6]

When Will wrote his memoir between 1910 and 1914, he wrote in longhand with a pencil on lined paper. Will created only eight chapter divisions, a practice he abandoned about halfway through the manuscript. It was obvious that he meant these breaks to correspond to changes in the routine of the journey, such as leaving the ship and starting on the pack trail, or when arriving at a destination and starting a new phase of the operation. However, he created more breaks in the first half of the memoir than were actually necessary. As editor, I have combined some of his earlier chapters into longer segments that concur with changes in the mode of travel, and I have dedicated whole chapters to the three camps in which the party stayed for more than just a few days, specifically Windy Arm, the Little Salmon River, and Dawson.

Will made no attempt to create paragraphs, and the only punctuation marks he used were periods (and those rather sparsely). He apparently cared little for commas and his occasional colon was always inaccurate. A handful of times, he accurately employed the use of dashes. As an editor, I did not want to impose my style on his, but his run-on sentences and lack of paragraph breaks demanded some sort of organization. Will had a tendency to change topics in mid-sentence, which sometimes made it difficult to decide where one paragraph ended and the next began, so I introduced paragraph breaks as well as I could. I also added commas for the convenience of the reader. Because Will's grammar is not always consistent with modern standards, my use of commas does not necessarily follow particular rules. Rather it serves to set aside clauses and break up his rather long, run-on sentences. I have added some hyphens, which he did not use, also to help the reader.

In addition, after a considerable amount of internal debate, I decided to do the sort of copyediting that would be required of any draft manuscript before its publication. If Will had published his manuscript soon after he wrote it, the publisher would probably have done a great deal more copyediting than I have. I tried to use his words as faithfully as possible, but some sentences, as constructed, were difficult to understand, and they were almost always run-on. Often all I had to do was remove an "and" and start a new sentence. Sometimes, the removal of conjunctions required the addition of a verb to the next clause. Only occasionally did I rewrite a sentence. The most extreme example of the type of changes I made was in a sentence Will wrote on April 1 at Log Cabin. "On the other hand, as had been stated, the Too Schi Trail was in a deplorable and dangerous condition, but many parties were reported as having reached Windy Arm in safety but had encountered a great amount of trouble in doing so." I changed it to, "On the other hand, as had been stated, the Too Schi Trail was in a deplorable and dangerous condition. Although many parties had encountered a great amount of trouble in reaching Windy Arm, they were reported as having done so in safety."

Will was obviously well-educated for a person of his time, but he made a number of consistent spelling errors. To avoid irritating the reader, I have corrected those errors and note them here. Those words he consistently misspelled include: accomplice [instead of accomplish], apetite [appetite], Argonots [Argonauts], coarse [course], dissapointed [disappointed], gestulations [gestures], labour [labor], neccesary [neccessary], and supplys [supplies]. Sometimes he used the word "cañon," and sometimes canyon: I corrected all to "canyon" to be consistent. He was inconsistent in the spelling of "Chamberlain," sometimes spelling it as "Chamberlin." Again, I changed all instances to the former. Will usually spelled out the numbers of a year: e.g., "eighteen eighty three," instead of 1883. I universally changed the long form to 1883 for the convenience of the reader.

Occasionally, Will would use words incorrectly; for the most part I have retained his words when the meaning is still clear to the reader. For instance, he often used the word "twilight" in connection with the hours before sunrise instead of restricting it to the post-sunset hours. I changed the word to "dawn" only when it was not obvious what time of day he meant.

As editor, I made one other major change to Will's memoir. The account of his trip on board the S.S. *Cleveland*, March 1 to 7, included long passages detailing the islands and course of the journey. As an introductory chapter to the account, this naming of channels, passages, and landforms become tedious reading. At the suggestion of experts who read the manuscript for Washington State University Press, I have deleted much of Will's rather monotonous recital of the geography. Those who are interested in that detail are referred to the original manuscript, which Sandra Dunn is donating to the Seattle Unit of Klondike Gold Rush National Historical Park.

Will's diary, as opposed to his memoir, was his daily notation of events, kept at or near the time they occurred. As such, these notations were not intended as exercises in proper grammar or spelling. In Will's diary spelling, grammar, and, in particular, capitalization and punctuation rules were neglected in the interest of speed. Will used his own form of shorthand to write a series of notes to himself, which obviously were meant to jog his memory at some future time, perhaps as he wrote letters home.

My original intention was to transcribe Will's diary exactly as it was written, but after attempting the first page, I realized that both the future readers and I would not benefit from a straight hand-to-type transcription. Therefore, I have corrected his spelling (except in place names) and grammar (except where it captures the flavor of the times). I have changed his capitalization, which was entirely random, except where I believe he meant to capitalize for emphasis (e.g. Home, Wilds of Alaska, dear little Wife, Father), and added punctuation where it helps the reader understand his thoughts. Usually, his entries were without punctuation, making for one, long, run-on entry, often creating a mixed message until it was dissected for clauses.

Curiously, while Will was quite liberal with capital letters on words, he used a small letter "i" to refer to himself. I let my computer have its way; the obstreperous machine insisted on changing the lone "i" to "I", and it does make for easier reading.

Many of the place names Will referenced had not been standardized at the time he wrote. For example, Will spelled Skagway with its original version, "Skaguay." The town's newspapers used this spelling well into the year 1898, even though the U.S. Post Office established the town as "Skagway" on November 11, 1897. Because Woodin uses the latter spelling in his memoir, he was obviously aware of the name change at a later date. I did not change this spelling in his diary entries. Likewise, I maintained Will's spelling of "Klondike" in the diary. Strangely enough, he used the more archaic word, "Klondyke," in his memoir. For the sake of consistency, I have used the more modern form of the word. I have changed his sometimes inconsistent spellings of other place names to their modern use. For example, Will spelled Chilkoot as Chilcoot; Chisana as Suschanna, Lovatt Gulch as Lovitt Gulch, and Tutshi as Too Chi, Too Schi, Tut Shi, or Tut Schi.

Will mentions "Malen" (also spelled "Malin") often in the diary, a person not introduced in either that version or the memoir. Will's diary entry for May 14, 1898, connects the nickname with Jim Daugherty, Jay Woodin's hired hand. The nickname "Malen" is never explained: it may have been Daugherty's middle name.

The research for a number of people in this account was made more difficult because Will either did not know their correct names or he deliberately changed them. The incorrect spelling of names can be readily excused, as often people at the time did not spell their own names consistently. However, it is readily apparent that Will changed some people's names about whom he had less than admiring things to say (more will be said about this practice in the introductions to each chapter). When I could determine the accurate spelling of a person's name, I have used it instead of Will's inconsistent spellings. Will's original spellings of names are referenced in Appendix A: Biographies.

Will stopped making daily entries after August 31, 1898. This was when he became ill two weeks after he accompanied his Uncle Hiram up Eldorado Creek to visit a claim. He probably contracted his illness on the creek, as his uncle also came down with the same symptoms. He did not take up writing again until October 8, when he had returned to Seattle. At that time, he attempted a day-to-day recollection of the intervening time. It reads more like a narrative than a series of daily entries, much like his memoir. I have edited this section much the same way that I did his memoir, introducing paragraph breaks and punctuation in the same manner I did the latter document. I prefer this summary in his diary to his later memoir because he wrote it when the events were still fresh in his mind. While the memoir account does elaborate on a few points, it is not as candid as the summary in the diary.

Will did have a tendency to complain in his diary, but his candor helps us see him as an untried, innocent young man facing the hardships of the world for the first time. His diary, much more than his memoir, helps us understand his year of misery, trials, and disappointments on his great adventure to the Klondike.

The excerpt below is an example of one of Will's original diary entries. Comparison to my transcription in Chapter 1, page 11, demonstrates how I have edited the diary:

Seattle Mar 1 1898

Mr. Green Jim Daugherty Bill Chamberlin Father & I have been laying at The Yesler Dock up To This Time 2 P. M. Waiting for The Cleveland To Sail We are all going To Skagway Alaska but do not know When we will get away i quit The Factory Two weeks ago Today Oh how my heart aches To leave The dear ones at Home but am going out To Try My Fortune in a Wild & new Country which is full of dangers and Hardships Dear little Blanch was down at noon and Bid Me Good By Left Seattle at 445 P.M. Amid a thong of People to see us off at The dock We were out awhile when a dog went overboard So They reversed The engines and went back and go him and board again and proceded on The way again We all retired at 7 P.M. after a hard day's work

In the text that follows, I have written introductions to each chapter to provide context for the reader or observations about the significance of Will's account. This discussion ties the contents of the chapter to the various themes of the adventure: how the men on the trail and river networked with one another, how they viewed their personal and class connections, the depredations and dangers of the journey, the significant historical events they witnessed, and the economics of the endeavor. Each chapter introduction is followed by Will's own words, displayed in a larger font in order to make it clear what words are his and what are mine, as the editor. His narrative from the memoir appears in normal print; his diary entries have been interspersed and inserted as italics. I have added brief explanatory notes in brackets or in sidebars so that they do not interrupt the flow of the narrative. Appendix A offers short biographies of the friends and new acquaintances Will met during his adventure, organized alphabetically. A transcription of Will's short story, "The Toll of the Yukon," is placed at the end of Chapter 5 after his memoir account of the same incident. Minor commentary and reference citations from my research have been inserted as endnotes.

Chapter One

SEATTLE TO SKAGWAY
JULY 14, 1897–MARCH 7, 1898

W ILL WOODIN'S FIRST CHAPTER introduces the Klondike gold rush, explains why his father decided to participate in the adventure, and describes their preparations. It also takes the reader from Seattle, Washington, where the Woodins lived, to Skagway, Alaska, where they embark on the overland portion of their journey north. The primary themes of this chapter are the preparations for the trip and the identity of the traveling partners.

The backgrounds of the major actors in Will's drama are typical of the men who were emerging from farming and working-class social status to that of the new middle class. Will's father, Jay Abram Woodin, was born on October 2, 1852, in Spring Creek County, Pennsylvania, to Abram and Anna Bassett. Jay's parents moved to Gratiot County, Michigan, in 1855, where they purchased the forty-acre farm on which both Jay and later Will would grow up. On January 22, 1873, Jay married Catherine McMahon. They had eight children, four girls and four boys; Will was the oldest. In a memoir of his childhood in Michigan, Will discussed his father's work. While Jay tried to farm like his father, Abram, he obviously preferred lumbering. Even after moving to the Seattle area in 1890, Jay continued to work in the lumber industry as a carpenter or a contractor.[1] It was his knowledge of building boats and working with lumber that made him a natural leader for a party that would build two boats and a scow for the trip on the Yukon River.

Jay prepared for the enterprise by spending a couple of months in Skagway during the fall of 1897, packing goods on horses over the trail for others. It was then that he no doubt decided to use the White Pass Trail rather than the shorter, but steeper, Chilkoot Trail. Jay's work in the lumber industry and as a contractor necessitated a thorough familiarity with draft horses, as they were used to haul lumber to construction sites. Jay and Will's most important partner was James Daugherty, referred to as "Jim" in the memoir and "Malen" (probably his middle name) in the diary. On May 14, 1898, at Windy Arm, Will writes in his memoir that "Daugherty, due to his own carelessness, sawed the end of his thumb off." His diary of the same day noted "While rip-sawing lumber this afternoon, Malen

The Woodin family, ca. 1900, left to right, top row: Louise, Claude, Birdie, Hiram, Carrie, and James; middle row, Will and Nellie; bottom row: Katherine McMahon and Jay. *Sandra Dunn Collection.*

sawed the end of his thumb off, so is crippled for some time to come." This entry, when combined with the memoir, above, makes it clear that "Malen" was Jim Daugherty.

A James Dougherty (with an "o") was listed in the 1897 Seattle City Directory as a teamster working at the Skookum Box Factory, the same lumber company where both Will and Jay worked.[2] As Jay was interested in retaining a man who was experienced with horses, the teamster James would have been an ideal companion

House where Will Woodin was born, Gratiot County, Michigan, photo taken ca. 1930. *Sandra Dunn Collection.*

for the trip. A James Dougherty, born in February 1862 in Michigan, was the son of John and Mary Dougherty, Irish immigrants, who were recorded in the Central City, Colorado, census of 1870. If "Malen" was this man, he could have been inspired by tales of his father's search for gold in the Colorado gold rush. He would have been thirty-six years old at the time of the gold rush. Daugherty married his wife, Hattie (Harriet) on August 13, 1895, in Victoria, British Columbia.[3]

Will referred to the fourth member of the Woodin Party as "Ed" Green in his memoir and simply "Green" in his diary. The "Ed" Green of Will's memoir was probably William L. Green, an express delivery man from Seattle. This Green was known to be associated with George Milham, who figures in Will's short story, "The Toll of the Yukon." Besides himself and Green, there are several other Williams, Bills, and Wills in this narrative. It is therefore suspected that Will changed Green's first name to "Ed" in his memoir to avoid confusion.

William L. Green was born in December 1855, probably in Prairie du Sac in Sauk County, Wisconsin. His farmer father was also named William and his mother was Mary G. Palletro. By 1880, his father had been to sea as a captain and had retired, but died by 1887, when William L. and his widowed mother were enumerated in Seattle. By that time, he had become a teamster, and by 1890, he

Skookum Box Factory employees, 1892. Jay Woodin is second from the left in the front row: James Woodin is fourth from the left in the front row; Will Woodin is fourth from the left in the middle row. Clipping is from an unidentified and undated newspaper. *Sandra Dunn Collection.*

was an express man, two closely related occupations. Except for the time he went to the Klondike, he would remain an express man for the rest of his life. Green never married, and his widowed mother lived with him until her death in 1906.[4]

The fifth member of the party was William Chamberlain, also called Bill or Will. Very little could be discovered about him, as his name was common in the Seattle area in the late 1890s and it was impossible to determine which of several individuals he was. A William Chamberlain, miner, was listed in the Polk and Company business directory for Nome, Alaska, in 1901. The Bill Chamberlain who joined the Woodin party could have gone on to Nome after being disappointed in the Klondike, but afterwards, he disappeared from the historical records.

Besides introducing these important members of the Woodin party, Will also visits a recurring theme of how the party depended on people they knew from "home." Of particular interest to him was his fiancée, Anna Blanche Graves, with whom he corresponded throughout the trip. Blanche, who went by her middle name, was the daughter of Helen and Willard Graves. This couple had come to the Seattle area sometime between 1880 and 1885 from Michigan. They had one daughter, as well as three sons: William D., Minor, and Victor E. Their father, Willard, became successful in the real estate business in Seattle. By 1911, he had contributed more than $20,000 to political campaigns that focused on cleaning up vice in Seattle's seamier precincts. Between 1897 and 1900, Blanche worked as a "tailoress" for Steffen Andersen, a "merchant tailor," and her younger brother William took various jobs such as clerk and driver.[5] The two youngest boys did not yet work, but Will received letters from them, as well as from Blanche, and obviously enjoyed the correspondence.

The younger men of the party visited a friend named Peter Goodrich in Wrangell on March 5, 1898. Goodrich appears to have been a childhood friend, Bert Goodrich, about whom Will wrote at some length in a childhood memoir. In addition, Jay Woodin knew the hotelkeepers with whom they stayed in Skagway. On March 6, 1898, they took beds at the Seattle Hotel, located at 313 Fifth Avenue. According to an advertisement in the *Skaguay News* in November 1897, the hotel was operated by Alexander Birnbaum. In late September, they spent several days with Lewis and Lucinda Lyman, who operated the Rainier Hotel. Will describes both establishments and the simple way they were operated, in delightful detail. For more information on these individuals, see the Biographies appendix.

Perhaps the most important point of the following portion of Will's memoir is his discussion of their preparations for the trip. To supplement his discussion of the supplies they purchased, Appendix B provides a detailed list of supplies that the newspapers and guidebooks of the time suggested. The Woodins would have referred to these lists when making their preparations.

Here, then, is where Will's adventure begins. (Will's memoir is set in roman type, italics indicate diary entries, brackets indicate editor's comments.)

＋≈≈＋

On the 14th of July 1897, the S.S. *Excelsior* streamed through the Golden Gate into San Francisco Harbor and tied up to one of the many piers forming its magnificent waterfront. On board the steamer were a score or more bewhiskered miners, joint owners in one half million dollars in gold dust, freshly taken from the now world's famous land of gold, the "Klondike." These men were the first to arrive with any such success and also with authentic reports of the great discovery of the precious metal in this region.

People were pessimistic and discredited the truth of the statement of these men regarding this fabulous find of riches. The reports were looked upon by the majority as sensational, even after the gold dust was put through the necessary smelting process and weighed up to the above amount in pure gold bullion. The majority of people were also skeptical to the extent to discredit the report of the new arrivals that the find was fabulous and that millions would follow from whence this came. This was proven to the satisfaction of all when three days later, the 17th of July, the S.S. *Portland* arrived at Seattle with something over one million dollars in the precious dust. The arrival of the S.S. *Portland*, as would be imagined, caused an immediate reaction of public opinion.

Skepticism vanished overnight and in its stead, excitement grew at a rapid rate over the wonderful gold strike in the northland. Friends and acquaintances of the returned miners received first hand a solemn vow that fortunes could in a single day be taken from the marvelously rich earth in the Klondike region. Coming to Seattle in 1890, I had seen the little city rise proudly from the ashes of the great fire of the previous June; had seen great activities in its rebuilding in the years to follow, which all were as nothing compared to the scene of activity that took place on its streets in the autumn months following the arrival of the gold ship *Portland*.

Even the days of "49" in California, I doubt, boasted of more exciting scenes. The nation, as the reader well knows, was in the summer of 1897 showing evidence of recovery from the panic of 1893. Seattle, not excepted, was awakening from her four-year sleep, showing signs of returning prosperity in more ways than one. Old and abandoned saw mills were being remodeled and lumber manufacture resumed in all the Puget Sound cities, while large new plants were being built, denoting a returning demand for building materials. Starting of the mills necessitated the opening up of many logging camps employing hundreds of men. Vast mining propositions were promised on both sides of the Cascade Mountains, and development was showing decidedly good results. In fact, business in general was taking on new life and bid fair to continue.

But alas, the arrival of the *Portland* immediately brought on a reaction throughout the state as well as locally. Mines were abandoned, unable to further exist with the great exodus which began to take place. In fact, every part of business suffered in consequence and for a time it appeared that Seattle would be deserted and forsaken by its male population entirely, so great were the numbers preparing to join in the mad rush to the new gold fields.

Seattle in this respect was not alone. The whole world did its share, which was quite evident to a resident of this city. Within a very short time following the arrival of the *Portland*, one could have seen thousands of new faces on the main streets of the city, each anxious, restless countenance indicating their motive and presence here. At this stage, the citizens and businessmen of Seattle began to realize that their city was about to enter a new epoch of existence, and from a practical standpoint, it was to be the principle outfitting and starting point for the newly discovered gold fields. Her two great transcontinental railway lines [the Great Northern and the Northern Pacific] and her many steamship lines, which ply between Seattle and all principle parts on the Great Pacific Ocean, connect here with the whole world in transportation as well as commercially. In distance she was at once recognized to be many miles nearer to the gold fields than any other principle port on the Pacific, and consequently, recognized as the most admirable starting point to the north. Outfitters and business of all sorts were unable for a time to cope with the orders for outfits and supplies which had so suddenly sprung into existence and for which they were not prepared to fill.

The sorts of supplies necessary to be taken to the interior were not ordinary and were never carried by the trade. Weight was a great consideration in completing an outfit, consequently a great variety of evaporated, condensed and canned goods were substituted for the raw goods and which reduced the weight to a great extent, but on the other hand I found in my experience the constant use was a menace to one's health. The manufacture of these goods was a new issue and factories suddenly sprung up, and by the spring of 1898, an inexhaustible supply was on hand for the Argonaut.

From the arrival of the *Portland* there was a decided increase in traffic to the north, which now became a serious problem to accommodate the unexpected exodus by the steamship companies already operating regular steamship lines. New companies were quickly organized and all manner of boats were pressed into service such as old colliers, freighters, schooners, etc., to compete with the companies already formed, and which caused a sharp competition in transportation rates, and which were quickly taken advantage of by the not very cautious Argonauts.[6] But in no instance has there been recorded a serious accident to any of the second or third raters plying between Seattle and Skagway; in several instances the first class steamers have suffered, but no lives lost in any case.

The second week in August saw the autumn travel at its height, and it was not an uncommon occurrence to witness three to four large steamers depart in one day for the north, and in more than one instance this number was exceeded in a single day. It was figured by many to beat his fellow traveler by one day would enhance his chance in the mad rush for gold, but principally it was to cross the treacherous coast range of mountains and float down the great Yukon River before that mighty stream became frozen and unavailable by the severe Arctic winter which sets in early in the autumn. From this course many belated ones were forced to winter either at Seattle or Skagway to await the coming of spring, and not a few returned to their homes not wishing to face the dangers and hardships the frozen, treacherous-looking trails presented to them. But notwithstanding the dangerous and lonely trip over the ice a few undertook it during the winter following the great discovery and reported safely at Dawson City none the worse for the trip.

It was when the fall rush was at its height my Father became afflicted with a desire to take his chances among the thousands already on the way and concluded there was but one cure, and that was to go. So leaving a fairly profitable manufacturing business in the hands of a partner, he departed on the S.S. *City of Seattle* for Skagway on August 11 [1897]. Upon arriving there, the situation was gone over with great care, and he finally decided to abandon the journey to the interior at least until the following spring.

A glance was sufficient to see that a small fortune could be made freighting outfits for the masses now going in before navigation closed. So eager were the people to reach the head of navigation that any price for packing was paid by them without a murmur, and actually it was outrageous the prices some packers extorted from the public. A short time following his arrival, he fell in with an old friend from Seattle, and they at once struck up a partnership to enter the pack train business from Skagway to Lake Bennett. Buying four horses and necessary articles used in packing, they at once began operations, and their efforts were crowned with success from the very start. The two carried on their packing with continued success until they finally had to give way to the severe winter, which began now to show itself, and to cross the blizzard-covered mountain tops became a menace to one's life.

Selling their packing outfits at a good, round figure and settling other affairs, Father departed for home and arrived on November 2nd, more than satisfied both financially and in the experience he had received on the most trying portion of the journey to the "Klondike." He was now more desirous than before of making the trip to the interior and very soon came to the conclusion to prepare at once for the journey and to leave on the first steamer for the north in the spring. From all indication the spring rush would far exceed the one now practically over for the season.

At occasional periods during the winter, parties braved the perilous trail over the frozen river from Dawson City and arrived safely at Skagway, thence to Seattle. Their glowing accounts of the richness of the gold-producing creeks adjacent to Dawson City flew to all parts of the world immediately, and as would be supposed, did not tend to discourage the minds already formed to make the trip early in the spring. On the contrary, it fired the ambition of many more up to the time uninterested as far as taking an active part was concerned.

Up to this time, Father was undecided which one of his four sons would accompany him on the trip and finally came to the conclusion that I, being the elder [at 24], should share the trials and hardships with him. I agreed quite heartily, as I had a great desire to see the northern country and also was desirous of increasing my bank account. This point being settled, I severed my position in my Father's manufactory [the Skookum Box Factory, a lumber company and box-making firm][7] the middle of February, and we began preparing to sail on the very first steamer we could secure passage to the north. The following two weeks, we found to be busy ones and found the purchasing of an outfit to be no small task. We also found that great care was to be taken in selecting nothing which was not absolutely necessary. But even with the care taken, we realized before reaching our destination many articles could have been dispensed of. Some were actually nonsensical, and much sport was created over our decidedly poor judgment in their purchase.

This was a failing in general among the inexperienced Argonauts, and many were the useless articles palmed off on the gold-seeker by the wily outfitting merchants at great profits to them, and which proved of no use to the travelers. On the contrary, these articles proved a great detriment as weight and compactness was a great item of concern. The outfitter, by the way, was not altogether at fault in this matter. This sort of trade had come into existence so suddenly that he was as ignorant or nearly so as the purchaser himself in regard to articles necessary for the trip into then practically an unknown land. But taking all into consideration under the circumstances, the Seattle merchants were conscientious in their advice and dealing, and few were the complaints from the purchasers.

The ordinary outfit consisted of white flour, navy beans, evaporated apples, pears, potatoes, peaches, condensed milk, and eggs, tea, coffee, rolled oats, bacon, sugar, candles, canned meats, necessary clothing, sled and other minor necessities too numerous to mention.

Having completed our outfit of the above named necessities, with the addition of two horses to do our packing, we were ready to depart on short notice about three days before the scheduled sailing date of the steamer we had been so fortunate as to secure passage with. The vessel was the S.S. *Cleveland,* an old collier which had plied between Seattle and San Francisco in the coal trade. She had been quickly transformed after a fashion to accommodate man and beast below decks and carried a limited number of first class passengers in the cabin above. As far as comfort was concerned, it was out of the question, but little did people care for that in their eagerness to reach their destination.

She was scheduled to sail February 27th, so upon this date our freight and horses were all checked aboard and our troubles at this end were at a close. After bidding farewell to those at home we were ready to go aboard at a moment's notice, but as the time of their scheduled departure drew near, we saw at a glance they were not going to sail on time, and they did not. On account of the enormous amount of freight the company had contracted to carry this trip, over two days elapsed before the cargo was complete. Unable to learn the exact time of departure, we were constantly on hand which, with loss of sleep and anxiety, became very monotonous and all greeted the first blast of the whistle with approval. At this signal the passengers streamed aboard and at 4:45 p.m., March 1,

1898, the hawsers were thrown from the pier, and the *Cleveland* backed out of the slip, and turning her prow to the north, glided out of Elliott Bay into Puget Sound on her long Voyage.

Seattle, March 1, 1898. Mr. Green, Jim Daugherty, Bill Chamberlain, Father and I have been laying at the Yesler Dock up to this time, 2 p.m., waiting for the Cleveland *to sail. We are all going to Skagway, Alaska, but do not know when we will get away. I quit the Factory two weeks ago, today. Oh, how my heart aches to leave the dear ones at home, but am going out to try my fortune in a wild and new country, which is full of dangers and hardships. Dear little Blanche was down at noon and bid me goodbye. Left Seattle at 4:45 p.m. amid a throng of people to see us off at the dock. We were out awhile when a dog went overboard, so they reversed the engines, and went back and got him, and boarded again and proceeded on the way again. We all retired at 7 p.m. after a hard day's work.*

The steamship had gained a point opposite Magnolia Bluff point, when the cry of dog overboard was heard from the crowd on deck, and sure enough, some frantic canine had become loosened and had leaped overboard and was making for his native land as fast as his strokes could carry him. Either superstition or sympathy overcame the Captain, for he gave the signal to reverse the engines and went back, and willing hands fished his dogship from the briny deep and the vessel proceeded on its way, everyone satisfied with the course taken by the Captain.

After feeding our horses and arranging things for the night, we made a passing acquaintance with men of all descriptions and professions, Doctors, Lawyers, Preachers, etc. and hailing from every state in the Union, nay, the whole world. Many from Seattle were aboard and not a few that we were personally acquainted with.

I regretted very much that the departure of the steamer could not have been in the morning. It would have given an opportunity to see the beautiful scenery on the upper sound between Seattle and Victoria, B.C., which is fast becoming world renowned. As it was, after two sleepless nights and busy days, we were ready to retire at an early hour, unmindful of our unusual surroundings and strange motion of the vessel.

The run to Victoria during the night was uneventful, and we arrived there at seven o'clock [March 2], just as we were rising from a very much needed and refreshing sleep. The stop here was to accommodate the

miners in procuring licenses from the Canadian Government to do mining and cut timber for boats. These licenses were necessary for miners
to present if challenged, but during our stay in the N.W.T. [North West
Territories], we were never approached in this regard.

As we were to lie here a part of the day, we set out early to see the
city, which is situated on the southeastern extremity of the island bearing the name of the great explorer Vancouver. The greater portion of the
city is built upon solid rock and in fact the entire island is of a rocky
formation which affords very few if any harbors on the Straits of Juan de
Fuca, which sweeps in from the Pacific on the southwestern coastline,
and which is very dangerous and treacherous to mariners. But on the
eastern coast there are many fine harbors, and Victoria in particular has
a magnificent one. There are many points of interest…in the Capital
City where many beautiful parks are a sight to see. The city is beautifully
laid out and has many fine buildings, among the latter are the post office
and Dunsmuir Castle,[8] which is constructed after the fashion of the historical old castles of old England and surrounded by beautiful grounds,
a sight rarely seen in America. Last but not least of the buildings that I
shall mention is the group of Parliament buildings, which are centrally
located and surrounded by well-kept grounds, and for architecture are
the grandest it has ever been my lot to witness.

Our time being limited, but with a great desire to see more, we has-
tened back to the steamer and found her about to leave, which she did at
11:15 a.m. After leaving Victoria harbor behind, we entered the Straits
of Georgia, which for beauty and picturesqueness would be difficult to
find anywhere in the world to equal it. One can almost imagine himself
on board a steamer ascending the St. Lawrence River in that portion
called the "Thousand Isles." All the afternoon our steamer dodged in
and out among the little formations of rock and soil sparsely covered
with a growth of small firs and a green covering of grass which were picturesque to look upon. The afternoon was rainy, but perfectly calm, and
it was not unlike river navigation.

Due to the stormy afternoon, darkness set in early and shut out to
view the ever-shifting scenery, which my eyes had feasted upon during
the afternoon. The chill of the night drove us all below, to satisfy an
appetite which the fresh sea breezes had created. After a hearty meal was

disposed of, we all retired to the forecastle where an entertainment of music (of which there was an assortment), recitations, etc. were enjoyed by all until a late hour, we retired for the night.

March 2, 1898. I with my mandolin and a fellow from Detroit, Mich. had a banjo and a guitar player from St. Paul and violin player from Butte, Montana. We all played together pretty well. We kept it up until 10 p.m.

The following morning [March 3] found us steaming through Seymour Narrows, an extremely narrow piece of water separating the northern portion of Vancouver Island and British Columbia mainland and connecting the Straits of Georgia with Queen Charlotte Sound. At certain periods of the incoming or outgoing tide, it is dangerous to attempt this narrow passage by many steamers, as the waters rush through the canyon-like passage at a rate equal to a mill race. We were informed by the Captain that during the early morning, he had brought the steamer to a stand-still and waited until the greater force of the tide had spent itself, whereupon he had entered, and at the time we came upon deck, we were travelling at a good rate of speed. Jutting rocks increase the danger, and upon one of these the United States man of war *Saranac* was wrecked in 1875, which to my knowledge is the only serious wreck in the narrows.

Our steamer glided swiftly through this narrow and dangerous passage into Johnston Strait at nine a.m. which is another link in the chain of sounds, straits and narrows of the Inland Passage to Alaska. After entering the straits, a decided change can be noted immediately. The passage becomes wider, consequently the swift current we had just experienced disappeared entirely, and the body of water appeared like an inland sea bathed by the bright, warm sunlight, which had made its appearance early this morning. The sunshine so unlike the day before had its effect on the passengers and brought all to the deck to breathe the fresh salt air and view the beautiful scenery through which we were now passing, and which is unsurpassed in the whole world. The south shore line of the Strait rises abruptly to a great height possibly between four and five thousand feet, and this time of year was covered by a mantle of snow nearly to the water's edge, and as the sunlight fell upon it presented a most beautiful sight. The opposite or northern shore differs vastly from the southern shore, as it is not as abrupt and many little arms of the Strait branch out in all directions losing themselves among the thickly wooded hills in the foreground. In the background the mountains rise to a considerable height and during the warmest summer months, snow may be seen on their summits. The strait appears to have many channels formed by its many picturesque islands, and it was very amusing to guess while at a distance which course the steamer would take when she came up with them. Chances were usually against the guesser in this regard.

We passed the S.S. *Albion* during the forenoon, bound for Seattle with apparently a small passenger list, which gave us a passing greeting and then was soon lost to sight among the islands left astern. In the middle of the afternoon, we passed the little village of Arctic Bay on the Bay of the same name, which has a pretty little harbor and is composed of a number of shack-like buildings. The inhabitants are both white and Indian, and the chief employment is fishing during the season.

As it was not necessary, the steamer did not stop here, but kept on its course, and very soon thereafter it became apparent that our river-like voyage was at an end for a time at least. In place of the narrow passage we had traversed all day, we suddenly came from the lee of an island into an open sea, the land being many miles from either side. Upon inquiry we found we were entering the waters of Queen Charlotte Sound and at 4:15 p.m., and as darkness was settling over the water, we entered the open sea. The sound is an open arm of the Pacific about thirty miles long, and during stormy weather is very rough and dangerous. Good weather favored us as we came upon the open water, but for all of that, the action of the incoming swells upon the steamer gave her a disagreeable motion, and the passengers with sensitive stomachs experienced the first disagreeable sensation of sea sickness while on the trip. Those who a short time before had eaten a hearty meal had about all they could do to retain it. The motion of the vessel had no effect upon me, however, and at an early hour I retired. But before sleep closed my eyes, I was conscious of an increased falling and rising motion of the steamer as she rode head on to the incoming swells.

The following morning [March 4], I was awakened at six o'clock by the violent rising and falling of the vessel, and lost no time in dressing and hurried on deck wondering if we were still on Queen Charlotte

Sound. Upon inquiry, I was informed that we were crossing Milbank Sound, another arm of the open sea about six miles across, and which gets very choppy and rough in stormy weather. This morning an unusually heavy swell was running and many passengers were loath to leave their beds, and a very few answered the call for breakfast.

In less than an hour we were in the shelter of Princess Royal Island, which, with the British Columbia mainland, creates the Finlayson passage. The island is quite large, being at least twenty five miles long and the elevation is, I should estimate, over fifteen hundred feet. The slope on the side we were passing is very steep, and in many places abrupt, and at this time of the year was covered with snow nearly to the water's edge. In several places on the side of the mountain could be seen spaces many hundreds of feet wide where it was devoid of timber while the greater portion was thickly wooded. The vacant spaces we were told were caused by avalanches of snow or landslides, and the mark of devastation is well-done, large trees being clipped off as cleanly as by the woodman's ax.

Upon entering the Passage, the passengers again took an interest in life and their surroundings, and by nine a.m. found the majority on deck enjoying the magnificent scenery we were now passing. The passage is picturesque and beautiful for which it is unequaled on the whole voyage to Skagway. The passage is about twenty-five miles in length, and at a number of places is very tortuous, made so by the many islands, and many times it appeared to me that the steamer would be brought short up against the towering hill ahead, as no channel appeared to right or left. But just before dashing into the land, as it seemed, the pilot would give a quick turn to the wheel, we would fly around and pass safely between two islands, either one of them within a stone's throw from the side of the steamer. The weather being admirable, the sun coming out bright and warm, added a fascination to the trip through this passage, which is not usually the case. The fog usually obscures the beautiful scenery from the eyes of the traveler, and also is a menace to navigation.

Upon the entrance to the channel, we passed the steamer *Lakme* going south with quite a list of passengers. Hearty cheers of welcome were given from both steamers as she sped on her way, and she was soon lost sight of among the islands. Late in the forenoon, we entered

Grenville Channel, a canal-like passage something like fifty miles in length, and after traversing a few tortuous miles at the entrance, it develops into a straight, uniform passage the entire distance to Chatain Sound. In width, it varies from one to three or four miles, but the towering hills which slope to the water's edge are very deceptive. One would think these hills were but a few hundred yards from the steamer, and they give a wrong impression of the channel's width. The same mark of nature's own destruction shows itself as in the earlier part of the day regarding avalanches, and quite frequently during the afternoon, we would pass great spaces completely stripped of all growth.

During the afternoon we encountered a greater number of craft than at any time since leaving Victoria, passing three scows loaded with lumber towed by two powerful tugs, no doubt bound for Skagway. Also another tug had in tow a schooner going south, and as she passed us, had her sails set in full in a manner that the canvas might dry by the warm sun. She presented a beautiful sight. Far to our right as we neared the entrance of Chatain Sound, we sighted a small steamer, but too far away to make out her name with the glass.

The remainder of the afternoon we are in the shelter of the Dundas group of islands before entering Dixon Entrance. This body of water forms the southern boundary of Alaska and British Columbia. At nine p.m., we passed the wreck of the steamer *Corona*, which went on the rocks during the winter and a number of lives lost. The darkness prevented us from seeing the wreck distinctly as the steamer flew by the dangerous spot. Soon after, all turned in after enjoying the most interesting and from a weather standpoint, beautiful days on the voyage.

March 4, 1898. Caught an awful cold last night and am doctoring tonight. Hope I am all right when we reach Skaguay.

The crossing of Dixon Entrance had been the main topic among the passengers, they having been informed that it was the roughest piece of water on the entire Inland Passage to

> The steamer *Corona* hit a rock on January 24, 1898, and immediately began to sink. The 245 passengers safely evacuated, but all cargo was lost. The ship sailed from San Francisco on January 20, 1898, and was headed for Skagway and Dyea. The tragedy made national headlines when the news came to Victoria, British Columbia, five days later.[9]

Skagway, but on this occasion it was quite the contrary. Nearly all had retired and sleep had overcome many before the steamer entered the strait and few knew anything of the steamer's progress during the night, so calm was the water. Dixon Entrance is a broad open sound or strait between the Columbian and Alexandria Archipelagos, through which passes the southern boundary twice between Alaska and British Columbia. It has been called channel, sound, strait and entrance: usage seems to have settled upon the above name. Dixon Entrance was discovered by the Spaniards in 1774 and called Entrada de Perez. Dixon, in 1787, visited it and named it after himself, Dixon Straits, the name being applied to the waters east and north of Queen Charlotte's Islands. A few still call it by its Indian name Kaigain Strait.

Saturday, March 5, 1898. Awoke this morning, my cold feeling better.

After a splendid night's rest, I arose quite early the following morning [March 5] and found quite a sea running, but it caused little inconvenience, as we were soon in the shelter of Prince of Wales Island, the largest of the Alexandria Archipelago, and over one hundred and fifty miles in length. On leaving Dixon Entrance, the navigator has the choice of two routes, one to the west, the other to the east of the Gravina group, namely Duke Mary and Annette islands.

Our Captain had taken the former course, and as we came on deck, were passing the little village of Metlakatla, situated on the western shore of Annette Island, and in another hour, we were opposite the village of Ketchikan, which at the time I write, has gained quite a prominence as a distributing center for points on Prince of Wales Island, which is very rich in copper and other valuable minerals. Ketchikan is now one of the principle stops on the Seattle and Skagway steamship runs, but on this trip, there seemed no necessity for stopping, so the steamer kept to its course, and we were soon clear of Tongas Narrows, a short narrow channel on which Ketchikan is situated.

Soon after leaving Tongas Narrows and entering Clarence Strait, a disagreeable misty rain set in, shutting out all the beauty of the surrounding scenery, spoiling the entire day's pleasure. Early in the afternoon, we passed between Etoline Island and Lincoln Rock, so named by [Navy Lieutenant Commander A. S.] Snow in 1886 after President Abraham Lincoln, and I believe in 1901 an executive order was issued

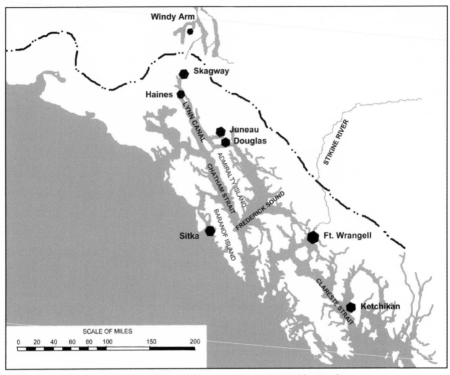

Southeast Alaska waters, Ketchikan to Skagway. *Catherine Holder Spude*

by the United States Government reserving the rock for light house purposes.[10]

The rain continued to fall the entire afternoon, and as we neared Ft. Wrangell, the wind that had sprung up became intensely cold, which made us realize that we were nearing the land of snow. As we passed around Waronkawskin Island (a name which has a strong flavor of Russia in it), we are in sight of the town of Ft. Wrangell, or Wrangell, as it is now commonly called, and in another half hour, are lying snugly alongside a brand new wharf on the village waterfront.

Wrangell is located upon an island of the same name, and is separated from the mainland by a narrow passage called Eastern Pass. The much-heard-of Stikine River flows into the bay a few miles to the north of the town. This is the largest river cutting its course through the boundary line and having its mouth in southeastern Alaska. At its source are located the famous Cassiar placer mines, which in the seventies and eighties were very successfully worked, and much of the yellow treasure was taken out.

Many who may read these lines will remember the horrors of the Edmonton Trail during the rush for the Klondike. It began at Edmonton, Alberta, and made its way through an unexplored region of British Columbia brought with all the danger due to man and beast. This trail crossed the Stikine at Telegraph Creek, a settlement of the once famous mines. The few who reached this point were without provisions or money and were forced to make their way down the Stikine to Wrangell, thankful to reach there with their lives. The only practical way to reach this part of the country has been by way of Wrangell, and to this much is due the advancement of the town in a commercial way.

Many glaciers on its course and tributaries feed the stream. The icy surfaces, in their flight downstream, come in contact with the chalky-colored hills, and upon reaching the river, cause it to become tinged with a milk-like color, and its cloudy path is marked for many miles from its mouth.

This being our first stop since leaving Victoria, we made all haste in going ashore, the Captain informing us that we would be here until ten p.m. at least. After being aboard the steamer in cramped quarters four days, it seemed good to stretch our stiffened limbs once more.

March 5, 1898. I went up to the post office and mailed a letter to little Blanche and Mother, and then went down to the Mill where Pete Goodrich [see Biographies] is working and seen him. He looks as natural as ever and is the same old Pete after the mill shut down. He showed us around the town. We took in the Gambling Dens first, which is done on a big scale here, lots of money made and lost here. Then he took us all into a War dance given by the Indians of the town, it was ghastly and interesting. When this was over, we went into a dance hall and looked at the White men dance with the Siwashes, a great sight. The Indian woman dresses both civilized and stylish. We stayed here until 12 o'clock and went on board after bidding Pete goodbye. A blinding snow storm is raging tonight and is very cold.

A schoolmate and lifelong friend of mine had located here a number of years previous, and after mailing letters home telling that all was well, we set out in search of him, and without much trouble, he was found, so after exchanging greetings, he informed us he was at leisure to show us around town, and we proceeded to improve our short stay here. We found upon observation that the town was growing at a rapid rate, and there must have been fifty or sixty buildings under construction, among them a fine hotel building three stories in height. A large sawmill is one of the principle industries of the town, and furnishes lumber for the adjacent country and boxes for the many fish canneries located in these parts, and the output is greater than any other part of the world.

The Indians comprise nearly one half of the inhabitants and their ancient landmarks, the totem poles, meet your gaze at every turn. The majority is thrifty and fairly well educated, and many hold responsible positions. During the fore part of the evening, we were escorted by my friend into a public dance hall and were much surprised to note the up-to-date dress among both sexes of the natives. The women especially were stylishly dressed, and I can assure you there were few wall flowers among them during the progress of a dreamy waltz or two-step, as all appeared light and graceful on the floor, and from indications were preferred by their white partners. We met upon the price of four bits, 50¢, and were admitted to a typical entertainment given by the Indians in the form of a war dance, and which was executed in a fascinating manner, which amused and interested us extremely.

An analysis of the 1900 census of Fort Wrangell indicates that there were twenty-seven Native Alaskan women living in the town, and they constituted more than half of the adult female population, which also included sixteen white, one African-American, and five women of mixed racial heritage. Adult white males constituted almost half (47 percent) of the town's population in the year 1900.

We finally ended our tour of inspection by visiting the gambling houses, which were unmolested by the town authorities who apparently favored a wide-open policy, judging from the number and amounts bet by the throngs which visited these houses no doubt nightly.

As the time for the departure of the steamer was growing near, we bade our friend goodbye and made our way to the vessel amid a blinding snow storm, which had already covered the earth to the depth of three inches, and bid fair to keep it up all night. Upon reaching the steamer, we at once retired.

Upon awakening next morning [March 6], we found ourselves at the northern entrance of Wrangell Narrows, having left Wrangell at six a.m., several hours later than the Captain had figured on owing to the great amount of freight dispatched. Wrangell Narrows is the most narrow, confined channel on the inside passage to Skagway, but on this particular trip, caused no inconvenience, the tide being in our favor. At ten thirty a.m. just after rounding Cape Fairshaw, we met the steamers *Humbolt* and *Packshaw*, both returning to Seattle after discharging the human cargo at Skagway. The former, a well-equipped passenger steamer, had on board a number of returning Alaskans. The latter, being an old freighter that was quickly fitted to compete in the passenger traffic exemplified by the *Cleveland's* class, was almost devoid of passengers. This difference showed that people at the Skagway end of the route had some choice in the manner of vessel they sailed in.

After leaving Dixon Entrance, the passage the remainder of the way to Skagway is completely shielded from the angry passions of the ocean which presents itself at times. Nevertheless, the disagreeable weather continued during the afternoon, much to our dissatisfaction and discomfort, for as we neared Juneau, the increasing low temperature kept us below decks most of the time. Shortly after darkness set in, the lights on Douglass Island became visible, and at ten p.m., we were lying beside the wharf in Juneau Harbor.

Twenty passengers and one hundred tons of freight were to be discharged here, and as some time would elapse in doing this, we took the opportunity to see as much of the town as was possible under the circumstances. As nearly all the passengers disembarked and filed uptown, we could see lights being turned on in the various stores in the business portion of the town, and finally the front doors were thrown open, inviting the trade of the transients at this unseemly hour of the night. And that they were fully rewarded for their trouble could plainly be seen as the passengers returned to the boat with their arms full of packages containing a variety of articles. The monotony of ship's food had caused a strong craving for fruit, and at one neat little stand, Father and I purchased a few dozen each of lovely oranges and bananas, the price being much higher than at Seattle, but we were glad to get them at that, and they were appreciated very much.

Juneau is located on the mainland a few miles north of Taku Inlet and is 899 miles from Seattle. The location is unequal and picturesque, lying at the foot of a mountain wall of solid rock, rising to a height of two thousand feet. The town spreads itself over a narrow ledge, which gradually slopes toward the wharves. A narrow ravine coming in from the north is the only chance for the expansion of the little city, and noting the building activity in progress, one would almost think in a very few years hence, building space would be at a premium. Among the many buildings under construction were two or three brick ones, two stories in height and of modern architecture facing up streets, which are forced to conform to the irregularity of the lay of the land.

Juneau is now the seat of Government for Alaska Territory, having been removed from Sitka in [1900][11] where it had been located since Alaska was purchased by the United States in 1867. This action on the part of the United States Government assures Juneau a popularity and prosperous future, and she is now recognized as the metropolis of southeastern Alaska. Her population in 1900 was given as 1,864, and when the census is taken in 1910, she will show a number close to the 3,000 mark.[12]

Across the Gastineau Channel lies Douglas Island, upon which the mining towns of Douglas and Treadwell are located, and as we looked across the channel from the steamer's deck, the many hundreds of glittering electric lights presented a beautiful sight, and forgetting for the moment that we were looking upon other than the lights of West Seattle across Elliott Bay from Seattle. The Treadwell Mines located upon the island are the richest quartz mines in the world. The vein is over four hundred feet wide, the ore being a low grade, but easily mined and milled with an inexhaustible supply in its twenty mile boundaries, the entire island being seamed with quartz lodes. The stamp mill is among the largest in the world, having in operation at the time I write, a total of six hundred stamps. I was much disappointed in not being able, under the circumstances, to make a visit to the island before resuming our journey, but resolved to do so as I returned from the north.

The night was disagreeably cold, the snow as our boots came in contact with it gave out a crunching sound, a very good indication of the low temperature. Our newly-purchased Alaska clothing, which we donned today for the first time, did not prevent us from feeling the cold keenly. Shortly after midnight we returned to the steamer and soon after, retired, as far as we knew, for the last time on board the vessel.

The steamer left Juneau at three a.m. [March 7]. As we came on deck at seven a.m. the following morning, it had gained a point opposite Point Retreat. A few miles beyond, we could plainly see where Lynn Canal was separated by a sharp point of land into two channels. Many miles to our left a small steamer could be seen entering the Chatham Strait, presumably bound for Sitka. Not long afterwards, a good stiff breeze from the north set in. As we came opposite Lincoln Island, a few miles farther on, the wind came down the canyon-like passage not unlike a hurricane, and we encountered a very rough sea until passing Point Bridget. There it settled down to a constant and steady breeze, continuing so until Skagway was reached.

Lynn Canal is a natural waterway extending from Point Retreat to Dyea Inlet, a distance of seventy miles and varying in width from three to ten miles. It is walled in on both sides by high, barren mountains around the summits of which hung a frosty mist (quite a usual sight). It has few indentations along its shores, the mountains taking a gradual slope from the water's edge, and many little streams and waterfalls find their way down the easy slopes into the channel. The trip up the canal was almost without interest, the mist shielding from view the beautiful scenery, which is doubtless to be seen on a clear day. The strong wind which was blowing seemed unable to remove the mist.

At twelve o'clock noon, we passed the point upon which Haines is located, and which separates Chilkat Inlet from Chilkoot Inlet. The passage narrows to half its former width and continues so until Skagway is reached. Not long after passing the point to our left, the little village of Haines could be seen nestling at the foot of the high hills in the immediate background and facing upon a pretty little bay. Ft. William H. Seward, a United States military post, is located here with two companies of soldiers being stationed here the year around.

As we neared Skagway, the cold wind increased to such an extent as to retard the progress of the large steamer, and we were an unreasonably long time in covering the remaining distance. A number of miles before reaching Skagway, the snow-covered mountains lying back of Dyea and Skagway came into view, and one can almost trace the two passes over their summits. As we came opposite Haines, they came into view, their entire surface being clothed in a mantle of white, and at their summits a fierce snow storm was in progress, at our distance appearing much like a fog. The Captain had stated earlier in the day that we would reach Skagway in plenty of time to eat our noonday lunch, but we were a little disappointed in this. However, when the snow-covered mountains came into view dead ahead, we came to a realization that our steamer trip was nearly at an end, and at once set about getting our luggage together preparatory to leaving the steamer. At a little past one o'clock we passed the little point of land between Dyea Inlet and Skagway harbor, and at half past one we ran alongside the long wharf, the wind whistling through the steamer rigging, threatening to blow everyone from the deck.

After the steamer became securely fastened to the pier (which she did after much trouble on account of the terrific wind sweeping down the Skagway River's canyon-like valley, laden with frost and particles of snow from the adjacent mountain peaks), the Captain and the local longshoremen disagreed in some manner or other in regard to the unloading of the vessel. The Captain remaining firm in his desires, it appeared for a time as though a general strike among the longshoremen would be the result. But finally some arrangement was brought about to the satisfaction of both parties, and the unloading of the mammoth vessel immediately began. This was much to our satisfaction, for upon gaining the wharf, we were told little time was to be lost in getting over the well-worn trail, which in places had begun thawing, threatening to impede traffic such as we had contemplated, that is in the use of horses.

The wharf we had made fast to is located snugly under the shelter of a perpendicular cliff of solid rock rising to an immense height and is reached from the city by a roadway built on piles about one half mile in length, this distance being necessary to procure a depth of water to harbor an ocean steamer.[13] After getting together our personal belongings and seeing them safely aboard on a express wagon bound uptown, we proceeded thither on foot, the cold north wind penetrating our heavy clothing, affecting our sensitive skins due to the sudden change of the temperature. This cold was in contrast to Seattle with its warm spring weather, which is characteristic of the Puget Sound country during the winter months. The change in temperature was too much for our sensitive bodies, but we became accustomed to the cold in a short time and fairly enjoyed the exhilarating mountain air.

As we were to spend the night in town, we at once went in search of hotel accommodations for the night, and found it to be no small task, the tremendous rush of transients being far in excess of hotel accommodations. Our search was finally rewarded by us securing rooms in a hotel operated by a friend of Father's from our home town [Alexander Birnbaum, see Biographies], and which he had named after the latter city [Seattle]. After stowing our baggage, we set out to see as much of the town as possible in the limited time the remainder of the afternoon afforded us, as early the following morning promised to see us on the trail if all went well.

The Seattle Hotel in Skagway is the two-story building behind the Brownell Hardware Store. Its sign hangs out over the street from the second-story window. Photo taken July 4, 1898 by Rev. John A. Sinclair. *Royal British Columbia Museum, British Columbia Archives, I-51623.*

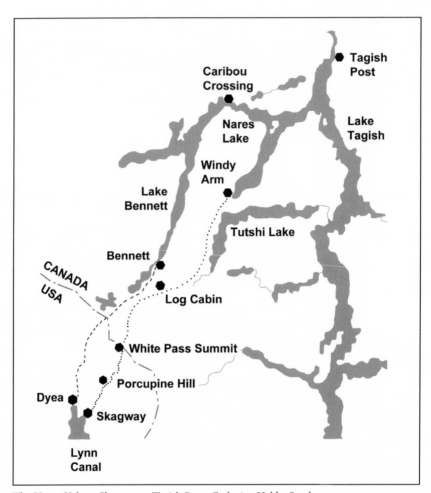

The Upper Yukon, Skagway to Tagish Post. *Catherine Holder Spude*

Chapter Two

THE WHITE PASS TRAIL
MARCH 7–APRIL 6, 1898

⊹⇒⋅⇐⊹

THE NEXT PHASE OF WILL WOODIN'S JOURNEY NORTH was the passage from tidewater over Alaska's Coastal Mountains to the headwaters of the Yukon River. The people headed for the Klondike had to cross one of two passes: the Chilkoot or the White Pass. The former pass was shorter than the latter by five miles, but the stampeders who used it climbed two hundred feet higher, much of it at an incline too steep for pack animals. As a result, those who wanted to pack their goods on oxen, mules, or horses were forced to use the White Pass. Tlingit people from the Chilkat River Valley had long used the Chilkoot Pass as a means of entering the interior to trade with native peoples living on the upper reaches of the Yukon River. They had avoided making any trails over the White Pass in order to control their trade routes. This second pass became important only after the establishment of Skagway by explorer William Moore and his subsequent reconnaissance of an alternative route to the headwaters of the Yukon.

Jay Woodin spent the fall of 1897 packing supplies over the White Pass and was thoroughly familiar with the route. He knew what he was doing when he decided to use horses to pack their outfit. Wealthier individuals usually hired packers who owned one or two dozen pack animals, so the forty-mile trip could be traversed in two or three days. The Woodins, with their two horses brought with great care from Seattle, required a month to transfer their outfit and the supplies that Jay Woodin intended to sell along the way.

Will never states how many supplies the five of them packed over the pass in March 1898. At the border, which coincided with the summit of the pass, the Canadians required each prospective miner to have a year's supply of food. Most sources suggest this amounted to about 1,500 pounds per person. In addition, the shared equipment, such as tents and cooking utensils, and tools for cutting wood and building boats and shelters (not to mention mining implements), could weigh another ton. For the Woodin party of five, these supplies and equipment probably weighed close to five tons. Because they needed to purchase hay and grain for the two horses, they had just that much more to pack.

In addition, Jay meant to sell goods in Dawson. Will's diary entries of March 23 to 30 detail a total of sixteen trips that the party made from their last camp on the west side of the pass to the summit. Earlier he had noted that each of the two horses could pull a 600-pound load. At 1,200 pounds per trip, the Woodin party appears to have transported almost ten tons of goods. This estimate is supported by the fact that it took them six trips to transfer all of their goods from the summit of the pass to Log Cabin, their last camp on this phase of the trip. Will notes that they were able to carry between 3,000 and 3,500 pounds per trip. It appears that Jay doubled the amount of goods they transported for the express purpose of selling the excess in Dawson. It is little wonder, then, that they took as long as they did to transfer their overly-large outfit over the pass.

This stage of the journey, from Skagway to the lakes at the head of the Yukon, was perhaps the hardest in terms of physical labor. Will's narrative recites the dangers of the trail from both the harsh climate and from other travelers. In these first few weeks of the adventure, he felt the absence of his mother, sisters, and sweetheart keenly. While some women did attempt the crossing, by far the majority, probably more than 90 percent, were men. The Woodin party, like all of the men traveling that trail that spring, learned to do those chores they usually left for women to do, such as cook, mend clothing, and wash laundry. As Will and his fellow travelers adapted to these previously unfamiliar skills, they turned to one another for companionship and sociability. They encountered old friends from Seattle and Michigan on the trail and made new ones. They shared duties equally, and helped other travelers who needed it.

For the most part, Will and his companions limited their new friendships and offers of assistance to members of their own class. These were men whose families had left farming within their lifetimes, and who were learning new occupations in an urban setting. While most of them had at least a primary school education, those who had finished high school were probably limited in number. They learned new skills on the job, not in a formal classroom setting. They valued group cooperation, the exertion of physical labor, and male sociability. And, like the growing middle class, of which they would ultimately become a part, they avoided violence, liquor, gambling, and the use of blasphemous language.

Will recounts another example of group solidarity after the Woodin party hauled its last load to the top of the pass. With several hours left in the day, the younger men helped a Presbyterian minister and family pack their outfit to the summit (see Rev. William Howie, Appendix A: Biographies). In a memoir of his childhood and family connections, Will noted that his cousin, Wallace Woodin, eventually became an assistant superintendent of Presbyterian Sunday Schools of the State of Connecticut. This notation suggests that the Woodins were Presbyterians, and so were naturally drawn to the Presbyterian minister on the trail. The Rev. Howie, in fact, is mentioned several times in the first few legs of the trip.

Once the party reached the headwaters of the Yukon, where they built boats and awaited the breakup of winter ice on the lakes and streams, the Woodin party restricted themselves to social interactions with men of similar economic and occupational backgrounds. The one exception occurred on Sunday, April 20, 1898, when Will, Jay, and Jim Daugherty provided dinner and a sled ride to a wealthy young man who had hurt his back. In his memoir, Will complimented the young man as "well bred and of unusual intelligence." Only in his diary did Will note that he took five dollars for driving the man's mule to the next cache, a job that took an hour. He wryly commented that it was "enough for one hour's work" (worth the equivalent of $140 in today's currency).[1] Will almost contemptuously noted that the young man was the "sort who was unconscious of the true condition of the trail and its difficulties, no doubt treating it all as a holiday jaunt." His statement betrays the class consciousness of the time. Accounts by rich young men of their quick travel over the White Pass left a biased picture of the ease with which that trail could be negotiated in the spring of 1898.

In fact, historians have often ignored the difficulties of the White Pass trail after it had been improved by George Brackett and his Skagway and Yukon Transportation and Improvement Company during the winter of 1897–98. The chief historian of the National Park Service, in preparing a resource study prior to the establishment of Klondike Gold Rush National Historical Park, stated that "The few accounts of travel over the White Pass in 1898 have a common denominator— brevity."[2] A follow-up study of the pass and its transportation corridors prepared for the park over thirty years later could list no detailed accounts of the use of the trail. Because the published accounts of those who went over the White Pass trail in the spring and summer of 1898 almost universally used packers, their experience of the trail was indeed short and unexceptional. Most of these men were able to cross the pass and proceed to Bennett in three to five days.[3]

One anonymous diarist who wrote for *Frank Leslie's Popular Monthly* in May 1900 passed over the trail on horseback, leaving Skagway on March 27 and arriving in Bennett on March 30, with only three nights on the trail. He complained of the terrible food he bought from restaurants and observed that he had walked "some of the very roughest trail and country I have seen or imagined."[4] Angelo Heilprin, who went to the Klondike in the summer of 1898, crossed the pass on horseback on July 30 and 31, making it to Bennett with only one overnight stay. He encountered no mud and complained only of the stench of decaying horse-flesh. He stated that it would have been a delightful ride if his horse had not come up lame.[5] Mary E. Hitchcock and her friend Edith Van Buren, who had gone to

Dawson on a river boat up the Yukon the previous summer, left the north in late September 1898. They walked from Bennett to the train stop at White Pass City on October 2 and 3, 1898, and stayed the night at a hotel at Log Cabin (Will and Jay had done the same only a couple of weeks earlier as they left the north). While the women complained of having to walk a steep grade and getting stuck in the mud, they mostly were excited by the adventure, and enjoyed their restaurant meals, pleased to be able to purchase lemonade and oranges during their hike.[6]

Contrast these published accounts to the extensive endeavor made by the Woodin party as related in Will's upcoming narrative. The Woodins started from Skagway on March 7 and did not establish a camp at Windy Arm until April 22, an effort that took forty-five days. The only similar expedition that has been published is that by college graduate Walter A. Starr and his partner Bill Brummage, who purchased two mules and four sleds and crossed the pass much as the Woodin party. They started in Skagway on March 1 and got their base camp in Bennett fully established by April 14, an effort that took the same amount of time as the Woodin party. Starr's diary entries, however, are quite brief, and detailed only the number of pounds hauled and the lateness of the hour in setting up camp, if applicable. A major crime committed on March 7 was treated with the curt statement, "A man named Beane was murdered and robbed on the trail about an hour after we passed his camp." Starr offered no commentary on the extraordinary event, unlike Will, who made observations about how the death affected his perceptions of social order and the dangers of the trail.[7]

It is possible that Will had more time to write than other diarists because he served more often as the camp cook than others. He was proud of his cooking abilities, as noted most eloquently in his memoir account of March 20, where he described the meal he prepared in some detail. These observations demonstrate the willingness that men on the trail had to take on the necessary chores usually reserved for women, and they felt no shame for it.

Unlike most diarists and letter-writers, the Woodin party did not observe Sundays by resting, although they would use the day as an excuse to sleep a couple of extra hours. They were so focused on reaching their destination that they did not take a full day of rest until April 3, after a particularly hard Saturday when they combated bad weather. They did not observe Sunday again until May 8, well into the next phase of their trip, when the pace of the work slackened somewhat.

Despite this disregard for the Sabbath, Will's diary entries and memoir account evidences the emerging middle-class attitudes about temperance in all matters. Drinking, gambling, and swearing did not characterize the experience of the Woodin party. While the mining camps have often been portrayed as being filled with men who frequently used profanity, Will used a cuss word only once in his diary

An example of Will Woodin's handwriting from his diary entry of April 4, 1898, showing his explicit use of a curse. *Sandra Dunn Collection.*

and not at all in his memoir. At Log Cabin on April 4, 1898 he noted, "Malen, Bill and Father were attacked !Farts—with snowblind." Because he printed and underlined the operative word, the context is clear that he means the word as an expletive, not an affliction.

Likewise, Will and his friends only once visited a saloon or gambling den, already recounted on March 5 during their sight-seeing with a close friend who lived at Wrangell. It is particularly noteworthy that Will discusses these institutions in that port city, but makes no mention of similar establishments in Skagway in March 1898. Newspapers of the time portrayed Skagway as wild, rough, and iniquitous, but that reputation was not deserved. Will's observation that the gambling houses were wide open in Wrangell is a stark contrast to later policy. Inspection of the 1901 through 1910 Alaska-Yukon Polk & Company business directories indicates that that city had only three or four saloons after 1899 when Congress imposed very high license fees for liquor sales in Alaska.

Other firsthand accounts of that spring in Skagway reflect an overall absence of lawlessness and violence. Kirke Johnson, who wrote to his mother several times between March and May of 1898, stated on March 17, 1898, "I didn't find

Skagway what the papers picture it. In fact in regard to law and order it isn't any worse than Chicago or Denver. There is no law here except the U.S. marshals, but from appearances there is none other needed. Of course a man wants to keep off the Trail at night and keep away from the gambling houses, anyway it is as safe here and things are as quiet as they are in any western city."[8]

Like Johnson, Will did not find much violence anywhere in the north except once on the White Pass Trail. In his March 9 diary entry, he recorded a shooting. *Saw a man pulled off the trail on a sled. Was shot up the canyon last night for his money. They got $200.00.*

Other diarists also discussed the murder, and probably because it was so unusual as to merit a remark. Walter Starr, who was on the trail at the same time as Will, named the man as "Beane."[9] Unpublished diarist Frank W. Purdy wrote on March 8, "Last night there was a man by the name of Bean from California killed or else he committed suicide. He was killed about one half mile above what is called Rescue Camp. We were first coming from where we had been hauling our stuff when we heard a shot fired. We didn't mind it any thinking that it might be a blast fired where some Company was building a road. After we got along a ways farther, we met a man with his sled who said he heard the shot and someone scream, but we didn't think nothing more about it."[10] A discussion of this event and an analysis of its relationship to popularly perceived violence in Alaska and Yukon appears in the sidebar at the end of this chapter.

The real dangers of the trail did not come from depredations by other travelers. Will's account of the snowstorms and blizzards encountered in March and April are detailed as to temperature, visibility, and the effects on their progress. When it was not snowing that spring, the stampeders faced the prospect of their pack animals and sleds becoming bogged down in mud. The storms, therefore, served as a blessing as well as a curse.

In addition to the physical danger imposed by the environment, Will's account emphasizes the loneliness faced by the men on the trail. When he wrote his memoir about fifteen years after the trip, he made very little fuss about how lonesome he had been. But in his diary of 1898 he often recorded how badly he missed his fiancée, Blanche Graves, and his mother and siblings. Will's affection for Blanche is obvious. In his diary, he referred to her as his "little wife" indicating his intention to marry her when he returned. In like manner, on April 22, 1898, at Windy Arm, Will noted that he received a letter "from my little Brother-in law Minor." Minor Graves was thirteen years old when Will went to the Klondike. However, he never mentioned Blanche or her siblings in his memoir, probably to spare his second wife cause for alarm at how frequently he pined for her predecessor. He married Blanche on December 1, 1900, but she died only four years later, on August

29, 1905, three months after the birth of their son, Harold.[11]

The loneliness on the trail, hazards from storms, difficulty of the work, establishment of a daily routine, and Will's relationships with family, friends, and those he encountered on the trail all form the basic themes of the trail phase of the Woodins' trip. Keeping those themes in mind, let us rejoin Will as he renews his narrative at Skagway on the afternoon of March 7, 1898.

Blanche Graves, ca. 1900. *Sandra Dunn Collection.*

Skagway is located in the valley and at the mouth of the river bearing the same name. The valley is walled in on both sides by mountains of quite an elevation, which, at the time we arrived, were covered by snow from summit to the base. Strange to say, there was little snow to be seen about the city as the strong wind which prevails the year around had made a clean job of it, blowing it into the bay.

Skagway presented a busy scene this day. Men from every clime and country on earth went to make up the throng that hurried to and fro getting their outfits together preparatory to "hitting" the trail as soon as possible. The approaches to the three wharves were continually lined with the loaded wagons, which were bearing the tons of freight and supplies as it was hoisted from the vessel's hold. It was taken into the city, where it was distributed to its owners. Few days passed during the spring that did not see two to three steamers anchored in the harbor or lying alongside the wharves, and arrivals and departures occurred regularly every day. Upon arriving, they poured forth their human freight into the city, and although a great number were transients, they tended to keep the city in a thoroughly prosperous condition.

It was quite evident that Skagway was to be the most practical start-ing point to the headwaters of the Yukon, and also had an unusual advantage in the fact that horses could be used in packing over its trail. This cannot be said of the Dyea Trail, which has its starting point at the mouth of the Dyea River located around the point of land about six miles west of Skagway. A spirited rivalry existed between the two towns during the rush this spring and the citizens of Skagway never could be heard to voice a favorable opinion of the Dyea Trail and Chilkoot Pass. We were informed that this trail, after traveling the first six miles, became unpractical in the use of horses for packing because of the rough and unbroken rocky terrain and, not least, the extreme inclines to the summit. As a Skagway citizen remarked, the Chilkoot trail was more than steep, it fairly leaned backward. In the struggle for the Alaska and Yukon traffic, Skagway has many advantages, and at the time I write and for years past, has been the gateway for nine tenths of the traffic leading to the interior. With its railroad for the present making its terminus at White Horse, it will continue to be important in this respect. But for all of that, Dyea and Chilcoot Pass will go down in history as the more famous of the two, and those who have experienced the hardships of scaling its summit will no doubt remember it to the end of life.

We noted, while touring the town during the afternoon, a tendency toward permanency. During the winter, the majority of the population resided in tents, which were now being displaced by substantial frame buildings. On all sides, music of the saw and hammer could be heard, notwithstanding the piercing cold wind, which was blowing, and which was the cause of us returning to our hotel at an early hour.

The hotel we were stopping at [Alexander Birnbaum's Seattle Hotel] was run on the American plan and was primitive in the extreme. The food was wholesome and appetizing and was enjoyed by all after the monotony of the ship's food. In the sleeping quarters, we found instead of separate sleeping rooms with comfortable beds, a long room which on both sides ranged three tiers of bunks, leaving an alley-way or corri-dor between, each arrival furnishing his own bed clothing.

Before going farther, I must return to the beginning of my story, and state that before leaving Seattle, we had grubstaked and arranged for a man to accompany and help us with our unusually large outfit through to our destination. Grubstakes were not unusual during the Klondike rush, and to those who do not understand this form, I will explain. He who receives a grubstake, or in plainer words, provisions, clothing, and in fact, all the necessities of life, works for those concerned. The man grubstaked is to share alike in all he discovers or receives with the man who grubstakes him. Few of the latter, however, have gained fortunes by this sort of contract.

Jim Daugherty, a tall, rawboned man measuring six feet in his stocking feet, had signified a strong desire to accompany us on those conditions. Having known the man many years, we put the fullest confidence in his ability and good judgment in this sort of a venture, he being a man of unusual experience in roughing it.

On the steamer from Seattle upon which we had come were two friends from the latter city and an old gentleman from central Michigan who were desirous of cooperating with us the remaining distance to Dawson, a preposition [sic] we readily agreed to. We found the association to be of unusual advantage to all concerned throughout the trip. This sort of an arrangement in every case was not a success in the fact that the hardships and discouragements of the trail that were brought to bear upon an individual were not of the brightest, and an even temper was not easily retained at times. Consequently, many of such parties disbanded before completing half the distance. In our particular case, aside from a few little disagreements of a comical nature and of which I will later mention, our companions were of a congenial nature, and at the end of our journey parted with the best of feeling toward one another.

Will Chamberlain, or "Bill" as he was called by us, was a man of sunny disposition, never complaining as long as rations came regular. He was of the optimistic kind, always looking on the bright side, never even referring to the reverse, and it was wholly due to him that the following days of hardships did not bring defeat and despair to our company.

Ed Green, a man of sturdy proportions and partner of Chamberlain's, was an acquaintance of ours in a passing instance. He was a man experienced in the hardiest kind of labor, similar in a great respect to that which now faced us, and without his services we would have been badly handicapped.

The third party, a Mr. Wells, a man of unusual education hailing from, I think, a small city in the central part of Michigan, completed our party. Mr. Wells, being a life-long friend of Father's, lived but a short distance from where Father had spent his boyhood days and also my birthplace. His gratitude was far-reaching in being able to accompany us, and I am sure his company was appreciated by all, and his good judgment helped us out of many a tight pinch, which we had unconsciously been placed.

Therefore, upon our arrival at Skagway, our agreement and arrangements were clear to each of the party, and it would have been difficult to find a more completely equipped company than ours on the trail.

Being anxious to "hit" the trail in good condition early the following morning, we did not loiter around town long during the evening. An early hour found us retiring to our primitive sleeping quarters, and I fell asleep almost immediately.

Early the following morning, March 8, 1898, we were made conscious by the call from Chamberlain to turn out, and all jumped from their berths in a bound, feeling much refreshed after the night's rest. After bathing our hands and face in the ice cold water placed at our service, we repaired to the dining room and did full justice to the appetizing food set before us. After dispatching the meal, the horrors of two trails would not have daunted our courage, so ambitious did we all feel, and we at once began our first day on the trail.

Daugherty, Green and Chamberlain were dispatched to the wharf to get the outfit in readiness to load into the sleigh, which Father had gone in search of, and which was to convey the goods to the canyon, a distance of seven miles from the city. From there the narrow rocky trail would not allow the use of the ordinary bob sleigh universally used in the eastern states, consequently our narrow sleds and a single horse attached were to be pressed into service from this point. Father was fortunate in procuring the necessary conveyance without much trouble, and at 10:30 a.m., arrived at the canyon with the first load amounting to four tons in weight, saving us much valuable time and labor.

We at once began packing and sledding the outfits to the foot of Porcupine Hill, having an elevation of three hundred feet. This hill will no doubt be remembered by those who packed over the Skagway Trail as

Men with pack mules carrying supplies on the White Pass Trail near Porcupine Hill.
Alaska State Library, Klondike Gold Rush Collection, P232-026.

one of its greatest obstacles, and many a man gave up in despair upon reaching it. Certainly it was discouraging to pack an outfit over its summit, as horses were of little use unless equipped with pack saddles of which we had none, therefore requiring us to pack our entire outfit on our backs. The information gained upon our arrival at Skagway in regard to the breaking up of the trail proved to be quite true. The evidence [of this condition] showed only too plain, as great stretches were entirely devoid of snow, and the remainder in a slushy soft condition. We found that Porcupine Hill cut off the cold north wind, and the sun which shone all day caused it to thaw considerably here, while at Skagway it would be very cold. It was plain to see that every effort must be taken by us or other means would have to be applied in getting over this extremely bad stretch of track in a very short time.

In view of this fact, we nearly disabled ourselves this first day, we not being accustomed to this sort of labor. When darkness set in, we were glad to make our way to our humble headquarters, the tent where we found Ed Green waiting supper. I must say that not a crumb remained when each had had his fill, causing a magical effect of cheerfulness to be felt for the morrow. After discussing our future prospects to some extent, we retired to our comfortable beds built upon fragrant pine boughs.

Early the following morning [March 9] found us on the trail, hard at work again. The trail was in fine shape after the chilly night, and much more could be accomplished the first few hours of the day than all the remainder. After nine o'clock the sun would find its way above the surrounding mountain tops and threw its warm rays into the narrow gulch. At any other time, it would have been heartily welcomed, but now it was looked upon in distrust and determent to our plans, as it was quickly and surely destroying the trail. The day was a repetition of the day before, and at night our bodies ached from the severe exertion we subjected them to during the day. Also, the headway made was discouraging in the extreme. Night found the trail in a deplorable condition, and it seemed that the next day would see it impossible.

March 9. Worked like slaves all day today packing to the foot of the hill again today. Never worked so hard in my life. Pulled our goods in hand sleds, could pull only 100 pounds at a load. I would give it up if we had [not] got horses coming up on the steamer Scotia, *but they haven't got here yet, and* [we] *have got to get out of here as soon as possible on account of the thaw, which is early.*

Many horses were shot during the day, the faithful animals having broken their limbs in the treacherous crevices in the rocky trail. Their dead bodies could be seen at frequent intervals, the entire length of the cruel trail. Cruelty to the faithful animals on the Skagway trail probably has no parallel in history, the poor creatures being destroyed by the hundreds in the mad rush of their masters.

During the day we met a man pulling a sled toward Skagway upon which lay a comrade in a serious condition, having been shot for his money the night before at a point some distance up the trail. The vagrant, securing $200 for his cowardly act, made good his escape, and it was well that he did, for if he had been captured, he would have been dealt with as is customary in a new and lawless country. This was the first case of the kind on record during the spring rush and tended to place all on the defense for a repetition of the affair. The trail was a rich field for the robbers and sneak thieves, but discretion was to be used in operating as a man's life was worth but little if caught in the act. In our particular case, we were not molested by them in any way during the entire trip to Dawson. But others were not as lucky, they having their outfits diminished by the heartless scoundrels after packing them to where they built their boats. [See page 61, "Violence on the Trails."]

The remainder of the week was but a repetition of the two previous days, nothing serious happening to deter our progress, but each day found the trail at this point in more deplorable condition. Where it was in good shape when we came, it was now worn down to the soil and rocks, making it harder for both man and beast.

March 10. Thought I would drop dead at night. Was so Tired, had to pack it all on our back.

March 12. Got into camp about 6:30 p.m. Had to put up tent, build fire and get supper after. This was the night that I thought I would die sure, but went to bed alive.

March 13. Today is Sunday, but did not observe it, as we usually do at Home, but pegged away all day, but all doing fine since we got our horses, making 2 trips apiece with the two horses everyday carrying 600# to the load. Mr. Green sick all today with the belly ache, did not work.

March 16. Both horses hauling up above Toll Gate. I am in camp all day today cooking, I done so well yesterday I guess. Father went down to see about O'Brian's outfit, this morning [and] did not return tonight. Must be getting the goods to the lower canyon. Still thawing fast in the afternoons.

March 17. Made three trips above Toll Gate today, which finishes our outfits. Father returned at 9 o'clock last night with a load of O'Brian's goods. Hired three horses and two men to help him haul O'Brian's goods through. Got my first letter since we came to Alaska. It was from my darling little Blanche. I don't think she will forget me. We were all in bed when they came. I had to get up and get their supper. Oh, it is nice.

March 18. Father fired his men and horses. They weren't used to the trail, so got along too slow. So all of us went down and hauled on to Porcupine Hill. It was just like putting our outfits over it again. I packed all day onto the Hill on my back, but wasn't I tired by night. Are going to try to get them all up tomorrow. The roads won't last a week longer. Brought two loads through to our camp at First Bridge. Got 3 miles from camp and a heavy snow storm set in and kept it up until long in the night, a God-send, but a very disagreeable night in camp, tent leaking all over. As such is life in Alaska.

March 19. The boys all went down to work on the Hill again today. Will get done about noon if nothing happens, but guess something has happened, for they are not here, and its 4 p.m. They made me stay in camp again today and cook something up, and have been busy all day, and a very long day, too. Have thought of the dear home I left behind me three weeks ago, and also my little intended wife. May God be good to me so that I may provide a good home for my darling and [God] shield [her] while I am absent. I don't ask for much, but may He grant this to me. I may not deserve it. I suffer enough, for it is now 6:30 p.m. and the men have not returned. Yet something must have happened to them. Am lonesome and homesick. Don't know what to do, but to write here, thinking of my dear home and darling. Suppose she has just finished supper and is washing her dishes. What will she do after that? Is she thinking of me, too? Can't tell, such will be my life in the Wilds of Alaska. I must keep up, by all means. I think of the Mission I came on. If I don't succeed, what use is it for me to return? This is what I think of. Will I be one of the lucky ones? Some of us must lose. Who will it be? Well, they came at last at 9 p.m. all right. Had supper and all turned in early.

On our last load Saturday evening [March 19], we stowed our camp equipage apart, moving it to a point on the trail eight miles beyond, judging that this distance would allow us to make two trips daily from our cache on the summit of Porcupine Hill. We found more snow on descending the opposite side and consequently the sledding much better. Darkness had set in when we reached our new camping ground and after the hard day's work we were compelled to set up the tent and cook our evening meal, which we were almost too tired to do justice to.

This careless failure caused much sickness and suffering to the gold-seekers working hard all day, stopping at noon only long enough to eat a meager cold lunch of baking powder bread and cold beans. Whereupon reaching their tent at night worn out by the day's toil, they would retire to their beds without tasting warm food throughout the day. This, combined with careless exposure, was the cause of much illness. It was not an unusual sight to see men being hauled on sleds to Skagway as they suffered from spinal meningitis, a disease that seemed to be an epidemic in camp. The cause was from nothing more than the victim going to his tent covered with perspiration, carelessly throwing himself on his lounge, and sleep overcoming him before he realized. The reaction being so great in his tired, weakened condition, he was easy prey to this and the many other diseases man is subject to. It was a fixed rule with us, and was carried out to the letter, that three warm meals be served during the day, regardless of circumstances. I believe it was responsible for the health and vigor evidenced in our party through the trip to Dawson.

Our location now was about seven miles from the summit of White Pass and was called the First Bridge, no doubt a familiar phrase to those who traversed this trail. The following day [March 20] being Sunday (the observance of which was ignored), found one of our number sick and unable to leave the tent all day. So leaving him in camp, we started at an early hour for Porcupine Hill. When night came on, had made two round trips apiece with our two horses, moving twenty-four hundred pounds of freight, a result far beyond our expectations. This progress tended to raise our spirits, which the experience of the first few days had been the cause of lowering to a very low degree.

The following day [March 21] proved equally successful in moving the large outfit between the two points. Ed Green, who was ailing the day before, was today able to take his place on the trail, relieving our minds regarding his condition of yesterday. His illness had given us some worry, but proved of no consequence.

It is marvelous what a great difference is felt in the temperature in the short distance between the two points. Below Porcupine Hill the sun shone bright and warm, and caused us to discard a portion of our warm outer clothing, which had become uncomfortable to work in. On this side, our coats were a necessity of comfort. It is true that every step forward increased our elevation, which was partly responsible for the increased cold. As we neared the summit, the surrounding mountains rose to a greater height, and shut out the sun for the greater portion of the day.

The camp at the First Bridge was surrounded by some of the most beautiful scenery I ever looked upon. Being elected to remain in camp today to assume the role of chef, I had an opportunity of gazing upon our surrounding, which previously I had not time to do. The village of tents was hardly discoverable, so little contrast was there between them and the snow. It lay on the right hand bank of the Skagway River, which now was, of course, in the grasp of ice and snow of the now fast-disappearing winter. Later, upon being relieved of its icy embrace and contributed to by the hundreds of rivulets finding their way down the mountain-sides in spring, it would become a raging torrent.

The village of tents grew at a rapid rate after our arrival, and every day saw a number of new camps added to the already large settlement. Each day had seen many vacant sites, the occupants having moved their camps to the next relay camp some distance up the trail, after moving their outfits between Porcupine Hill and the First Bridge. This system of moving outfits was adopted by all, the cache and camp being separated from one another by a distance which the trip to and from could be made in a single day. After having safely cached all of the outfit at headquarters, the camp would be moved an equal distance beyond, and the same operation repeated as before. This operation necessitated the handling of the freight many times before reaching our destination.

The morning of March 17 saw Father on his way to Skagway to procure a few necessary articles, which we had forgotten in our haste. He also went to receive any mail which was there, as this would be the last opportunity at such close range, if not at all. He returned the following evening at a late hour, finding us all in bed, but the announcement of letters from home caused each to crawl from his warm blankets to read their contents. The reading of these, our first letters from home, had its effect. Each of us experienced a tender regard, the like we had not felt before for the loved ones so far away, a feeling we had tried hard to avoid since leaving them, knowing that many months would elapse before setting eyes on them again. After the belated ones had satisfied their hunger created by their long tramp during the day, we all retired to our blankets in a happier mood since striking the trail.

The following afternoon as we were nearing camp with the last load for the day, we were overtaken by a terrific snow storm, which actually shut out objects to view at a few feet distance. The storm continued far into the night, causing much inconvenience and discomfort to man and beast. The heat of our camp stove rising to the ceiling of our tent dissolved the heavy spring snow as fast as it fell, and caused little streams to penetrate the thick ducking. This melted snow drenched us as thoroughly as though we had spent the night on the outside. The next morning found us stiff and sore from our night's experience. We found the contents of our camp in a deplorable condition. Aside from these defects, we suffered little from the effects of the storm, and little time was lost in complaining of our sad plight. The fall of snow during the night had put the trail in fine condition and much was gained by it. Loads could be doubled and hauled with much more ease than the day before, and it was taken advantage of by all in camp. Night found many caches complete at this point.

Sunday, March 20th, found us still at the First Bridge, but with our enormous outfit complete and safely cached at this point, and upon seeing the enormous amount of freight together for the first time, we did not wonder that twelve days were consumed in moving it this far. One quarter of the distance to the lakes had been accomplished with a great amount of labor and with fair success. With dismay, we viewed the pile of goods to be moved in this same manner over the remaining distance of forty-five miles by means of unseen trails that were possibly far worse than any we had traversed. I am not quite sure but what discouragement was prevalent in camp that night. Determination and stick-to-it were our mantras, however. The hundred and one different mishaps that we had to contend with were at all times discouraging, and tried our patience to the limit. But we came to succeed and succeed we would, if our health remained good. It was not so with others.

After reaching this point, yes in many instances before reaching here, many of the gold-seekers would become tired, homesick or discouraged by the terrible condition of the trail already traversed. With the prospects not very bright for the remaining distance, they would stick a "For Sale" sign on their outfit, and sold it for about the same price which had been paid for it in Seattle. The first steamer from Skagway would find them aboard, bound for their homes, poorer but wiser in regard to the difficulties and hardships necessary to overcome in reaching the land of gold. This class of people was composed principally of those who had spent most of their lives at indoor, genteel occupations. They were not familiar with—nor had they constitutions strong enough to stand—the rough and strenuous life. But for all of that, there were among this class of men who had the true grit and determination, and it was wonderful the amount of hard work they could accomplish in a day, success rewarding them in the end.

Still another sort was in evidence on the trail, and he was the man financially able to have his outfit packed by contract to the source of the Yukon. Every day we were either met or passed by many pack trains, each composed of from six to twelve, or in some cases twenty, mules or horses marching in tandem style, each faithful animal grunting under his heavy load. In the rear would come the owner of the outfit, clad in his natty duck suit and leather leggings, either afoot or astride as his physical condition deemed necessary. This sort of man was unconscious of the true condition of the trail and its difficulties, no doubt treating it all as a holiday jaunt.

During the day we had occasion to meet one of the latter class as we presumed from all appearances. As the boys were returning from the hill during the forenoon, a well-dressed, pleasant-appearing young fellow approached Father. Stating that in some manner he had injured his back in the canyon below Porcupine, he asked Father to assist him and his small outfit consisting of two or three hundred pounds of provisions and horse to our camp. Thanking Father profusely upon him granting his request, they made a comfortable seat for him on his own sled, while one of the boys led the horse the entire distance to camp.

March 20. Had an extra man for dinner. He hurt his back in the Porcupine Canyon and our boys helped him to our camp, and I drove his mule to the White Pass Hotel and had fine luck. Left here at 1 p.m. and got there at 2:10 and he gave me $5.00 for it, enough for one hour's work.

My success as cook had been recognized and appreciated from the start, and today being Sunday, I had made a special effort in preparing an extra good bill of fare for dinner. Their arrival and bringing a stranger with them caused me no embarrassment to ask him to dine with us. My bill of fare was quite out of the ordinary, the famous bacon and beans not being in evidence. Instead, the first course of the meal was started by serving soup prepared from our stock of evaporated vegetables and adding the desired amount of water and seasoning. I fried bacon to a golden brown, and by adding water and flour to the grease, made a gravy that tickled the palate. The dessert coming last, but must not be considered least, consisted of baking powder biscuits of snowy whiteness spread with real butter and evaporated plum sauce, which went well together. Pie prepared from the sauce and fruit, along with a cup of delicious tea, concluded the meal. Now, friends, the preceding is not an effort on my part to impress nor solicit renown in the culinary or pastry art, but simply to show what can be done if desired on an ordinary camp stove, the pipe projecting through the roof of a wall tent. These varied meals were prepared often by us and broke the monotony of the proverbial bacon and bean meal and gave us a feeling of yet being civilized beings. [In his diary entry for the day, Will admitted, *I must put it down as my first attempt at cooking.*]

Dinner over, the boys proceeded to the hill after their last load, while I was to accompany our strange friend to White Pass Hotel, three miles distant, where he had concluded to remain until able to continue his journey unassisted. Seating himself once more upon his sled and myself leading his horse, which was a noble little animal, we started for the hotel. By using care, we arrived without a single mishap in one and one half hour afterward. I had taken a particular liking to this young fellow, whose manner, despite the pain he was suffering from his injury, was of a jolly, sunny disposition. He also was a man well bred and of unusual intelligence, which was plainly shown on his handsome, manly face. Little was said by him in referring to his home or mission in the north, more than to say that he hailed from Boston and that he came north to share in the search for the hidden treasure. His sincere appreciation for our act of kindness showed only too plainly on his face. After seeing him comfortably housed in the primitive hostelry, I left him. My return to camp was done in much less time, and I arrived in ample time to prepare the evening meal for the boys, who had not yet returned.

Monday morning, March 21, found the sleds loaded with great care, as Daugherty and Chamberlain were going to make an attempt to reach the summit during the day. The day had broken stormy and forbidding. Snow filled the air and was driven by a terrific, cold wind, which, despite our heavy clothing, chilled our bodies to the very bone. We all had our doubts about the boys reaching the summit in such a storm, but they were determined to make the attempt. With a joking reply to our parting advice, they were off soon, and disappeared in the blinding snow storm.

Noon found them again in camp, it being utterly impossible to gain the summit in the storm that grew worse as they made the ascent. Instead of hauling their load back to camp they had, upon investigation, made a cache at a point on the trail called Third Bridge. There were three of these bridges crossing the Skagway River. They were distinguished points for the fact that at each were located relay camps of the travelers. Meeting a friend or acquaintance on the trail, you or he would inquire where yours or his camp was located. The answer would be at the first, second or third bridge, as the case happened to be. The answer was as intelligible to one another as the same instance applied to a street in a city known to both.

March 21. I am cooking again. Keeps me busy, makes me homesick to stay alone, but have Skookum dog with me today, so am not entirely alone.

The remainder of the day and all of Tuesday [March 22] was spent in moving the balance of our outfit to the new cache at Third Bridge, a place that gave us a greater advantage. From this point, two round trips to the summit could easily be made in one day, the distance being several miles less than at the former camp.

March 22. Am cook, guess they are stuck on my grub, for they keep me at it and is very tiresome and a lonesome job, but is nice for a change from the hard work on the Trail. The boys are taking two loads to the Summit and succeeded this time. Experienced a terrible snow storm coming back. This the first trip to the summit, but had good luck otherwise. Made a try to the Third Bridge Cache this afternoon, got in at 5 p.m. Have expected mail all day today, but were disappointed. The mail man did not come.

On Wednesday morning, March 23, we rolled out of our warm blankets at four a.m. During the night, the thermometer had taken a decided drop. Upon arising, we noted that it registered fifteen degrees below zero, the coldest weather by far that we had experienced while on the trail. The occasion of the unusual hour in rising was for the purpose of attempting to reach the summit if possible. The failure of a few days previous was still fresh in our memory and had a tendency to place us in doubt as to the successful outcome of this, our second attempt. The weather outlook boded us no good, and the snow filled the frosty air, driven by a brisk wind from the north.

After a hearty breakfast of flapjacks and bacon with delicious coffee, we felt more fitted to the arduous task before us, and at once began preparations for the final climb. The sleds were loaded, and the goods securely tied and strapped to them to prevent any delay by their coming loose on the rough trail. Extra outer clothing was donned, which was gladly appreciated before the round trip was accomplished. Six o'clock saw us leaving camp with Daugherty and Chamberlain acting as teamsters. I brought up the rear and filled the capacity of escort.

The trail leading to the foot of the summit was found to be in fine condition made so by the fresh snow which had fallen during the past few days. The sleds, as they easily slid over its well-packed surface, emitted a squeaking sound, which indicated the low temperature otherwise very much in evidence. With the exception of one or two sharp inclines, Porcupine Hill in particular, one does not notice or realize the latitude [sic] attained on the Skagway trail, the ascent is so gradual. But from our latter camping place to the Ford, a well-know locality at the foot of the White Pass, the climb is quite noticeable. Several hundred feet are attained in traversing the three miles, this being the distance between the two points.

A few words in reference to the Ford might not be out of the way, if not uninteresting. It received its name during the rush the previous autumn, and was a point on the summer trail where the Skagway River was crossed on stepping stones by man and beast. Here many of the faithful animals perished in doing so. Now the snow covered their dead bodies to a great depth: in fact, there was little indication of the river bed, the snow filling it to a level with its banks. The Ford became quite a prominent point during the spring rush, it being the last camp this side of the summit. It became a relay camp for those who wished to discard a part of the goods on their overloaded sleighs before starting this, their final and steep climb. A hotel and feed stable of a primitive sort was also located here, and was well patronized by the thousands of hungry travelers passing its doors.

It was still early morning when we reached the Ford. As our sled was not overloaded—a point we considered before leaving camp—we did not stop, but pushed on to the foot of the steep incline a third of a mile beyond. Here the trail narrowed to a width that, in some places, was barely possible for the narrow sleds to pass one another. At other places, it was utterly impossible to pass without placing oneself in danger of being precipitated to the bottom of the canyon far below. The narrow trail winds itself in and out along the mountainside, each step increasing the elevation. The climb continues until the summit is reached, a distance of one and one third miles. The explorer, Mr. Ogilvie, claimed that the elevation gained nine hundred feet over that distance.

The storm that was in progress in the early morning grew worse as we slowly made our way up the steep incline. When we reached the narrow gorge on top, it struck us with full force. It had developed into a blizzard, the like we had never experienced before. The raw north wind filled with snow and particles of ice caused us much discomfort as it came in contact with our faces, and caused them to sting with pain. As a result, we pulled our fur caps over that part of our anatomy, leaving the eye holes as the only openings to the raging storm.

After traversing the canyon for perhaps one half mile, we came out upon a broad expanse of snowy waste. Not far beyond could be seen the British flag waving in the stiff breeze from the top of its flagstaff. Here was located the Canadian Custom officers and quarters. It was necessary for all parties to cache their entire outfits at this point to await the examination and a levy of duty by those officials before proceeding on their journey. Six hours had been considered in making the trip owing to the terrible storm and unfamiliarity of the trail. Otherwise, we were fortunate and felt encouraged as we made a cache of the contents of our two loaded sleds.

The sight that met our gaze here will probably never be seen again on a singular occasion. On both sides of the trail and extending about a quarter of mile each way from the Custom office, outfits of the thousands of gold-seekers were snugly piled, separated from one another by only a few inches. Some were awaiting the action of the Custom officials, while others were reloading their sleds and descending to the lakes far below. Many, as in our case, were just making their first trip to the summit with hundreds more to follow. Notwithstanding the blizzard weather, the camp presented a scene of activity. The corps of custom officers detailed by the British Government to collect duties on all foreign purchased goods was kept very busy at their task. At any time of day, dressed in their close-fitting duck uniforms, they could be seen flitting here and there examining outfits.

After caching our two loads of goods in a locality some little distance south of the flag and seeing that it was protected from the storm, we turned our horses back toward camp. Great difficulty was encountered in descending the narrow portion of the trail, it being one solid mass of moving horseflesh and freight from top to bottom. Our descent was made by small degrees on account of the infrequent places of allowing two sleds to pass one another. We finally reached the bottom, and the wide trail from there to camp allowed the horses to make good time in covering the remaining distance. We arrived at camp at one thirty p.m., the descent being made in one third of the time it required to ascend.

The week that followed [March 24–29] was full of hard work, and each day saw the large pile of food grow smaller as two to three round trips to the summit cache were made daily, despite weather conditions. The cold spell continued throughout the week, and on the summit the morning of the twenty fifth, the thermometer registered twenty-five degrees below zero, this being the coldest weather encountered on our seven months' sojourn in the northern country. Good fortune attended us the entire week, and aside from the hard work and some hardships, little transpired to break the monotony.

Will's diary entries during this week detail the trips from the Ford to the Summit and are notable only for their repetition of weather conditions. Only two incidents stand out above the others, which he neglected to mention in his memoir.

3rd Bridge, Skaguay Trail, March 26. Made three trips over the summit today. Weather moderate on Top today, little snow. Very cold though tonight in camp. Mr. Green returned from Skaguay with lots of mail. I got two from my little Wife. Green got one and Daugherty one. Haven't got any from home yet. Don't know what to think of it. Makes me homesick to get letters from little Wife. Will have company tonight, a friend of Green's will stay all night. Is going to the summit, won't be back to our camp until 10 p.m. Green stayed with him last night.

3rd Bridge, Skaguay Trail, March 28. Made two trips to Summit again today. I drove the little mare all day today. Had good luck. Bill and Malen cook and char boy. Moved the last of our provisions to the summit. The horse feed and camp outfit is all that remains here now. Was coming down the trail from the summit when somebody caught me around the neck and hugged me like a bear and when I managed to squirm away from him, Ollie Jones [see Oliver Jones in Biographies] *stood before me. I never was so surprised in all my life to see him here. He was freighting over the Summit from Skagway with his brother-in-law, Lee Loomis* [see Biographies]. *Gave me two letters, one from Blanche and one from Will G. Did not have time to talk with him, but he will be on the trail all the time.*

At noon on the twenty-ninth of March, the boys returned from the summit for the last time, having taken, with the exception of the camp, the last of the outfit on the two sleds during the forenoon. They had decided that the start to our new camping ground would be made at an early hour the following morning. High spirits prevailed in camp, gladness showing on each one's face in the thought that today ended the labor on the most difficult end of the trail, and we planned on spending the reminder of the day in a way we had not dared to since leaving Skagway. Each one was in perfect health, the exhilarating mountain air and out-of-door life having added flesh and an appearance of ruggedness, which with our four weeks growth of beard, few of our friends would have recognized us.

On board the S.S. *Cleveland* from Seattle was a minister of the Gospel, accompanied by his wife and aged mother, a woman of perhaps sixty-five years of age, bound for the Klondike, Rev. Howe [William M. Howie, see Biographies] by name, made his introduction by preaching a sermon the Sunday we were aboard, which was appreciated and enjoyed by all. He was a medium-sized man of a vigorous makeup and the patience and perseverance shown in overcoming the trials and stumbling blocks, which so often presented themselves on the trail made him a prominent figure. I speak of this man and family for the reason that we had made their acquaintance on board the S.S. *Cleveland* and later on had met him on the trail each day as we plied to and from, and it appeared that whichever trail we chose they were sure to follow us. They were intellectual and interesting and of a kindly nature, which made them many friends and many little favors were shown them along the trail.

The day of which I speak, one of our boys had discovered their camp in our locality, they having just arrived with their camp equipage, their outfit having been hauled to this point the day before. During a conversation which he and Chamberlain had entered into, it was quite evident that the man was well nigh discouraged, and well he might be. Handicapped as he was by wife and aged mother and a twelve hundred pound outfit to be sledded by his own strength over the steep mountain pass now directly ahead was enough to discourage a stronger heart. But he was loyal to the task he had set about, and without rest was going to push ahead as best he could.

Our afternoon of recreation was to be put in paying the assessed duty on our goods at the Custom House on White Pass. We had intended to give our little ponies a needed rest this afternoon and make the ascent on foot. But when Chamberlain returned from Mr. Howe's camp and explained what he had discovered, a desire to help the man was unanimously voted and carried. So hooking the ponies to the sleds once more, we drove down to their camp and, to their amazement, began loading their outfit. His pleasure knew no bounds when informed of our intentions, and during the entire procedure, he proclaimed his heartfelt thanks for our kind act. We were soon on our way, the entire outfit (with the exception of the camp) on our two sleds, and three hours afterward it was safely cached on top of the mountain. A more thankful and happy man than Mr. Howe could not have been found on the Skagway trail that day.

Some little trouble was experienced in getting Custom Officers to examine our goods but owing to the great number of applicants ahead of us, we were detained until nearly darkness. With our duty paid and the clearance papers in our packets, we returned to camp satisfied the most difficult section of the trail was behind us. That assumption soon proved to be untrue.

Canadian Duties

Kathryn Winslow, in her book about adventurer Howard V. Sutherland's trip to the Klondike, described the Canadian duties in detail. She stated that, ordinarily, they averaged about twenty-five percent of the value of the goods being taken into the country. The duty was levied on all provisions, clothing, hardware, tools, mining equipment, dogs, horses, and cattle. Sometimes items were taxed by the pound, sometimes by a percentage of the original, "new-goods" cost, and sometimes a combination of the two. The table below presents some of her examples of how the duty varied by type of item.[12]

Table 1. Duties assessed by Canadian Customs in 1898, as described by Winslow, *Big Pan-Out*, 79.

item	measure	percent levied	additional duty
lard	pound		$0.02
butter	pound		$0.04
baking powder	pound		$0.06
sugar	pound		$1.00
canvas bags and sacks		20	
dogs		20	
firearms		20	
grains, flours, meals		20	
horses		20	
maps and charts		20	
bacon		25	
tinned meats		25	
candles		28	
ammunition		30	
edged tools		35	
hardware		35	
sweaters and knitted goods		35	
tobacco pipes		35	
Union suits		35	
tobacco	pound	12.5	$0.42
wool blankets	pound	25	$0.05
socks	dozen pairs	25	$0.10
cigars and cigarettes	pound	26	$2.00

March 29. The boys all went up to pay the duties on goods. Came to $160.00 in all. Gave them [the customs officials] *a tip of $5.00 and they put them* [the goods] *through for that, where it would have cost them* [the boys] *$450.*

We broke camp at an early hour the next morning [March 30], each horse hauling light loads, which were to be added to upon reaching our cache on the Summit. The morning was grand, not unlike one of those beautiful winter mornings so common in the eastern states. It was very clear and cold, and as we breathed the pure, invigorating mountain air, it seemed to give us new life and vigor. The sun came out and its rays, as they struck the surrounding snow-covered cliffs and hills, made them appear studded with diamonds, so brightly did the particles of ice sparkle.

Reaching the cache on the summit toward the noon hour, we loaded our sleds to their capacity, and without stopping to lunch, we slipped down the trail leading to Summit Lake, a small lake lying at the foot of the mountain slope. Summit Lake was the first of a chain of lakes each being connected by short portages, the waters of which finally went to make up the great Yukon River: therefore Summit Lake is the source of that great river.[13] The lake was soon reached, and its six miles of snow-covered surface was traversed in little less than an hour, which brought us to a canyon connecting Summit with Middle lakes. This canyon or gorge is about one and one half miles in length, which in the summer or open season is no doubt full of rapids and cascades impossible for craft of all kinds. At this time, it was frozen and filled with snow. Here and there the jagged rocks showed themselves above the surface, causing us no little amount of hard labor and trouble. This mile and half of trail proved to be in a more deplorable condition that any we had yet passed over.

The afternoon had ushered in a most disagreeable, nasty snow storm, and had it been rain, could not have drenched us more thoroughly than it did. The trail not being in a smooth condition due to the rocky formation on which the snow had long since disappeared on account of the excessive travel, our sleds were several times overturned. It therefore became necessary to unload and reload every article before going farther. This required much time and patience, and the good humor in evidence the night before was entirely absent as we wiggled our way through this hell-hole. We finally emerged from the narrow, contracted passage to a valley that widened as we progressed. The trail here was quite passable and grew better as we neared Middle Lake.

About halfway between the two lakes, a road house had been established to accommodate the many tired and hungry travelers passing this point. Rescue Camp was the name applied to the road house, a very suggestive name, but in what manner it was acquired, I was unable to learn. It was nearly four o'clock when we reached here, and not having eaten a mouthful since early morning, we were more than glad of an opportunity to procure any part of a lunch. As it was necessary to leave the poor horses in the storm, our lunch was meager, composed of a piece of pie accompanied by a cup of steaming hot coffee, the effect of which was wonderful to our bedraggled condition.

Soon after leaving Rescue Camp, we came upon the large snowy expanse of Middle Lake. Due to the splendid road, it was crossed in a little less than an hour. At the lower end of this lake, a short portage connects it with the next, namely Shallow Lake. Some little trouble was experienced here, but the distance being short, it was soon overcome, and left behind. A stretch of four miles of splendid sledding lay before us, this being the distance traversed on the latter lake. The chain of lakes we had traversed during the greater part of the day lay in a valley varying from one to four miles in width, running a little northeast to southwest. Away to the west lay the high, snow-covered mountains forming the Chilkoot Pass, while to the east they were not so precipitous an altitude. Far above us to the east lay the horrible summer trail which in the previous autumn had, with the aid of man, been the cause of the destruction of hundreds of faithful animals.[14] In the valley below lay extensive meadows of luxuriant grass, which thrive during the summer months, affording grazing in abundance for those inclined to use them. Very little timber is in evidence and the majority of the entire valley is a barren, rocky waste, and for summer travel is quite impractical.

After traversing the entire length of Shallow Lake, the trail follows a hog back resembling very much an old railroad bed. After nearly a mile, a steep grade puts in its appearance, which is necessary to climb before reaching our next relay camp. After the hard long tramp of the day, it seemed cruel to force our faithful little ponies to pull their heavy loads up the steep incline, but it was, after many resting spells, accomplished. The next and most important move was to find a suitable locality to pitch our camp. This was easier said than done, as it was eight o'clock, darkness having set in more than an hour before, and the starlit sky affording us the only light with which to search.

Fortune finally favored us in our search, and much to our satisfaction a spot close to the trail was discovered that had been vacated by a party but a short time before. This good fortune saved us much time and labor, as the snow lay to a depth of from four to five feet, all of which needed to be removed from a space large enough to set our tents. The cleared space from the former occupant's tent was of the same dimensions as our own, and after the erection of our tent, little space remained between its walls and the snow banks, which served as an admirable protection from the cold winds. Notwithstanding the fact that all this saved us much time, it was 9:30 when our horses had been sheltered and cared for, and our own appetites satisfied. So far this had been the most strenuous day experienced while on the trail. Twenty-one miles had been travelled in a nasty, wet snow storm, which had drenched our clothing to our very skins, causing us much discomfort therefrom.

However, we were becoming more accustomed to the discomforts and hardship, which were necessary to cope with. After the evening meal was eaten, we rolled into our blankets, giving little thought to our wet clothing in our fatigued condition, and were soon lost to conscientiousness [sic] in a sound and refreshing sleep lasting until four o'clock the following morning [March 31].

Log Cabin, as the locality was commonly called, was located on the Skagway trail, sixteen miles north of the summit of White Pass. The name had been derived from the fact that a lonely log cabin stood here in the wilderness serving as a road house and traders' headquarters, the former for the convenience of the few prospectors that penetrated this region before the discovery of the Klondike, the latter was done with the Indians. During the previous autumn, the name was applied to the locality by the gold-seekers and many outfits were stowed here, the owners returning to their homes to wait until spring. The British government established a Post Office here in 1900 and continued to call it Log Cabin, which name it carries to this day.[15]

During the winter, a number of cabins were built, and at the time of which I speak, there were at least one dozen, large, substantial structures of this sort. Several were occupied as mercantile houses and outfitters, and anything from a hairpin to a steam engine could be purchased if so desired. A number of buildings bore the sign "hotel" or "meals and lodging," each one having in connection a stable for the shelter of their patron's stock. The British government had, for the protection of the public and to keep a watchful eye out for her affairs in general, established a Mounted Police Station. The officers were comfortably housed in one of the largest structures.

Log Cabin had the distinction of being the most important camp between Skagway and Lake Bennett, and few who chose this trail did not make a camp here or in the near vicinity. It was here where the Too Chi Trail branched, keeping the northeastern course to Too Chi Lake, thence to Windy Arm, a large bay or inlet of Lake Tagish, while the Skagway trail made a sharp turn to the left, which continued in a westerly direction, converging with the Dyea trail at Lake Bennett. A majority of the people were continuing on the Skagway Trail to Lake Bennett, while a number were taking their chance on the Too Chi trail, regardless of the warning posted by the Custom Officer at Tagish Post regarding the almost impassible condition of the route.

This latter trail was taken on account of the extremely crowded conditions at the Lake Bennett Camp, and reports received from there were to the effect that little timber remained suitable for boat building purposes, a report if true put a serious outlook to the late-comer. Regarding our choice, we were quite undecided at first and concluded to take it under advisement until the time came for us to make our next move.

After our long and hard day's work of yesterday, the morning [April 1] found us up at four a.m., and after a hearty breakfast was eaten, we left for the summit. Green and Chamberlain took one horse, while Daugherty and myself managed the other. The frosty night had made the trail hard and slippery, and good time was made to the summit. The return trip was but a repetition of the day before, the principle trouble and delay being met with in the canyons, their condition being more deplorable than the day before. Thirteen hours was required to make the thirty-two miles in the round trip. At seven p.m., we drove into camp with our three thousand pounds of goods intact, realizing in our wet, tired and hungry condition that a strong constitution combined with patience was required to continue in this manner.

The day that followed [April 2] was more successful, and thirty-five hundred pounds of goods were added to our Log Cabin cache that night, dispelling to a certain extent the discouragement created the day before. Green was taken suddenly ill during the evening, complaining of cramps in the stomach, which were not relieved until 12:30 a.m. the following morning, making it impossible for one of us to get any sleep before that hour. This was responsible for a late start to the summit, it being seven a.m. before we began the long journey.

The long morning ride of sixteen miles to the summit was quickly accomplished, seldom ever taking more than three hours. On the long, level stretches of the lakes, we would comfortably seat ourselves on the sleds, and starting our little ponies on an easy trot that continued until reaching the canyons, where we would walk the treacherous, worn-out trail. The cool, refreshing, morning air infused us with renewed life and hope, and in spite of difficulties and hard labor attached to the return trip, we enjoyed it immensely. It will ever be remembered by me as one of the very few pleasures granted us on the Skagway trail.

This particular morning was unusually cold and frosty. The sled runners emitted a squeaking sound as they flew over the frozen trail, and the ponies needed little persuasion in keeping a good gait in their efforts to keep warm. As for ourselves, we took turns in riding while the others kept up a healthy circulation by running behind the sled. As the forenoon advanced, the weather moderated surprisingly, and when we reached our cache at the summit, it gave every evidence of a coming snow storm. The sleds were quickly but securely loaded, and at 11:30 a.m., we turned our backs on the summit and made our way down the easy incline to Summit Lake.

Here the gathering storm burst forth in all its fury. Objects were visible from but a short distance, so full was the air with snow. Added to this discomfort, a strong breeze from the north came sweeping up the valley, the force of which we caught square in the face, causing us no little inconvenience in our progress. As the old proverb goes, "it never rains but what it pours," was today in our opinion proven quite true, for as we entered the canyon from Summit Lake, our sled under its heavy load had spread its runner, making it necessary for us to unload. This was done, and repairing the sled as best we could, one half of the goods were reloaded while the remainder was cached on the spot to be picked up at some future time. It was thought the division we had made could be hauled on the disabled sled, and after a cold lunch of bread and beans were eaten, we proceeded on our way, and under the circumstances were fairly successful.

The snow continued to fall and before reaching the incline leading to our camp darkness set in making it very difficult to proceed farther with our loads. So unhooking the tired little ponies from the sleds we made for camp in the most deplorable condition we had yet experienced, wondering the while if any reward could be just for the hardships that were necessary to undergo.

In view of the fact that the day had been an unusually hard one, we voted unanimously in making the following day [April 3], which would be Sunday, a day of rest, much needed by man and horse. So accordingly, our former prolonged Sunday morning sleep was indulged in, it being close to midday before we became conscious of our surrounds once more. After the breakfast was prepared and eaten, the remainder of the day was spent in overhauling sleds and repairing them. After a month's hard usage, our clothing began to show the effect and necessarily needed patching and mending, which was done in a clumsy, awkward fashion, but was finally accomplished to our satisfaction. This done, pencils and paper were put to use and long letters by each of us were written to the dear ones at home.

The days that followed were much the same, full of hard work and long hours. The frequent snow-falls had been a godsend, and good fortune favored us in moving our large outfits over its surface, and on the evening of April 6 found our entire stock of goods cached at our camp at Log Cabin.

[Typical diary entries of those days included the following:]

Log Cabin, Skaguay Trail, April 2. Started for Summit again this morning at 7 o'clock a little late on account of being up last night faced another storm coming from the south. Snow falling fast and thick. Put on 3000#

at the caches at Summit and got started back at 11:30. Got as far as the canyon, ate our cold lunch of bread and beans and started through the Hell Hole. Just got started and broke a sled, so had to drop half of our loads. Took us 2½ hours to get through. Stopped at Rescue Camp and got a cup of coffee and proceeded on our way again. Had good luck until we got to the grade that leads to the Log Cabin and left the rest of our loads on account of darkness.

Log Cabin, Skaguay Trail, April 3. Today is Sunday and laid abed until 9:30 this morning, the first day all of us have taken a day's rest together since we left Skaguay four weeks ago. A terrible storm is raging today. The snow falling fast and thick, and wind blowing a gale. The road will be good tomorrow or I am a liar. Went down and got our loads this afternoon that we left below, and roads are good already. Had good luck with them. Wrote a letter to my dear little Wife, after we got back, the best pastime I could indulge in.

Log Cabin, Skaguay Trail, April 4. Made a trip to summit and back today got in early, had fine luck all day, I drove the little mare today. Malen, Bill and Father were attacked !Farts – with snowblind [sic] but Bill recovered, but Father and Malen laid up today, could not make the trip, so I drove the little mare and Green and Bill, the Horse with two sleds. The Canyon was all right. Came through in 1/2 hour. Am too tired these nights to write much. Am working too hard.

And none too soon. The last trip showed plainly the effect the warm sun had made on the snow, and in many places the lake had become overblown from the thaw that had set in. It was quite evident that many difficulties were in store for those following, and many gave voice to the effect that the trail over the lakes would not last another week, and if so, would prove disastrous beyond comparison to those concerned.

> The term "overblown" is common in areas where lakes melt and then freeze again. As the ice melts, the wind will blow and move the broken slabs of ice. These slabs can become tilted, which creates a rough surface. In addition, snow blowing in from the neighboring shores will fill in cracks between the slabs, and weak spots in the ice cannot be seen. This "overblown" condition makes for almost impossible travel on the lakes.

During the week, snow blindness had struck the camp by storm, confining many men to their tents on account of it. The epidemic claimed Father, Daugherty, and Chamberlain as victims, and they were unable to leave camp all of one day. Thereafter, a precaution was taken by the use of colored goggles, which was a relief, and no trouble from this cause was again experienced on the trip.

Our goods safely cached here, a serious problem was at once to be solved. Which trail was to be chosen in continuing our journey to the head of navigation? The Lake Bennett trail would be closer by many miles, but report had come during the week that little timber remained close to the lake, it being necessary to go miles to secure suitable timber. Doing so would take up much of our valuable time and cause a great amount of labor. The immense crowd that had congregated there had swept the sparse forest before them in their frantic rush for boat material. On the other hand, as had been stated, the Too Schi Trail was in a deplorable and dangerous condition. While many parties had encountered a great amount of trouble in reaching Windy Arm, they were reported as having done so in safety.

During the week we had thoroughly considered both propositions from a practical standpoint, basing our choice on the most favorable reports gathered from those who each day were coming in contact with the two trails. It was finally decided that the most favorable reports came from the Too Schi trail, despite the fact that it was doubly as long. Therefore the trail to Windy Arm was chosen without a dissenting voice among our party, and preparations were at once made to make an early start the next morning.

Violence on the Trails and in Skagway in 1898

The murder of Peter Clancy Bean late on the night of March 7, 1898, was reported in several newspapers on the West Coast and throughout the Western mining country. Bean (whose name sometimes appeared as Beane) had left Skagway on the morning of March 7 pulling four hundred pounds of goods on a sled. He cached these goods at the base of Porcupine Hill, ate his dinner, and then left for Skagway at eight p.m., even though the weather had turned bad and he was advised not to go back. He wanted to get an early start from Skagway with his next load on the morning of March 8. About an hour later, one mile from Porcupine Hill, and six miles from Skagway, his still-warm body was found lying in a pool of blood on the frozen surface of the Skagway River. He had been shot twice, once in the left breast and the other grazing his face, which was covered with powder burns. His open pocketbook was found near his body, suggesting robbery as the motive for the murder.[16]

The packer who found him took his body to the camp at Porcupine Hill, where someone then went into Skagway to report the murder. U.S. Deputy Marshal H. D. McInness went to Porcupine Hill the next morning to investigate the crime. The deputy found $400 and a draft for $300 on a Seattle bank in his money belt, $33.70 in cash in an inner pocket, and a miner's license obtained in Victoria. According to David Faulkner, a passenger on the steamship *Rosalie*, no shots had been heard during the night (he obviously did not know that Frank Purdy and his party had heard the shots).

While Faulkner opined, "They [the robbers] are probably from the ranks of hundreds of desperate men who hang around Skagway's dens of vice," the local authorities concluded that he had not been targeted, but was simply at the wrong place at the wrong time. Bean had been in Skagway for a few days and he had been very careful not to show any of his money.

It was common for the West Coast newspapers to inflate the dangers of the Skagway and Dyea Trails in order to encourage stampeders to buy their outfits before they left for the Klondike. Port cities like Skagway and Dyea usually offered competitive prices for goods and eliminated the complexity and cost of shipping. To offset those advantages, merchants in coastal cities exaggerated the rough frontier conditions in Alaska so that travelers would instead spend their time acquiring supplies in "safe" and "civilized" urban centers. Newspapers in Seattle, Tacoma, Portland, San Francisco, and Victoria uniformly seized on the murder of Bean as an example of supposed lawlessness in Skagway and on the trails, and the following days were filled with examples of imagined crimes. In Skagway, a drunken man was found dead, having fallen from a wharf. The Seattle newspaper blamed this death on thieves, although other newspapers later reported it as an accident. The Victoria newspaper stated that more than twelve people had been robbed and killed on the trail the week of the incident, events of which Will and other diarists at the time make no mention.

It was actually the robbery of Alexander McLean, "a prominent resident," on the streets of Skagway on Sunday, March 6, that stimulated retaliatory measures by that city's "respectable element." On March 8, they issued "notices warning all concerned that all gambling rooms, 'flimsy' and 'sure-thing' games in the city or on the trail, must close, and all objectionable characters leave by four o'clock the same day." The disreputable element was largely curtailed for the next couple of months, despite legends that arose in later decades of con artist and crime boss Soapy Smith becoming "King of Skagway."[17]

If the extent of violence was purely speculative on the part of newspapers far removed from Skagway and the trail, both travelers and citizens took it upon themselves to curb future criminal activity. In that light, Will's comments on the shooting of Peter Clancy Bean reflect the general feeling that such violence, if continued, would result in vigilante actions to bring it to a halt. In fact, stampeders on the Chilkoot Trail, in January, had publicly whipped a man for stealing from another man's cache, and obviously the general sentiment was that travelers to the Klondike could and would not tolerate such lawlessness.

Chapter Three

THE TUTSHI TRAIL
APRIL 7–APRIL 22, 1898

✦⊱━⊰✦

So UPON THE FOLLOWING MORNING [April 7] we were astir at an early hour. All hands with the exception of myself were to accompany the initial trip over the unknown chosen trail. It was, much to my chagrin and disappointment, my turn to assume the role of cook and make myself useful in general around the camp for the day. The start was made at the break of dawn, for past experiences had taught us that we needed all the daylight allotted us in meeting the many difficulties and drawbacks that were continually met with, and especially over an unknown trail. The sleds were not heavily loaded as it was thought wiser to make an inspection of the trail before taking unnecessary chances in losing or injuring the provisions we had toiled so hard to get this far.

As the others filed down the trail and were lost to view among the thick timber, a sense of lonesomeness took possession of me in a way that I had not felt before. A realization of the undertaking we had gone forth to accomplish seemed to present itself to me in a different light than I had looked upon it before. Facing the perils and hardships of an unknown country, sacrificing the comforts of a civilized home, which now seemed so far away, were the thoughts that during the day were forced upon me. And all for the greed of gold! My mind lingered on the latter. All the thousands going in search of the glittering metal would not be successful. Some would, and return to their homes blessed with the comforts that their well-deserved fortunes would buy them; but the great majority would return broken in health and wealth, a great many having sunk their last dollar in an outfit in their gamble for gold.

This train of thought that occupied my mind was only relieved by the return of the boys at 5:30 p.m., they having made the round trip of ten miles in twelve and one half hours. The trip had been successful, but their account of the condition of the trail was discouraging in the extreme. Their reports were that as bad as the already traveled trails had been, there was no comparison in the deplorable condition this one presented to them. No turning back now was the word. We had made our bed, and we must sleep in it.

The following day, Father remained in camp, which gave me an opportunity to accompany the boys on the second trip. The morning was chilly and the ponies hauled the well-loaded sleds over the frozen trail with little effort, but this state of the trail was confined to the first few hours of the morning. After nine o'clock, under the bright rays of the sun, the snow would soften and become a slushy path of mud and water covering the runners of our sleds and, at times, reaching nearly to the beams.

After leaving Log Cabin, the trail leads through a thickly wooded and level country. It continues about three miles where we encountered a grade of great proportions, which was necessary to descend to reach the Tut Shi River bed. This grade caused us no little amount of trouble and labor in descending, it being so steep and slippery that it was necessary to provide means to keep the loaded sleds from crashing into the heels of our ponies. To prevent such a mishap, the "snubbing" process was adopted, an action that proved successful. However, on two or three occasions, a sled, going at a good speed, veered to the side of the road. In doing so, it overturned its contents, which went flying in every direction.

To make the snubbing process clear to those who are not familiar with the word, I will say it is accomplished by the use of a long rope. One end is fastened to the rear end of the sled, while the remainder is passed in a half hitch around a nearby tree. A man stationed at the tree pays out the rope as the sled descends the grade. At will, he could bring horse and sled to an abrupt halt with little effort on his part. When the rope had run to its full length, the process was repeated until the level ground was reached. Imagine the time that was necessarily spent in this procedure each day, even if all went well. Caution was to be taken in every descent, or as before mentioned, over would go a sled, causing a loss or injury to provisions, the cases or cans bursting as they came in contact with the rocky surroundings. Many horses here were crippled so as to be of no use, by a rope parting. Carelessness on the part of the man at the snubbing post could be responsible for an uncontrolled sled crashing with great force into a horse, causing serious results, and in some instances broken legs.

I recall an instance where a party with a hand sled heavily loaded with an outfit attempted the descent without using the snubbing post. His attempt proved disastrous. All went well for a time, but as he came to an unusually steep grade, he lost all control of his sled. Instead of turning to one side, which would have stopped the progress of the flying sled, he kept straight on, for what reason he could not explain when asked. The sled gained speed at every step, and we stood spell-bound, expecting every moment to see him fall and the sled pass over his body. He did fall, and as he did so, the sled struck a chuck hole, changing its course. Like a flash, it darted into a tree standing alongside the trail, and for a few seconds, flour, beans, baking powder, and bacon filled the air.

The poor fellow had luckily fallen into the soft snow off the trail. As he picked himself up and viewed the remains of the once complete outfit, an expression of grief overspread his countenance, pitiful to behold. Here he was, as he explained, after days and weeks of toil from early morn till late at night, with an outfit depleted one half, and which had taken his last dollar to purchase. This was only one instance among a thousand of the heartrending scenes enacted on the trails of the gold-seekers, but its effect impressed me stronger than any I witnessed.

All hands assisted him in collecting the remains of his outfit. As his sled had been demolished, a cache of the goods were made on the spot. He was of the never-give-up sort, and at once set about repairing his sled. Every day thereafter, he could be seen toiling on toward Windy Arm, which he reached as soon as we did. The last seen of him was on the streets of Dawson City, the owner of a claim which bid fair to net him a snug little fortune.

After descending the "Big Hill" (as it was commonly called), the trail followed the frozen Tut Schi River its remaining distance to the lake of the same name. Here the supplies were cached and a return to Log Cabin was made. Over good roads, the round trip of twenty miles could have easily been made in one half day, but under existing circumstances took from twelve to sixteen hours. Many nights, camp was not reached until nine or ten o'clock in a condition more dead than alive. The trails already traversed had been in a horrible condition, but my first trip over the Tut Schi trail caused me to look back on these as bicycle paths in comparison with this almost impassible trail. I have since wondered at our success in reaching Windy Arm over this trail.

On the following day, April 9th, we got an early start with sleds well loaded. Chamberlain and Daugherty drove the ponies while Green and myself put in the entire day filling chuck holes and mending the road in many other ways necessary before it became passable. Many others volunteered their services in this manner and by doing so much time and trouble was saved. For instance when a heavily-loaded sled came to one of these indentations on the trail, it would plunge with great force against the opposite side, dislodging the outfit on a well-loaded sled and necessitating an overhauling and reloading. On more than one occasion, a sled became utterly demolished by coming in contact with these holes. It therefore became necessary to fill the holes with new snow, a measure which answered the purpose for a time. The constant heavy travel made it necessary to repeat this process each day, but as before stated, we saved much time and labor by it.

Green and I busied ourselves until darkness set in, when we became concerned in the non-appearance of Chamberlain and Daugherty on their return trip from the lake. If trouble had not overtaken them, the three hours they were gone would have brought them back to where we were at work. Something must have happened to delay them, and no doubt our assistance was needed. So acting on this surmise, we set out down the trail toward the lake guided by the moon, which was shining full and bright, casting shadows from the nearby timber across our path.

We must have walked about three miles, when to our right an army of men were seen repairing a bridge which spanned the river. It had been a rude affair, but served the purpose very well. Three logs served as stringers, while smaller timbers were laid crosswise making a crossing of the corduroy sort. The river's course here cut its way between high banks, therefore making it necessary to cross on a bridge in order to save a couple of miles of travel. It was a mile down the river before a level crossing could have been made. The warm spring day had played havoc with the rude, temporary crossing. The ends of the logs had rested on the snow and frozen ground at either bank, but due to the warm day the bearings had become softened. The stringers had dislodged, and the entire structure had slid to the snowy surface of the river below. New logs of greater length had to be cut, and the tired and hungry men, anxious to get to camp, had fallen to with a will. As we arrived, the new crossing was nearing completion.

We were informed upon our arrival that, fortunately, no one was injured in the collapse of the bridge, which had occurred three hours before. A party had barely escaped by reaching terra firma not a moment too soon, no doubt saving himself and horse broken limbs or a more serious injury. Soon after our arrival, the crossing was completed, and all haste was made toward camp, which was reached at ten p.m., man and horse nearly ready to drop from fatigue and hunger.

The next day [April 10] was filled with mishaps and disappointment, and the boys were unable to reach the lake with their loads, but were compelled to cache their goods three miles from there. The trail was becoming terrible and almost impassable in places, and if the thaw continued in another two or three days, would render it impossible to follow the river bed. We all now became thoroughly alarmed regarding the frightful condition of the trail. To become stranded now was not pleasant to think of, but every indication pointed to just such a predicament unless the weather changed, and at this time of year, we had no hope of it doing so.

So under the latter impression, we were astir early the following morning [April 11]. Green was appointed to repair the worn trail, Daugherty and Chamberlain manned the two sleds, and Father and myself loaded our hand sled with five or six hundred pounds of the outfit. After getting into the harness, we all started down the trail with a realization that every effort must be used to cover this most undesirable and treacherous highway in the shortest possible time. The ravages of the warm sun were quickly transforming the trail into an impassable barrier. The case of our becoming cut off here meant disaster to the whole trip, and this fact tended to infuse new ambition into our already overworked bodies.

At about five miles from camp, a hand sled trail left the horse trail at the right, saving by doing so some little distance in a short cut. It was, of course, impractical for horse travel on account of the narrow ledges and narrower gulches encountered. Here we made our cache, having made the five miles by noon, and in our fatigued condition, we deemed it wiser to return to camp than to proceed farther that day. Having far better success than the day before, the boys arrived in camp unusually early, and we all sat down to the warm meal that Father and I had prepared. All were in a more cheerful mood than for some time previous, as the morrow would see all of the outfit, with the exception of the camp equipage, at Tut Schi Lake (if all went well). So with this pleasant knowledge, we retired early to our beds, sleep overcoming us at once. It was disturbed only by the dawn of another day.

The day [of April 12] broke cloudy and warm, and all appearances indicated rain. We were fearful lest these indications would be borne out, for a rain now would be the last stroke in the complete destruction of the sled trail. Not waiting for the weather to choose its program for the day, we loaded the last of our outfit. The same course as of the day before was taken, that is, Father and I hauled the hand sled to the forks of the trails. Before reaching the latter point, a damp, disagreeable snowstorm set in. It impeded our progress and saturated our clothing to the skin, a condition, I assure you, we did not enjoy.

The return trip in our wet clothes was one of misery. To make matters worse, before we reached camp, the temperature fell below zero, and a raging blizzard set in, shutting out from our gaze objects at a short range, so thick was the driven snow. The boys, having reached the lake with fair success, came in soon after our arrival, but in a condition similar to our own. Despite our wet and disagreeable condition, we were happy to know that our outfit was completely and safely cached at Tut Schi Lake, and that the morrow would rid us of a section of the trail which had caused us so much toil and hardships to get over.

The little settlement had not decreased in numbers apparently, but each day saw a like number moving down the trail, as we intended doing on the morrow. Of the former, we were in doubt of their reaching the Arm before the trail became impassable, but on the following day, a brighter outlook was apparent.

The terrible blizzard continued all night, and upon rising the next morning [April 13], it showed no signs of abating, but on the contrary, it had increased in violence. We saw at once that moving our camp today was out of the question. So gathering enough firewood, we busied ourselves at various occupations during the day, which in our anxiety to proceed seemed like a long one. Nevertheless, the delay afforded us an opportunity of a much needed rest. As evening drew near, the storm grew less in velocity, but the snow continued to fall with the usual velocity. With the exception of moving our camp, we were done with the miserable trail, but it was gratifying to know that those behind would now, with the new fall of snow, be able to reach their destination with ease.

James McKnight [see Biographies], *a Seattle friend of Father's, and Green will stay all night with us. He came from Windy Arm since morning on his way to Skaguay to sell his horse. He is through with his goods, and will build his boat at Windy Arm.*

The following morning [April 14] found it still stormy, but considerably less than the day before, and a vote was put before the house whether we should move or not. After a much heated argument, we decided there was insufficient cause for us to remain here longer, and the vote was finally carried unanimously to move at once. Having risen at four thirty, everything was in readiness to leave at eight, so bidding adieu to our camp of nearly three weeks, we filed slowly down the Tut Schi trail for the last time. [Will's diary entry of that day details the "heated argument."]

Chamberlain was against it [a move] *and Green for it. Something was said that made Chamberlain mad, and for a time we all thought there would be a scrap, but Green took back what he said, so all was right in a minute.*

The snow driven by the stiff breeze pelted us in the face as we forged ahead, but we were quite unmindful of that fact, so great was our desire to leave this most undesirable stretch of trail behind. The storm of the past couple of days had not been of much benefit to the trail. It is true that much snow had fallen, but the strong wind had stricken the majority from the path, heaping it in snow drifts at the side.

Lake Tut Schi was reached at 3:30 p.m. At our cache we fed our ponies and ate a cold lunch, and at 4:00 p.m. were again on our way. It was with gratitude and satisfaction that we looked back and could say that we were done with that portion of the trail that had given us so much genuine toil and hardship, and also that the end of our sled journey was close at hand. To where we were to make our next camp on the opposite side of the lake was a distance of twelve miles, which was covered by seven thirty. We made the twenty-two miles in just eleven hours. The first ten miles consumed seven and one half hours, while the latter twelve took but three and one half to cover on account of the level and fine condition of the lake trail. On a pebbly beach devoid of snow we pitched our camp. After eating a much needed supper, we retired, tired but with a new-born ambition from the fact that the morrow would see the first of our outfit landed at Windy Arm, the source of navigation.

Lake Tut Schi is of considerable size, it being about twenty miles long and varying from one and one half to two miles wide. It is beautifully situated, being entirely surrounded by sandstone hills rising to a great height. At places these hills rise sheer from the water's edge, making a landing impossible. But the majority of the shore line has a wide, pebbly beach, from which the land takes a gradual slope, meeting the mountain proper a great distance from the lake.

Daugherty's horse being slower than Chamberlain's, we did not get to the portage between Too Shi Lake and Tagish. We did not get to camp until 7:30, one hour later than them, but they had picked a fine camping place in the pebbled shore of the lake, and no snow on them. So I got supper while they put things in shape for the night, ate supper at 9 o'clock and turned in as soon as possible after a good day's work.

As we arose not as early as usual the next morning [April 15], we were greeted with one of the most beautiful sights our maker ever presented to man. On each side, the stately mountains clad in their mantle of white were bathed in a golden yellow hue from the morning sun, which was just showing itself above the far eastern peaks. The atmosphere was as clear as a bell, and looking far away to the west from which we had come, we could see the higher peaks glistening like diamonds where the bright sun struck. The river valley we had left the day before was easily visible, as also was the river valley to the east through which the waters of Tut Schi Lake flows into Taku Lake and finally goes to make up the mighty Yukon.

Our destination, the end of Windy Arm, now lay three and one half miles due north, but in order to reach that point, the mountains must be crossed, a task that necessitated no small amount of labor. In view of this fact and on account of the low altitude—which here was about five hundred feet—the locality where our camp now stood was chosen by the trail makers as the most feasible place to cross to the other side. From close observations, it was the only one of like altitude on this side of the lake.

Descriptively, nature apparently had upon a former period cut a valley to connect Lake Tut Schi with Windy Arm. Then, changing her mind, she had placed between the towering mountains this ridge, which in its uniformity was perfect. The trail led up the hillside in a straight course, an angle of forty-five degrees being attained the entire distance to the summit. There, immediately, the descent began in a more gradual degree until within a mile of Windy Arm, when it become perfectly level to the water.

During the day, Chamberlain and Daugherty made a trip with the ponies to our cache at the lower end of the lake, and returned early with record loads. Father, Green and myself busied ourselves in completing our camp, and when finished, we proclaimed the most model camp we had yet erected. The remainder of the day was spent in repairing our sleds, which were now almost worthless from their long and rough service, and which, with a little repairing, we figured would serve us the short distance that remained.

On the following morning [April 16] at an early hour, we began our labors with a will that only the nearness of our destination could arouse. But as night came on, our ambition and strength was at a very low degree. After one trip to the summit of the ridge, it became quite evident that horses on this grade would be of little use, it being as much as they could handle to pull the sled with one hundred pounds. So it was finally decided to pack the outfit on our backs to the summit, and there one horse could be kept busy hauling to the final cache. Green and myself were detailed to pack to the summit, and when night came on, we were quite ready to cease work.

The climb is about one quarter of a mile, and the altitude obtained in the short distance is five hundred feet. During the day, we each made twelve round trips to the summit with a pack averaging eighty pounds each trip. Many breathing spells were made, I can assure you, before the summit was gained, and when camp was reached that evening, we could truthfully say that we were never so fatigued since we were born. Daugherty had without much haste made two round trips to the Arm and had found the trail in fair shape but very steep for quite a distance after leaving the summit, and a careful watch of the loaded sled was necessary lest it would be overturned as it slewed from side to side on the slippery trail.

The days that followed were much the same, full of work of the hardest sort for man and beast. But of this, we were unmindful in the realization that our efforts were soon to be crowned by success. Our faithful little ponies were beginning to show the effects of the strenuous toil they had been subjected to. They had been given the best care that circumstances afforded, but they were fast becoming reduced in weight, and after a day's work were hardly able to stagger to their primitive stalls for the night.

Too Schi Lake Trail, April 16. This is 8 p.m. and bushed. We have been sick since 3 o'clock. Made 12 trips to the Summit on the portage of Too Shi and Tagish lakes on my back. Bill made a trip to the lower end of the lake and brought in 3500# at one load. Malen made two loads to Windy Arm, got 1700# to the two loads, thank God that ends that 1700#. Will soon be at our destination with all the goods by next week, Saturday April 23 if all goes our way.

N.W.T., Too Schi Lake Trail, April 17. Green and I packed all day today to the summit of the hill again today and nearly dead. Malen and Father made a trip to Tagish Lake in the forenoon and afternoon. Bill hauled #3500 from the far end of the lake, a good day's work.

April 18. Bill hauled the last of the goods from the lower end of the lake today. Got in at 2:30 p.m. The best time made yet. Malen and Father made two trips to Windy Arm again today, but nearly bushed the little mare. Green and I got in another day packing up the hill. From the other end of the lake has been the quickest move we have made since we have been on the trail. Made it in 4 days [hours?], 12 miles each way.

April 19. Both horses on the portage trail. Green and I following the horses today, as it needed two men to each sled. The trail is so bad. Bare ground nearly all the way in the afternoon when it thaws up, but is fine early in the morning. The Portage is 3 ½ miles long from Too Shi to Windy

Arm. Today is first I have been to Windy Arm and lots of interesting sights met my gaze, and will tell more about them later when I have more time.

April 20. Hauled two loads to Windy Arm this forenoon. Green and I went over with them and made arrangement for our camping ground for the next six weeks to come. We laid our foundation to our tent with logs, the same as a log house, then put our tent on top, which makes lots of room inside. Had to shovel so that when it begins to thaw and dry, it will be a fine floor. We worked hard all day until the boys came with their loads in the afternoon, then went back to camp with them. Father cooking, not feeling well, and I have not felt so bad since I left home as I have today. Am sick to my stomach.

Four days were required to move the outfit from the lower end of the lake, and on account of the long and level stretch, it was accomplished in less time than any move we had yet made. The night of the seventh day [April 21] after our arrival here, found our outfit, with the exception of our tents and the bare necessities of getting the morning meal, safely cached at our destination at Windy Arm. All were in the best of spirits now that success was ours, and during the evening meal, much planning for the future was indulged in.

After supper was eaten, I decided to step outside and view for the last time the beauty of our surroundings, which at that moment was bathed in the glory of the setting sun. While strolling aimlessly on the pebbly beach, I discerned not a great distance on the lake to the east a large, dark-colored animal. He had left the shore below our camp, and when I discovered him was making little haste toward the opposite side of the lake. I raised a cry not unlike a Comanche Indian, and in less time than it takes to tell it, there were a score of men and a like number of dogs in hot pursuit of Mr. Animal of whatever specie he might be. The party leaving camp had gained quite a distance upon him before he became aware of his pursuers. Upon doing so he shot ahead with increased speed and was soon out of gun range, disappearing in the timber on the opposite shore of the lake. None had gotten close enough to decide exactly what the animal was, but some claimed it was a cinnamon bear while others were quite sure it was a wolf.

As we were outside the tent looking out over the eastern part of the lake, I happened to see an animal making a bee line for the farther shore, so I raised a cry and in less than ten minutes about 20 men armed with rifles were on his trail, but he was too swift on feet for them, and soon outdistanced them and was lost to view. Some of them that were close enough to see him say it was a cinnamon bear, while others say it was a wolf.

From this time on wild game was plentiful, and if one would take the time and trouble by going two or three miles from the trail, the hunter's search would almost surely be rewarded by bagging a caribou, bear, or mountain goat. In this regard, we felt we could not spare the time, as much work was yet to be done, and according to the laws of nature no specified time was at our disposal. If the season be early, the ice would leave the lake before our boats would be finished, while on the other hand, the congestion might detain us beyond the usual time, giving us plenty of time after all work was done.

Chapter Four

WINDY ARM CAMP
APRIL 22–MAY 29, 1898

✦

ONCE THE WOODIN PARTY ARRIVED at Windy Arm, they set up a camp that would serve them for thirty-seven days. There they built the boats that would carry them on to Dawson. It was in this camp that the camaraderie and social life of the journey becomes most evident.

Will's account of the stay at Windy Arm focuses on an extensive network of acquaintances and relationships between his party and the other men they encountered on the trip. The people he most admired were co-workers, relatives, and neighbors, either from Seattle or central Michigan, where he grew up, or men of like background that he met on the trail. For those of us who now rely so heavily on instant communications provided by email and social networking, it is hard to comprehend how they all knew where their old friends would be. Nevertheless, Will had seemed unsurprised to find a childhood friend in Wrangell, Seattle friends running a hotel in Skagway, and, as will be shown, an old Michigan neighbor at Windy Arm. These connections brought familiarity to life in the wilderness amongst hordes of strangers.

Will mentioned the Michigan neighbor, William H. Wells, when he described the composition of the party in the beginning of Chapter 2. There he said that the older man joined the party while on board the *Cleveland*. However, his diary entry on May 15 indicates that Wells did not ask to join the Woodin party until they were all settled at Windy Arm. Will often commented on Wells's unpleasant personality. It is likely that he had a falling-out with a previously-formed party.

The Woodin party met others at Windy Arm who would continue to offer help and companionship all the way to Dawson. At the end of their stay, on May 29, Will remarked that "we had met and made many staunch and true friends" at the Windy Arm camp. Once they settled into this longer-term camp to build their boats, there was much opportunity for socializing in the evenings. A number of the men with whom they gathered to sing and swap stories included those they knew from Seattle. Most had worked for the Madison Street Car Company, the Skookum Box Factory, or local express companies. The men that the Woodin party socialized with at Windy Arm included Zacharia F. Hickman, John and Henry

75

Advertisement for the Skookum Box Factory, *Seattle City Directory*, 1897, page 837.

Foster, John and James Allen, Edward A. Hering (not Herring, as spelled by Will), Myron E. Clough, Calvin A. Johnston (not Johnson as spelled by Will), and Isaac Newton Hooper (see Biographies). All worked in semi-skilled occupations typical of this first generation of men who had left the farm for city life, and all possessed skills that gave them an advantage in the rough living on the trail, packing horses, and building boats.

Another group of men with whom Will socialized included George "Bert" Eastman of Omaha, Nebraska, and his partner, Bruce Ives; Tom Murray of San Francisco, California; Al "Larry" Larimer of Marion, Indiana; Jack Gilchrist, John Malady, and "Dutch" Myres, all of Wabash, Indiana; "and several others," as Will explained on May 28. "I have not learned their names, but I give the most intimate ones." The only people who could be researched from this bunch of pals were George Eastman, who appears twice in Will's narrative, and his partner Bruce Ives. Eastman was a twenty-nine-year-old carpenter from Omaha, and William Bruce Ives was his twenty-five-year-old cousin from Ogden, Utah (see Biographies).[1]

It is during this phase of the trip that it becomes apparent the Woodin party cut their costs by hiring out as labor. Will had earned five dollars taking an injured young man to a hotel while on the White Pass Trail, and Jay used his two horses to pack for a man named O'Brian on the first segment of the White Pass Trail in early March. The presence of lumber mills at Windy Arm offered more familiar employment to the men who had worked at the Skookum Box Factory in Seattle. During the week of May 20 to 27, in particular, Jay, Will, Green, and their new partner, Wells, all worked at Giffert's Mill in exchange for cut lumber. The company paid them seven dollars apiece for each day they worked, and applied it towards the three hundred feet of lumber they wished to acquire.

Will's account, especially during this leg of the trip, demonstrates how the stampeders relied on their friends and extended families to minimize the risks of going north. Not only did they often encounter and socialize with men they had known elsewhere, but they relied on the contacts and connections to provide a source of income and a safety network. Other accounts, both published and unpublished, stress the accomplishments of the individual, alone, combating the fierce environment and economic difficulties. People of the middle or upper classes tended to value individual achievements over group solidarity. What is different about the Woodin account is his underlying assumption that he was part of a broader community of men who relied on one another.

Besides recounting the social events with friends at Windy Arm, Will mentions several fatalities during this phase of their journey. His only account of a death prior to Windy Arm was that of Peter Clancy Bean, who was robbed and murdered on the Skagway trail on March 8. The evening socializing at the lake provided an excellent opportunity for spreading news. Will's accounts of a shooting accident, three drownings, and the death of an older woman from pneumonia fill out his previous discussions of the hazards from the harsh weather. These stories help put his own brush with death while at Dawson into perspective. Going to the Klondike was not a lark.

In fact, the funerals for two of the individuals who died demonstrated how the community of men would gather in support of one another. Services for an elderly lady drew over a hundred mourners; two hundred men attended the funeral of a young man Will's age, who accidentally shot himself. In the absence of an official government body—there was no North-West Mounted Police station at Windy Arm—Will recounts how the miners appointed a coroner and a physician signed a certificate of death for the latter incident. These volunteer services were typical of the types of activities the so-called "miners committees" would provide in gold rush conditions. While the funeral of the older woman was conducted by her fellow travelers, the Masons in the community provided final rites for the young man.

It is during this phase of the trip that the differences between Will's diary and his memoir become most apparent. For instance, in his memoir, he attributes a wildcat rush at Windy Arm to May 12, not May 11, as noted in his diary. When he wrote in his diary, he did not think much of it; with the benefit of hindsight, he gave it much greater importance than he did at the time of its occurrence, and changed the chronology slightly to make a better story.

In another instance where Will ignored his diary in order to make a better story in the memoir, he indicated in the latter that the last day at the camp was Sunday,

May 29. He described a large going-away party held by the camp, in which fifty to sixty men indulged in music and feasting. However, his diary states that this event occurred on Saturday, May 28. As the funeral for a man who died in a hunting accident took place on Friday, May 27, he may have thought that his readers might not approve the camp having a party the day after the funeral.

With that introduction, let us rejoin Will at Windy Arm.

<hr />

The morning of April 22 saw us astir at daybreak, making preparations to break camp for the last time on the trail. After breakfast was eaten, the tents were lowered and with the other scant camp equipage divided between the two sleds, we were ready to depart for Windy Arm. Because the loads were very light and the use of the horses would be unnecessary after today, we decided to haul the sleds ourselves. This decision allowed one of the party an opportunity to return on the trail all the way to Skagway, if necessary, to dispose of the ponies. By leaving from here, he would save one day's time and three and one half miles of his journey, which if it became necessary to go as far as Skagway, a distance of sixty miles would have to be covered.

Father was duly appointed to accompany them, and left on his long journey at six thirty. If he had to go to Skagway, it would require the greater portion of a week to do so. It was with a heart full of sympathy and pity that I saw the faithful little ponies depart. They had been our success in our vast undertaking, and without their services, utter failure would have been the result. Physically they appeared little like the horses we started with. The long, rough trail, combined with the long hours, had nearly gotten the best of them. But for the best of care and kind treatment, they would have long before been numbered with the thousands that had fallen from overwork and ill usage at their masters' hands.

Soon after Father's departure and everything being in readiness, we began the assent of the troublous incline for the last time. Each sled was manned by two of the party, one pulling while the other pushed with good effect with a forked pole brought to bear on the rear of the sled. The three and one half miles was covered without trouble or mishap, and noon found us with our entire outfits snugly cached at the final camp and source of navigation. Without giving a few introductory words on this important point on the way to the Klondike would be doing an injustice to my story and the beautiful section itself.

Literally, I have been unable to find, after a thorough research, but a meager mention of the Tut Schi Trail and Windy Arm, and nothing regarding the hundreds of Klondikers who used that trail and prepared for the river course at Windy Arm. I will therefore give a brief outline of the section and enumerate the happening of the six weeks spent here before continuing on our journey to Dawson.

Windy Arm lies about forty miles due northeast of Skagway. No one packing an outfit between the two points disputed that sixty-three miles was the estimated distance of the trail we had taken. The arm is about twelve miles long and one to one and a half miles wide, and surrounded on both sides by tremendous, high sandstone hills. On the north side of the lake, these hills rise sheer from the shore and are almost entirely barren of any growth, with the exception of a few scraggly spruce and hemlock upon which the mountain goat subsist entirely.

It is quite different on the south shore, as one is able to skirt the shore at a distance of one hundred yards from the water nearly the entire distance to the lake proper. It is also thickly wooded with a spruce forest, and trees were found that measured twelve inches in diameter, being entirely clear of limbs for ten to fifteen feet from the stump. Of course, this size timber was scarce, the average size being about six inches in [diameter]. In many ways, these smaller trees were preferred by those whipsawing their own lumber, in the fact that they were more easily hoisted to the scaffold and also more easily sawed.

To the west from whence we had come, a valley receded for many miles through which a small stream bubbled profusely. It was fed by the adjacent mountain rivulets, and day by day after our arrival it increased in volume. At the time of our departure, it had gained a torrent, emptying itself into the lake not far from where our camp stood.

Windy Arm, in itself, is a body of water of some extent, but it is very small in comparison to the body of water of which it is a part, namely Lake Tagish. The latter name derived from the tribe of Indians who inhabit its shores, where they subsist on the fish from its waters and hunt in the adjacent forests. Its waters lie between the many mountain ranges, and its outline resembles very much an octopus or devil fish with its many arms reaching out from the body in different directions. Windy Arm is the third in length and area. It was so named by the miners at some previous date on account of the strong wind that constantly prevails and tears its way down the narrow canyon-like channel, bringing consternation and disaster to he who ventures without caution in its path.

The traveler coming from Lake Bennett has more cause to remember an experience with this treacherous arm than he who sails from between its perpendicular walls. Coming from Lake Bennett, the breeze might be moderate, whereupon rounding the point separating the Arm from Caribou Crossing [actually, Nares Lake], the unthinking traveler would be caught unawares. Before he becomes conscious of his predicament, the boat would be overturned and a watery grave for the occupant would be the result. Many lives were lost in this manner during the fall of 1897 and thereafter. More will be told of this section in the following pages, but now it is quite necessary that we should return to our arrival at Windy Arm.

The sight we beheld as Windy Arm came into view that memorable day will never be forgotten. The arm of the lake with its carpet of immaculate white snow and ice spread away to the northeast as far as the eye could see. Looking across this white expanse to the north, the eye would linger on the beauty of the stately mountain, dotted here and there in its garb of white with scrubby pines and hemlock growing apparently out of the solid rock. On the south shore, the mountain with its virgin forest reaching far up its slope, presented a beautiful sight.

It was along this shore that the majority of the gold-seekers had built their camps. For nearly two miles down the lake, their presence was in evidence by the curling smoke from their many stovepipes. At the head of the Arm, among the stunted growth of hemlock, birch and pines, many had made comfortable camps and built their boats close by. It was rather an inconvenience to carry the lumber from the distant forest, but those arriving first had claimed sites most convenient to the timber available. Thus it can be seen that those arriving last were forced to build their camps in the valley at the head of the Arm. It was here that we built our camp and boats.

About one mile down the south shore, two saw mills of small capacity, but otherwise answering the purpose very well, were being installed and began operations soon after our arrival. The owners were going through to Dawson with the machinery, where they would construct a permanent mill and manufacture lumber for the trade. Here the mill was of a temporary nature, built solely for the purpose of sawing enough material for the scows and boats necessary for the transportation of the machinery and their many effects. They did, however, before leaving the Arm, sell a great quantity of boat material to the many gold-seekers in the vicinity at fabulous prices, but not at all unreasonable when the cost and trouble of transportation was taken into consideration.

It was a busy scene that greeted us as we filed into camp, an activity so unlike anything we had ever seen before. Here and there among the green foliage of the stunted spruce were scores of camps of a substantial character, while nearby was the owner's cache well protected from the weather by heavy tarpaulins. Here and there could be seen men and horses arriving like ourselves from Tut Schi Lake laden with outfits, only to return again and again until completed. The sound of the hammer beat a merry tattoo as the wielder busied himself in erecting a comfortable camp, or as many were already doing, building their boats. In the forest not far away could be heard the wick of the whipsaw as the freshly felled trees were slowly reduced to boards of snowy whiteness and of many sizes and lengths soon to be converted into all manner of conveyances on the great highway to the land of gold, "the Yukon."

Upon our arrival [April 22] and after a hearty meal whetted by our exercise of the forenoon, we at once set about erecting a comfortable quarters for our long stay here. Previously for the complete protection of the perishable portion of our outfit, we had built a platform of logs with six pillars of logs, elevating it about two feet above the ground. A large tarpaulin thrown over the outfit protected it against the heavy rains and hot sun, which we experienced during our stay here. The living quarters were erected on practically the same plan, with the exception of the floors, which were hewn down, making a smooth surface.

There were two of these tents, one being used for a cook house and dining room, while the other was for sleeping quarters. When the night [April 22] came on, everything was in ship-shape, and it would have been rather difficult to find a more cozy and comfortable camp than ours. The stove was set in position, and a cupboard, table and benches were built for the kitchen. For the sleeping apartment, a bunk or rude bedstead large enough to accommodate the entire party was constructed. When finished, boughs from the hemlock were gathered and substantiated for mattress and springs, which made a most healthful and comfortable couch to sleep upon, and one, I will venture to say, a specific remedy for insomnia. The remainder of the day and all of the following day [April 23] spent in this work, and when finished everything was as comfortable and convenient as could be made under the circumstances, and it was with satisfaction we retired this Saturday night.

Windy Arm, April 22. The Mail Man came along and I got four letters, one from little Blanche, one from my little Brother-in law Minor, one from Dear old Mother, and one from Mother that was written last Sept. when father was up here. They all made me lonesome to be with them again, but it can't be. Blanche's letter nearly broke my heart, but I will forgive her, it is so terrible to think of somebody taking my place, but she may not have been to blame.

Will's references his "little wife" throughout his diaries and at least once to her brother, Minor, as his "little brother-in-law" are in terms of hopefulness, not reality. Will became concerned about Blanche's faithfulness when he read a letter from her on April 22, which suggests that she might have spent time in the company of another man. Will had proposed to Blanche Graves on May 9, 1896. His diary entry of that date, in Seattle, states: "Blanche and I sat in the back steps of 209 Birch St. and I presented the ring to her, but behold it was too large for her engagement finger, so I will have to have it smallered [sic]." On December 1, 1900, after returning from the Klondike, he wrote, "After six years of steady courtship, Blanche and I were married this evening at her parents' house at no. 965 John St. at 8:00 p.m."

The following morning [April 24] when we awoke, we found a most disagreeable wet snow falling. It was one of those nasty spring storms so much like the April snow of the far eastern states, and one which, if you venture out of doors, will soon penetrate to the skin. This happened to be Sunday, and with nothing urgent required for the day, we were loath to leave our warm beds until far into the forenoon. The storm had ceased, giving place to the bright, warm sunshine, which was having the desired effect on the snow and ice, but making it very slushy underfoot. After a breakfast of delicious mush and bacon and hotcakes browned to a golden hue, we decided to spend the remainder of the day in an unusual manner. Forty eight days had now passed since we left Skagway. Due to our inconvenient circumstances, our clothing, laundry and baths had been sadly neglected, therefore it was agreed to apply ourselves to this important task. When finished, the vicinity of our camp appeared not unlike a Chinese laundry, as several lines reaching from tree to tree were full of clothing drying under the warm sun.

The boys are playing cards with some of our neighbors here. There are lots of Seattle boys here. I will name those I know. Three Madison St. Car men, James McKnight, Chas. Lund and Thompson, and the two Lunn brothers, the photographers of Seattle [see Biographies for McKnight, Lund, and Lunns]. *I have finished a long letter to my little Wife, so will go to bed.*

Chamberlain had, out of curiosity, a burning desire to visit the large settlement at Lake Bennett, and during the day [April 24] had made preparations for doing so on the morrow. Nothing in particular around camp would be done until Father returned, and doubtless another opportunity would not present itself while located here. So at four o'clock on Monday morning he arose [April 25]. He cooked a hasty breakfast, rolled a lunch in his blankets together with his rifle, and hooked Skookum in the harness to haul a light sled. At five, they left camp, starting down the Arm on a dog trot, and were soon out of sight behind the prominent headland. His course led him down the Arm to Lake Tagish, thence through Caribou Crossing [Nares Lake] to Lake Bennett. It was a distance of forty miles each way and would require three days in making the round trip.

> "Skookum" is a northwest coastal Native American word meaning "big and strong." The party dubbed both their dog and their boat Skookum, which was also the name Jay Woodin had chosen for his lumber company in Seattle.

With our party depleted in numbers for a few days, those remaining at camp had a comparatively easy time of it. During their absence, Green and Daugherty ground the axes, filed the saws and prospected the woods. They blazed such trees as would be suitable for good boat timber, which by so doing everything would be in readiness to begin whipsawing immediately upon the return of the absent boys.

April 26. This is Tuesday night and the boys, Father, and Chamberlain have not turned up but I did not really expect them tonight, but Green at [illegible word]. *Green, Daugherty and I while away the idle lonesome hours at anything that we come to. Am cooking. I have not felt so Homesick on the Journey as I have in the last week. Nothing to put my mind to, but to think of the Darling home I left so far away, but must not give up now.*

April 27. Wed. morning and the boys are not here yet. Daugherty and Green have gone to hunt logs. Can't do much of anything until they come. Chamberlain returned at noon. Him and dog nearly exhausted from traveling on the ice. Brought six letters with him, one from little Blanche, three for Green, 1 for Daugherty and 1 for Chamberlain. Father has not returned tonight yet.

Chamberlain and Skookum reached camp at noon on Wednesday [April 27], having made the trip from Bennett City, a distance of forty miles, in eight hours, and from their exhausted condition, it was quite evident that it had been a hard trip. His account of the tremendously large city of tents was of much interest to us, and the trip to him was much appreciated. As he said, he was fully paid for the hard jaunt he had subjected himself to. Our hearts were gladdened by the receipt of a half dozen letters, which he had procured at the Post Office at Bennett City, and all vowed that his trip had been a complete success.

A week had now passed since Father left, but due to the unreliability of the trail, and his mission in general, little concern was felt. The next morning [April 28] a strong cold north wind was blowing down the Arm, reminding us that the northern winter was not yet over. After the morning meal was over, it was decided that a start should be made at the task that lay before us, and which had been delayed so long. With axes and saws over our shoulders, we proceeded toward the wood to enter into an unfamiliar task, which then was necessary to master in gaining our goal.

When night came on a large and substantial scaffold for whipsawing had been furnished all ready for use on the morrow. This was erected by setting four logs about six inches in diameter firmly in the ground. They were set in pairs, the two forming one pair being placed about five or six feet apart, while on top of each pair another log was placed, forming an arch about six feet high. Between the arches or scaffold a distance of twelve or sixteen feet intervened, and with two logs placed in a slanting position from the ground to the top of each arch, a good-sized log could be rolled to the top of the scaffold without much effort. Having rolled the log upon the scaffold, it was held in place while sawing by two saplings, one on each side, which also served a place to stand for the man working above. The log being in place, a man takes his place on top while his unfortunate companion grasps the lower handles of the whipsaw.

I say unfortunate, and feel justified in saying so from my own experience in the pit. I found it by far the most laborious task that has been my experience to come in contact with, and at the end of the first day's sawing, my feelings were that I could never pull another stroke. I was not entirely alone in this respect, as many complaints were heard of the lame bodies and blistered hands caused by this strenuous and necessary indulgence [industry?].

During the afternoon, Father returned from Skagway, which place he had to go before disposing of the ponies. He found conditions vastly changed since we left there, and some little time and trouble were experienced in disposing of the horses at any price. They had now, on account of the impracticality of the trail and the dwindling arrivals, become a drug on the market, and where two hundred and fifty dollars would have been paid for the two horses early in the season, only sixty dollars was realized for the two now, with a choice of much less being paid before the summer was finished.

April 28. Father returned from Skaguay this afternoon with a letter from my little wife again. He sold the horses, one for $15.00 and Fred for $40.00, quite a fall in the price of horses since we struck the trail.

Due to his long, hard jaunt, the following day found Father in an exhausted condition that confined him to the camp all day [April 29], but was able to get about on Saturday [April 30]. One entire week was required to whipsaw what we calculated would be sufficient material to construct the two large boats we had in mind, and on the following Friday night [May 6] we left the scaffold for the last time, having sawed during the week eight hundred feet of lumber. We had by this time become quite expert in the art of whipsawing, but were not at all sorry when the last board, with a ringing slap, fell on the serviceable scaffold.

Wed. May 4. I took the lower end of the whipsaw this morning and Daugherty the top. I thought I would take the easiest end for a starter again, and it is much easier than I expected it would be below and was not a bit tired tonight. Green and I had some words tonight as we were about to quit work. He is getting now so nobody can do or say anything without his criticizing it, so I called him down tonight, and we had it hot for awhile, for I won't stand it for a minute. I did not know I was to have an overseer in my travels through the N. W. T. [North West Territories][2] *and Alaska. Who can blame me? I feel sorry that I should have any trouble with any of the boys, but it was forced on me.*

Thurs. May 5, 1898. Whipsawing again today. Daugherty knocked out at noon, so I had to take the top again this afternoon and stood it fine. Am just getting on to it easy now. Malen and I finished up a log that we have been on two days. It scales 140 ft. and got done early. Weather cooler and has a tendency to rain but just a few sprinkles fell. Would like to see a little rain, it would take the ice out a flying.

The weather had, during the week, moderated to very warm spring weather, so warm in fact that in the whipsawing more comfort was derived when stripped to the undershirt, so strenuous was this exercise. The thermometer had in the middle of the day registered from sixty to seventy degrees for many days past and had therefore been the direct cause of maturing and setting forth millions of those troublesome and venomous insects—the mosquitoes. These little insects swarm in clouds, and are the greatest curse the northern traveler has to contend with. The snow, due to the extremely warm sun, was fast disappearing in our vicinity, and the surface of the lake in places became sloppy during the day. On the mountains, great snow slides could be seen to leave their lofty summits, and with a roaring, thundering sound would rush down the steep incline, making a clean sweep of everything in its path, and finally spread itself over a great area of the lake's surface to a depth of many feet.

Windy Arm, Friday, May 6. Tonight finished up whipsawing and got done early [at] *the saw. I and Malen have worked fine all day and seems as if we were just getting on to the work when we had to quit. We estimate that we have sawed in the seven days 800 ft. of lumber, have 51 boards from 1 x 6 x 24 to 30 ft. in length. It will average 1 x 7 x 28 ft. long and also 10 pc* [pieces] *that will make 200 ft. of 2 x 4s which we think will make two boats. So our hardest work is over. What patience percerperence* [perseverance?] *will do. What a lesson it is to a man.*

The next day [May 7] after a foundation was constructed, Green and Father began laying the keel of the two larger boats, while the remainder of the party transferred the lumber still at the saw pit to the scene of boat-building operations. Much of the lumber had been packed by us in coming to our dinners and returning to camp at night, and in consequence, it required but a portion of the day to complete this laborious task. It was with a genuine feeling of joy and satisfaction that we saw a start made on the boats, and we figured that with fair success, a week or ten days would find the two larger boats ready for launching.

It was now the eighth of May, and taking a record of the opening of navigation of former years, three weeks would yet elapse before the ice would be entirely out of the lake. This would afford us plenty of time within which to make our final preparation. Every indication now pointed strongly toward a repetition of former years in this respect, as reports reached us that the river below was open in many places. They caused no little excitement in camp, spurring the late-comers on in their boat building, lest they would be caught with unfinished boats.

The Holy Sabbath fell on the following day, and it was observed as we had not done since leaving our homes. A later morning sleep was indulged in, after which the entire day was spent in a genuine needed rest, all cares and worry cast to the winds. A light snow had fallen during the early morning, and unlike the day before, a chilliness filled the air that was disagreeable. It did not much retard the advance of spring, judging from the ever increasing volume of water in the little brook beside our tent.

During the afternoon, Daugherty and myself, out of curiosity, took an exploring tour, going on the ice for several miles down the Arm, thus gaining much knowledge of the lay of the land, and examining the formation of the nearby cliffs. The latter are formed of an inferior grade of slate with here and there a streak of quartz, while the remainder...was

"Yukon diamonds" is a term used in the north for cassiterite (SnO_2), a tin oxide often found in Yukon placers. Cassiterite is a tetragonal crystal, a shape that can appear to be octagonal to the layman, as it did to Will, and was sometimes used as a gemstone. Advertisements in U.S. newspapers referred to Yukon diamonds as the "nearest approach to genuine stones on the market." They appear in many colors, mostly black, brown, and gray. Purple cassiterite has been found in Sri Lanka.[3]

a rock of a soft crumbly sort. We discovered firmly embedded in the slate many small octagon-shaped stones, dark purple in color and clear, almost to transparency, appearing except in color like so many diamonds, so uniform were they. With the aid of a rock, we secured several beautiful specimens of these stones, and I retain many now as a memento of this locality.

To the south we could now see, without obstruction, the fairly level but rocky surface of the shore reaching away for a few miles. The mountains formed a background of extensive proportions, closing to our vision the country beyond, but receding as we presumed, to the shores of the south arm of Lake Tagish. We came upon a mass of ice, snow and debris that reached out upon the lake for two hundred yards and attained a height of twenty feet. The day before, it had slid from the mountain-side. We could see many of these avalanches on the frozen surface of the lake far below the point where we turned back. They showed only too plainly that the long severe winter was almost at an end.

On our return to camp, the appetizing smell of dinner prepared by Chamberlain greeted our nostrils. Our long walk in the cool, exhilarating air had created an appetite creditable to a bear. The remainder of the day was spent in visiting friends whom we had become acquainted with on the journey, and not a few who had been passengers on the *Cleveland* from Seattle. Socially, the day had marked a new epoch among the Argonauts in the little settlement. Thereafter, on many occasions after the day's work was done, gatherings of a musical nature or for the purpose of playing a sociable game of cards or other manner of entertainment was indulged in. Thus passed many pleasant hours, which would otherwise have been spent in a severe longing for home. Drawing from people from all over the world, some excellent talent was shown in many cases, especially in a musical line, there being several professionals in our settlement, who in case of failure in the goldfields, had brought along musical instruments of several varieties. When performed together, the harmony that came therefrom would have done credit to an up-to-date orchestra.

May 8. This is Sunday morning 10 o'clock. Just had breakfast and are going to take a general rest all day. Did not get out of bed until 8 o'clock this morning. A light snow falling when we peeped out of the tent this morning and is a little chilly outside. Little Windy Arm is a long narrow bay that forms the Southern part of Lake Tagish. The arm itself is one mile wide and about 8 miles long. It sits in a regular basin while the lofty Mountains rise from the water's edge to a great height. The formation is of slate and some granite and is far from being a solid formation. A very limited amount of timber lines the shores. They grow in patches and no tree attains the size of 2 ft. in diam. on account of the very dry summer climate. Much game is being taken in the mountain sides now and every day you can see hunters coming in with either bear, mountain goat, pheasants and red squirrels, and don't have to go far either. The little Village of tents called Windy Arm is located at the extreme southern end of the Arm, and rows of tents face the little stream that empties into the Arm on both sides. There are four Sawmills here now in this vicinity, two right in town, the other two are a mile farther down the Arm. The main occupation of the people at the present time is boat building. The population of the city is about 300 people, taking in the suburbs. Got tired writing and don't feel at all well this day, so took a walk in the woods alone. Sunday is a lonesome day to lay around camp. I first went up a little stream that flows into the Arm from the south. Thought I would do a little prospecting, so dished up some of the gravel, got some colors, but of no consequence, so came down to the lake and took the west shore down about a mile to see a snow slide that had slid off the mountain two weeks ago, a mass of snow and ice pile up before me. When I got there [I found it] reached out on the lake about two hundred yards. I turned back and got in to camp in time for dinner. After eating we all went over to a tent occupied by a Dr. Hill. He gave notice in the week that there would be a sermon at his tent today, but after waiting an hour we all got tired and Malin and I went up the East shore of the lake to see the Kalamazoo Mining Co's. mill. It is located about a mile up the shore. They have not started up yet on account of their boiler not working. They got in here before we did. Ed Herring [see Biographies] *of Seattle and his party are camped about ¼ of a mile from the mill, so I ran down to their tent, and who did I see but Father eating supper with them. We did not know he came down too. Visited awhile and came to camp, and I got my mandolin and went over to a neighbor's tent, a Mr. Doane by name, and stayed until 11 o'clock.*

Next morning [May 9] work was resumed on the boats, but was interrupted at noon that we might pay our last respects to the dead. The Reverend Mr. Howe's mother-in-law, due to her extreme old age and exposures of the trip, had expired on the Saturday night previous. Her illness was so brief that few in camp were aware of it, and her death came as a complete surprise to all, notwithstanding her age. A mention of the lady has been made in a previous chapter and much interest was taken in her welfare, and the decided pluck and good health she attained throughout the trip was the talk of all. The hardships and exposures had been too great, and she became an easy prey to the dreaded pneumonia, a disease that does its work quick and well.

The services were to be held at the grave and were to be preached by her son-in-law, the Reverend gentleman. When we arrived, about one hundred people had congregated to pay their respects to one gone before, knowing not who would be next to follow. A rude coffin of pine boards had been made in a plain fashion, lined with what under the circumstances was available, but answered the purpose very well, for a time at least. A site for the grave had been chosen on a prominent knoll overlooking the inland sea and its beautiful surroundings. A cavity of the proper dimensions had been hewn by slow and diligent work from the solid rock to a depth of security from wild animals. The ceremony was brief but impressive, and with the hundred or more roughly-clad, but intelligent spectators gathered around the opening formed a picture that will ever remain clear in my mind. The ceremony over, each with heartfelt sympathy for the bereaved betook himself back to his work, and appearance in camp soon after gave little evident that anything unusual had taken place in camp.

Her age was 62 years…Her daughter and her husband should have known better than to bring an old lady of her age up to face the hardships on the way to the Klondike, but people will learn after awhile.

Presbyterian Missionaries
in the Klondike

When the Klondike gold rush started, the Christian churches of the Pacific Northwest Coast were not immune from the excitement over the stampede north. In an article about the religious work being done in Alaska by the predominant Christian denominations, an unnamed Presbyterian "moderator" announced that he would take at least fifty clergymen to the gold regions by July 1898 "if he can find any to go." The January 1898 article stated that there were currently Presbyterian stations near Circle City, Chilkat, Wrangell, Hoonah, Juneau, St. Lawrence Island, Haidah, and Point Barrow, and Presbyterians had been active in Sitka for decades. A list of the Presbyterian churches and pastors in Yukon and Alaska between 1901 and 1910 indicates that, in addition to these missions, churches were eventually established in Atlin, Bonanza, Cordova, Dawson, Eagle, Fairbanks, Grand Forks (on Bonanza Creek), Haines, Skagway, and Whitehorse. It seems likely that Rev. Howie was one of the ministers who responded to the January 1898 call.[4]

The identity of the elderly woman accompanying Rev. Howie and his wife remains a mystery. In his memoir, in describing the events of March 29, Will referred to her as Rev. Howie's mother. In both his diary and memoir accounts of May 9, Will contradicts himself and states that the older woman was Rev. Howie's mother-in-law. However, both mothers had already passed on. Marion Miller Howie, who gave birth to William M. Howie, died on April 18, 1875, at the age of sixty in Vernon, Wisconsin. Susan Lackey Howie's mother, Rebecca Lee Rogers Lackey, died in 1887 in Washington County, Iowa.[5] This information suggests that Will was incorrect about how the older woman in the Howie party was related to the couple. It seems likely that she was a fellow missionary whom the couple called "mother," in much the same way that members of some religious denominations refer to their fellows as "brothers" and "sisters." A number of evangelical traditions follow this tradition.

Up to this date, the irregularity and delay of mail had been a great annoyance and disappointment to all. Letters would finally reach us that were written five or six weeks previous and bearing a weeks-old Skagway postmark. As there was no regularly appointed mail carrier, we were forced to endure this unavoidable service, much to our displeasure and regret. This condition became changed as the camp became settled, and duly appointed carriers were assigned to the tiresome and unpleasant duty of carrying the first class mail between our camp and Skagway, a distance of about sixty-three miles. A fee of twenty-five cents was the charge of sending or receiving a letter while newspapers were, on account of extreme weight, absolutely refused this service at any price. Consequently, many weeks at a time passed before news of the outside was gained from this source.

May 10. I am cooking today. Bill has the rheumatism and is laid up for repairs. Made my first batch of yeast bread tonight. Took me until 10 o'clock to bake them as I did not set the yeast until late. The mail man came from Skaguay and with a letter from my little Wife and answered while I done my baking this evening as I have a chance to send it out in the morning for 25¢. Are getting along fine on Green's boat. Have not started on ours yet.

By May 11, nearly three weeks had elapsed since reaching our destination. The several parties back of us who had chosen this trail had three days ago reached camp. The stragglers were compelled to pack their outfits on their backs a great part of the distance from Tut Schi Lake, on account of the entire absence of snow. Today a greater part of the distance showed little evidence of a sled trail ever existing. From early morn until late in the night, the saw and hammer could be heard as they were wielded by the hundreds of busy boat-builders, making a busy scene that was interesting and unusual to look upon.

May 11. It is quite exciting here the morning on account of a gold find up the little creek I visited last Sunday. The news got around that a man had got a spot that would pay $1 to the pan. So Green and Daugherty took a gold pan and shovel and went out, but came back at noon, but could not [make] even wages, but found good colors. They claim the man that has struck it is trying to keep it a secret and will tell no one anything in regards to it. There is surely something in it. I cooked this forenoon and have been whipsawing a little lumber this afternoon with Daugherty. Bill is feeling *better today, too. Laid the keel of Father's boat tonight, so will get a good start on it tomorrow. The weather is cool now, but the ice going fast, hardly any snow in sight, now. The mountain streams are swelling as the snow thaws on them, which is rotting the ice faster than the sun.*

On May 12, a report that gold had been found in the near vicinity of the camp caused a frenzy of excitement to reign throughout the population. Boat building was forgotten in the magic report, and a very short time found the settlement nearly deserted. The little stream that wound its way down the valley, emptying itself into the lake not far from our camp, was the scene of all the excitement. The particulars and reliability of the supposed strike was vague in the extreme. A man on the night previous [May 11] was seen to glide silently away from camp in the direction of the valley which lay to the south of us. He was armed with the customary prospector's implements, the shovel and gold pan, and his actions to us seemed of a suspicious nature, and of which we thought would bear close watching. No action by others was taken upon this occasion, but upon seeing the same party leave in his mysterious manner early on the following morning, people began to wonder. Their suspicions grew stronger each moment until finally he was followed, but search as they would, no trace of him could be found, so cleverly had he covered his tracks. This failure by no means served to quiet the excitement that had taken possession of the people, but on the contrary fired them to immediate action. During the forenoon along the little stream and its vicinity could be seen scores of men searching for the supposed paystreak.

Before the day [May 12] ended, the little stream had been thoroughly prospected from its source to the lake without finding gold, with the exception of a few very fine colors, so fine in fact that it was almost impossible to catch them. The search was finally given up in disgust and thereafter treated as a joke. Rest assured he who had caused the excitement was not approached for an explanation regarding the supposed strike for fear of becoming the laughing stock of the settlement. This excitement, however, gave us a very good idea of a stampede for a new gold strike. Many famous strikes have taken place in the northern country, making many of those taking part fabulous fortunes.

The occasion of one of these almost insane flights never fell to my lot while in the north, but a few acquaintances have taken an active part in some, which afterward proved to be very rich. I will here make a note of their experiences as they were told. The one in question began at Dawson and extended for miles and miles over the rough mountainous country to a tributary of the Stewart River. The excitement started in a manner similarly to the instance just mentioned at Windy Arm. A party having discovered good diggings and becoming short of supplies had returned to Dawson City to replenish his larder, whereupon in some manner or other, he became an object of suspicion. Upon leaving with friends about midnight, he was followed to his lair of golden treasure. Those following after, having staked good claims, returned to Dawson, spreading the news soon after. An exodus of no small proportions began at once. Little time was consumed in preparing for the long, rough trip. Barely enough food and blankets were carried to satisfy the hunger and protect the body from the cold mountain air, so much in evidence at the time of year I speak. The new strike was reported as very rich, which fired the ambition of all taking part to beat his neighbor, thus enabling him to a choice of the good claims. That is, if upon his return to Dawson City, the claim had not already been recorded ahead of him. This was, in many instances, the case, all his efforts having gone for naught. Many a pitiful tale of the lives wrecked physically and mentally could be traced to the insane endurance men subjected themselves to in these mad stampedes for gold.

May 12. Malen and I are working in the woods again today getting out what little lumber that we lack for ribs and boat sills. Green and father are rushing the boats along and are doing fine.

Since leaving Skagway two months previous, not a mouthful of fresh meat had been eaten by our party for the simple reason that it was very difficult to procure, and where procurable, the price asked was far in excess of our means. There had now begun a craving in our appetites for fresh meat, vegetables and other staple foods, so monotonous had become the everyday bill of fare composed of bacon and beans, sourdough bread and the numerous condensed foods in our possession. Therefore, imagine our pleasure when the news became circulated that a large moose had been killed in the timbered hills to the south of us. Two of the boys had, on the night before, while hunting between Windy

Arm and Lake Tut Schi, discovered moose tracks in the newly fallen snow. The tracks were easily followed, and after following for five or six miles, the hulking form of Mr. Moose hove in sight. He became an easy prey to the rifle in the hands of the young nimrods, and fell dead from the first shot.

Upon their return to camp, they invited a number of us in their immediate vicinity to accompany them to the carcass on the following morning and secure a portion of the meat, costing us only our time in going after it. Father volunteered to go for our share, and returned with a number of pounds of choice steaks, which I broiled at dinner time. Notwithstanding its wild taste, it was enjoyed more than any meal we had eaten while on the trail. Thereafter at frequent intervals, fresh meat, principally moose, was procured while we were at Windy Arm, but none was appreciated quite so much as the first we had eaten. [Diary: *I don't care much for it, but the boys do.*]

As the days went by, progress on the boats showed remarkable results, and another week, if all went well, would see everything in readiness to embark on our long river voyage. The snow had since entirely disappeared, and ice was fast going to pieces, and in many places, large patches of open water could be seen showing only too plainly that our avenue of departure would soon be in readiness.

During the week [of May 13-20], Chamberlain had been very ill, but was now able to do the duties about the tent. Daugherty and myself had consumed the greater part of the week in whipsawing odds and ends needed in the finishing touches, also masts were secured, paddles hewed to their proper shapes, and numerous other necessities that could not very well be overlooked. It was while busying ourselves in this manner on Saturday afternoon [May 14], that Daugherty, due to his own carelessness, sawed the end of his thumb off, partially disabling him for at least a week, but otherwise, causing no considerable inconvenience.

May 14. While rip-sawing lumber this afternoon, Malen sawed the end of his thumb off, so is crippled for some time to come.

Larimer, the mandolin player, got an invitation to come down to the Giffert Mill Co's settlement a mile below here on the lake shore to spend the evening with his music at a Seattle party's tent, Zach Hickman by name. They had a boys' concert there last Sat. night so heard about us fellows here,

*so sent for him, so he invited me to go with him. So we went up and had
a hell of a time playing and singing. Seemed like old times in Seattle, but
somewhat rougher. Lots of Seattle boys in attendance. The two Foster bros,
Jack* [Zach?] *Hickman, Allen bros., Ed Herring, Mr. Clough, Mr. Cal
Johnson of the P.S. Machine Depot of Seattle, Mr. Hooper, a barber of Seattle* [see Biographies]. *About 11 p.m., they broke up and we were invited
over to a tent a friend of Larimer's and gave us a spread and we came Home.*

The next morning [May 15] dawned bright and beautiful, and the
day proved to be the warmest we had experienced, the thermometer registering seventy degrees at one o'clock. It being Sunday, little work was
done, but full advantage was taken of the beautiful weather by taking
a long tramp in the forest, and along the shore line, investigating the
progress of the outgoing ice on the lower end of the Arm. The tramp in
the bright, warm sunlight was enjoyed immensely, and for the time we
forgot we were in the perpetually cold northern country of which we
had so often read.

In retracing our footsteps along the lake shore, we called on some
friends who had a camp about one mile below us, and were informed
that three men, in an attempt to cross the lake on the ice, had been
drowned sometime during the early morning. The previous evening,
despite many warnings, two attempts at rescue had been made, each
proving futile and nearly ending seriously. It was finally given up after
many protests from the onlookers until the following morning, thinking that during the cool night, the ice would become stronger and more
secure. This was the last seen of the poor fellows. Their whereabouts
were plainly told by the evidence they had left behind. Their loaded sled
was found on the ice not far from a gaping hole, with a hat floating on
the surface of the open water. Their depleted outfit was hauled ashore to
be kept until such a time as it could be delivered over to the North West
Mounted police, and if possible, notify their relatives of their tragic end.
This was a warning in the future to those who had any intention of ven-
turing on the ice, and no fatalities from this source occurred thereafter.
No attempt to recover the bodies had been made, and because of the
danger, none would be made until the spot could be reached by boat.
Nothing could be done by us, so a return to camp was made, and was
reached in ample time for our Sunday dinner.

Malin and I took a walk down the lake shore to kill time. We had not gone far when we heard there had been three men drowned while crossing on the ice through their own carelessness. So for curiosity we went down about 2 1/2 miles to where one man went in and could plainly see his hat, blankets and sled laying on the surface of the rotten ice. He was drowned about 100 yards from shore in plain sight of a camp of Klondikers, but they could not give him any assistance whatever on account of the ice. He had been warned the night before by God Almighty and campers for he had gone in twice the night before. The other two were seen to go through opposite this one, and did not appear again, and it is supposed they are in a watery grave now. The people take a warning at this. I wrote a letter to my little Blanche today and sent her an Alaska Diamond and a big end of spruce gum. How I wish I could have spent the day with her at Home but no I cannot be now. I have made my bed and will have to sleep in it now. Oh! I would not leave her again.

During the afternoon, much to our surprise and elation, a carrier entered camp with a large supply of a late issue of a Seattle daily paper. It was the first newspaper we had seen since leaving Log Cabin, weeks before, and I assure you, the supply was exhausted in a very short space of time, notwithstanding that fifty cents per copy was charged [the equivalent of fourteen dollars in today's currency]. We were fortunate in securing a copy, and as the contents were of vital importance pertaining principally to the Spanish American War, every paragraph, even to the advertisements, were devoured by our hungry eyes. The war had now been in progress about five weeks, but aside from a few unreliable reports, little information had been gained of its progress. Hence, little interest had been taken in our nation's serious affair, so engrossed had we been in our undertaking. But now when we read of the victories and splendid fight the United States was putting up, all else was forgotten and our hearts swelled with admiration and pride toward ours, the greatest nation on earth. During the evening, a demonstration of patriotism was shown in camp by a ratification over the glad news, and closed by singing the Star Spangled Banner, accompanied by several musical instruments.

The USS *Maine* was sunk in Havana Harbor on February 17, before Will Woodin left on his journey north. Spain declared war on the United States on April 20, 1898, while the Woodin party finished hauling their supplies to Windy Arm. The next day the Congress of the United States acknowledged that a state of war existed between the two countries, as it imposed a blockade of Cuba. The news, when it reached Skagway at the end of April, prompted a "Patriotic Parade" on May 1, after Jay Woodin had sold his horses and left the city. Apparently it took another three weeks for the news of the war to reach the camp at Windy Arm.

May 15. Had company this forenoon, a Mr. Wells of Ithaca, Mich. Father knew him well back Home. He wants to buy in with us to go down the river, but I don't care about him going. I think he is too much like Green, and I had all of that kind of experience I want for awhile.

Next day [May 16] while at work on the boats, an old gentleman nearing his sixtieth year accosted Father in a familiar way, and introduced himself as Mr. Wells of Michigan [see Biographies]. He had known Father many years before, having lived not far from our home in the state named, and was now on his way to Dawson. He had been informed that Father was on his way to Dawson, and wishing to overtake us, had been rightly directed to Windy Arm. Being entirely alone, his desire was to join our party and immediately made known his object in looking us up. With our enormous stock of supplies, we did not feel that we could very well accommodate another party in our boat, and circumstance afterward proved this a wise act on our part. The old gentleman was much disappointed when the facts of the matter were put before him, but he saw the logic of our refusal and did not force his cause farther.

It was here where Green and Chamberlain came to the old gentleman's rescue and offered him a berth on their boat, which he readily accepted. Their boat had been planned to carry double the amount of which their outfits consisted, so there remained plenty of room, and having three instead of two to man the boat would be a great benefit. So after a speedy agreement, the Green, Chamberlain and Wells Co. was launched, and in the trials and tribulations of the river voyage, his intelligence and good judgment helped us all out of many a tight squeeze.

The week that followed [May 17-22] was without unusual event, but a great quantity of hard work was done, by which much was accomplished toward the completion of the boats. It had become evident the forepart of the week that a shortage of material would necessitate more whipsawing. So the greater portion of the week, two of us had spent at this laborious pastime, sawing some of the choicest timber we had yet seen. Much of this lumber was used in the construction of two skiffs, which we thought advisable to build to be used as tenders. I will say that before Dawson City was reached, they had become an indispensable acquisition. The end of the week found the two larger boats nearly completed. The wood work had been finished, the calking had been done, and all that yet remained to be done was pitching the joints, which required little time to do.

Thurs. May 19. Have been caulking Green's boat all day today, that is Green, Father and Mr. Wells have it finished tonight. Next will come pitching and decking the bow a distance of six feet. Father's boat is now ready for caulking and probably will finish it tomorrow. Wells is now one of the Company. Has had some trouble with his party and has left them and bought in with us yesterday, so is helping with the finishing touches. He will sail with Green and Chamberlain, as there isn't room in Father's and our boat.

May 20. Have put in a hard day at whipsawing. Have been sawing on shares, that is one of McKnight's men, Thompson by name, and I are finishing up the finishing touches on the large boats, but finished up tonight, I guess but may run short yet. The boats will be ready to launch Monday next. Have the oars to cut out now. Oh! Won't I be glad when I get out of this place. I will die of homesickness if I don't. This end of the lake shore has undergone a great change since we came here. The shore ice has all gone out and boats have taken its place, at least a dozen boats go in the lake every day. We helped take two down last night and two tonight. Quite a snow storm this forenoon. Snow fell to the depth of 3 inches and had to give up sawing for 1½ hours. Never saw snow fall so thickly before, but disappeared as quickly as it came. Got a letter from Mother and my little wife tonight. How homesick it made me feel, but I must not give up now. Must keep up my courage and endure it now. What a long year it will be.

The ice that had up to this week held together was now a shifting mass of miniature icebergs being quickly ground to pieces as they came in contact with one another, forced thus by the incessant stiff breeze coming down the valley. This breeze had gradually forced the ice clear of the south shore, which had given an opportunity to those desiring to launch their boats without fear of having them demolished by the action of the enormous bodies of ice. Many boats had been launched during the week and the number was increasing daily. Sunday was spent applying the finishing touches, and when night fell, the two large boats were complete in every detail.

Upon rising on the following morning, Monday, May 23, no ice remained to be seen, having disappeared around the point of land some two miles down the Arm. This state of affairs had an electrical effect on the camp. It was an incentive to renewed action, as much work by many was yet to be done. To all appearances the way was clear for the voyage to begin this morning, but lack of knowledge of the condition of the Arm below us was to be taken into consideration. Few favored the idea of taking any chances of being caught in the ice jam, which possibly would cause a loss of outfit and life. But in spite of the advice and good common sense voiced on the folly of so early an embarkment, four parties did, during the day, take unto themselves the responsibility of an early start, and left with bag and baggage amid the cheers of the whole community, who had gathered at the shore to see them off. This had been the first departure from here, and I must say, as we witnessed the setting of the sails and saw them glide beautifully out of the little harbor into the broad expanse of the lake, a feeling of restlessness took possession of the camp. They were soon lost sight of around the point two miles distant, and from our observation here, little was to hinder them from continuing on down the lake. But advices a few days later were to the effect that they were tightly wedged in the ice about five miles from camp, although nothing of a serious matter had yet befallen them. Although this news put a quietus to those contemplating an early departure, the latter part of the week saw many leave each day.

We now planned that with all the work before us, we could not possibly get away before the first day of June. The two skiffs were yet to be constructed, sails to be made, more oars to be fashioned, and one hundred and one little incidentals would pop up not yet thought of, while the loading of the goods would be no small task in itself.

During the day, the two large boats were launched without mishap. It required the combined efforts of thirty-two men to handle our large boat [Will's diary of May 23 states that it took thirty-four men], which to my knowledge was one of the largest built at this point. It was of the dory type with a length of thirty-two feet, while the beam measured six feet across, and was capable of a tonnage of six to eight tons, and drawing twenty inches of water. As she struck the water with a splash, I, without the formality of champagne, christened her the *Skookum*, the Siwash Indian name meaning "big and strong," which I thought quite appropriate. With much less difficulty, the Green and Chamberlain boat was launched, Green naming it "May G." in honor of his wife.[6] The two boats were complete in their own particular type, and rode the incoming waves in an admirable way. Very little water had found its way through its well-built sides and bottom; when night came (and during the whole voyage) little trouble was caused from this source, which was not the case with all.

As soon as a boat was finished, it was the custom for a necessary number of men to turn to and cooperate with his neighbor by assisting him in moving his boat from the scene of construction to the water. In this way it saved much time and hard, heavy work, as many had built their boats a considerable distance from the lake on account of the congested condition nearer the shore. We took part in many of these moving "bee's" at the latter end of our stay here, which services were gladly and gratefully returned when our turn came.

The lake shore now presented a far different scene than at any time since we had arrived. About three hundred boats extended along the shore for nearly one half mile and were resting easily on their anchors. Some places they could be seen two and three deep, thus representing a party. An activity in loading preparatory to leaving had set in, and a busier and more unusual scene would be hard to describe. It is quite probable that another scene of a like character and extent will never be witnessed in a rush for gold.

May 23. Father is working for the Giffert Mill Co. this afternoon in payment for lumber for the two little skiffs.

May 24. Mr. Wells, Father and Green are all at work at Gifferts Mill today building a steamer for him in exchange for lumber for our two skiffs.

Bill and Daugherty are tinkering around at odd jobs such as getting out jib
poles, fish poles, pike poles and sawed a chord of wood to take along in the
boat, and also took the boat down and got part of our earned lumber at the
Mill. I am cooking. People are rushing their goods to their boats or cach-
ing on the beach making ready for departure as the time presents itself. The
boys from Giffert's Mill gave us a surprise tonight. A big gang came up and
we had music and singing for God's sake. Got a P.I. [Seattle Post-Intelli-
gencer] *tonight giving full details of the War in progress between the U.S.*
and Spain. The U.S. seems to be the aggressor so far.

Windy Arm, May 25, 1898. The boys will finish paying for the lum-
ber 300 ft. of it at $15.00 per hundred. They are allowed $7.00 per day
apiece… The boys got in only three fourth's day today. The mill Co. run out
of spikes and had to go hunt some.

As the month of May advanced, the weather grew warmer, which
greatly increased the greatest pest and inconvenience man is compelled
to endure in the northland, "mosquitoes." Wednesday [May 25] was a
very warm day, the thermometer registering 90 degrees in the shade.
The heat continued far into the night, accompanied by swarms of mosquitoes, which made it anything than pleasant with their vicious attacks.
Upon being repulsed, the mosquitoes would return with reinforcements
double in number, their object evidently being to exterminate us then
and there. This proved the first night of discomfort from these little
pests, but I can assure you it was not the last.

On Thursday evening [May 26] at about six o'clock, the report
became circulated that a young man of the community, while hunting
in the hills to the south of us, had accidentally shot himself. The wound
proved fatal before help could reach him. His comrade, upon seeing the
fatal results, had returned to camp, bringing the news, and soliciting aid
in bringing the body in. A sufficient party left immediately and returning, reached camp about ten p.m. The body was taken in charge of by
the Masons, of which order he was a member, and cared for in the best
manner under the existing circumstances. The young man was twenty-
four years of age and hailed from Boston, Massachusetts. His name I
never heard, not having been thrown in his company, as their camp was
some distance from ours, but I had upon several occasions seen him. He
was a striking fellow, being stalwart in stature and a handsome, honest

countenance that conveyed intelligence and a sunny disposition, one a poor mother and Father at home would mourn the loss of until their dying day.

May 25. Word was circulated about 6 o'clock tonight that a young fellow had accidentally shot himself while hunting and which proved to be true, as they brought the body in from Too Schi Lake about 10 o'clock tonight. He was a fine looking fellow, 24 years of age and was from some place in Massachusetts. Did not learn his name. This makes the third death here since we arrived here.

May 27, 1898. The funeral of the lad that was shot on the 25th occurred today at 10 o'clock and about 200 people turned out to attend it. The miners appointed a coroner and he gave in the verdict of shot accidentally while hunting and also a doctor gave his certificate so as to show his parents how and where he was killed. He was buried under the auspices of the Masons Order as he was a member, about 30 Masons here.

Two days later [May 27] after all technicalities compelled by law was complied with, such as a coroner's inquest and a licensed physician's certificate of manner of death, the funeral took place under the auspices of the Mason order, there being about thirty numbers in the community belonging to that famous old order. The entire camp turned out to attend the ceremony, which was an impressive affair conducted in a beautiful manner, after which the body was lowered to its resting place until such a time kindred advice came from his parents.

May 27. Went down to Gifferts Camp and took Cal Johnson [see Biographies], *an old Seattle friend, and then pulled down to 2 Mile Point, 2 miles from our camp. From here we could see plainly solid ice 4 miles below, but people are leaving in numbers now, by taking chances of getting around the ice. By this time next week Windy Arm will be a thing of the past.*

That evening after work, Father, Daugherty and myself made a trial trip in our large boat, and all were enthusiastic in the manner in which she behaved. In spite of her size and clumsy type she made good time with the leg of mutton sail going with the stiff breeze that was blowing. The run was made to the point two miles below camp, and from there could be seen four miles beyond, ice in great quantities, slowly working its way out of the narrow arm, which eventually, when caught by the current, would be whisked down the river until dissolved. The return to camp required considerable more time than the run down had taken, on account of the head wind that was encountered, but was partially overcome by resorting to tacking. The wind finally died out entirely, making it necessary to bring the oars into play, which we found out before reaching camp to be no boys' play. We finally reached the landing with aching back and arms, but were thoroughly satisfied with our initial trip.

The day had been clear and beautiful, and as we reached camp, our watches told us the hour was eleven o'clock. Notwithstanding this late hour, daylight yet remained sufficient to read newspaper print, and away to the west the wooded hills were bathed in the last beautiful tints of the sun, which had disappeared some time before. True to nature, the days were now fast approaching their extreme length, which became more pronounced as one neared the Arctic Circle. Now that but two or three hours of darkness was given us, a severe attack of insomnia had developed, which was difficult to overcome. Try as we would, some days elapsed before we could educate and content ourselves to retire before darkness set in. Even then, many wakeful hours were spent occupying our thoughts with the golden future and of the dear ones at home. Later on, with long hours filled with hard work, combined with the responsibility of the river voyage, sleep under any circumstance and conditions was regularly indulged in.

Sunday, May 29 dawned warm and beautiful. In fact, the weather was becoming settled, more like the spring weather in the central eastern states, and quite contrary to the opinion that many people held that Alaska and the North West Territories possessed a perpetual winter climate. This belief was general up to but a few years ago, and even today there are many people living in the East who sincerely believe that Alaska is one vast frigid waste the year around. It was but a few days ago that I had occasion to refer to the warm weather encountered while on this trip, when the party addressed actually scoffed at the idea of ninety degree weather in Alaska at any time of the year. No doubt he had not interested himself in the statistical reports of that wonderful country.

To return to my story, we had arisen quite early, and after the morning meal had been prepared and dispatched, all became busy with work planned for the day. The two skiffs had been finished during the forenoon and launched later in the day. Daugherty, Wells and Chamberlain loaded the triple outfit on board the "May G," finishing late in the evening. With her cargo aboard, she was lowered in the water sixteen inches, but deemed by all to be absolutely safe in dodging the rocks and sand bars that would surely be encountered on the way down. This, no doubt, would be the last Sunday we would spend at Windy Arm, and even now, many of our friends were planning to leave at an early hour on the following morning. Before another Sunday dawned, the camp at Windy Arm where we had met and made many staunch and true friends, and with whom we had spent scores of pleasant hours, would be but a memory of the past. Before another week expired, the throng would be separated and scattered along the great river, the exact whereabouts of one another would be impossible to determine, while many of the faces would be seen no more. As the time of departure grew near, it was evident that a feeling of regret was felt among the men, and this feeling was fully demonstrated during the evening.

During the day a farewell meeting had been arranged to take place at our camp. After the day's work was finished, the guests began to arrive, and they did not cease coming until fifty or sixty were present. The evening was spent in a glorious manner. Music, dancing, and singing made up a creditable program that was immensely enjoyed and appreciated, judging from the spirit evidenced. The revelry was indulged in up to a late hour, when three rousing cheers were given for those leaving on the morrow, after which the gathering dispersed to their primitive abodes. The few hours of night that yet remained were put to good advantage in a restful snooze.

Windy Arm, May 28, morning. All hands on the boats again today. Bill and Malin cutting and sewing the sails. We are trying to get out of here Wed. June 1st and guess will make it without any trouble at all. Night. Have all the wood work done on the two little skiffs and also all the caulking. All that remains now is the pitching and then our carrying capacity will be complete. Several boats pulled out today for down River. One saw mill will remain here only, that is Racins, all three of the others will move nearer Dawson. After doing up the work this evening went down to Giffert's Camp to give the boys a farewell Saturday night serenade, for by next Sunday all the camp will be deserted and we will be separated on all parts of the Yukon River or its tributaries. I will give some of the names of my acquaintances that were here tonight. Geo. Bert Eastman of Omaha, Neb. [see Biographies], *who I have fallen in love with and is a fine fellow, good natured and jolly. Tom Murray of San Francisco, Cal. who has played the banjo for us. Larry for short for Al Larimer of Marion, Indiana, the mandolin player, who is a sullen and disagreeable fellow, but can play a mandolin to perfection "and he knows it, too." He is traveling alone. Jack Gilchrist and John Malady, both of Wabash, Indiana. Gilchrest is a fine singer and has furnished with that part of the program since we have been here. Foster Bros. of Seattle, Allen Bros. and Zach Hickeman of Seattle, Ed Herring also of Seattle, Bruce Ives, Eastman's partner* [see Biographies], *"Dutch" Myres of Wabash, Indiana, and several others I have not learned their names, but I give the most intimate ones. "Larry," Jack G—,* [and] *I came down in a skiff, Home for we are all camped together at the lower Arm. Very windy and lake very choppy, nearly as light as day, for have no more night. It was 11 o'clock when I lay myself down to sleep, but could not get to sleep, my mind and soul was with my little Sweetheart so far away. If I could only have been with* [her] *tonight how happy I would be.*

We were astir at an early hour [May 29], and after the morning meal, all hands immediately got busy loading our outfit, which was carried on incessantly throughout the day. It was nine o'clock that night when the last of it was placed aboard. During the progress of loading, it was soon discovered that the boat was going to leak considerably. This trouble lay in the seams that, since launching, had remained out of the water. Exposure to the hot sun during the week had shrunk the lumber, leaving a chance for the water to ooze through the oakum-filled joints. This condition, however, would be only temporary, for as the weight of the outfit settled the boat into the water, the lumber would swell and eventually cause the joints to come closely together again. It was found, after bailing the water out on the following morning, that no more was coming in, and little trouble from this source was caused thereafter.

It was seen after all goods were aboard that the enormous weight of the latter settled the boat amidships into the water twenty inches. This fact caused us much concern, and not many days thereafter, we found out through experience that our suspicions were well founded. I actually believe that every sand bar and rock of any prominence in the great river was scraped in our descent. It was now too late to make any change in our plans, and so it was decided to take the chances and leave on the specified time agreed to, notwithstanding the handicap we were subject to. After putting everything in shipshape we retired for the last time at Windy Arm.

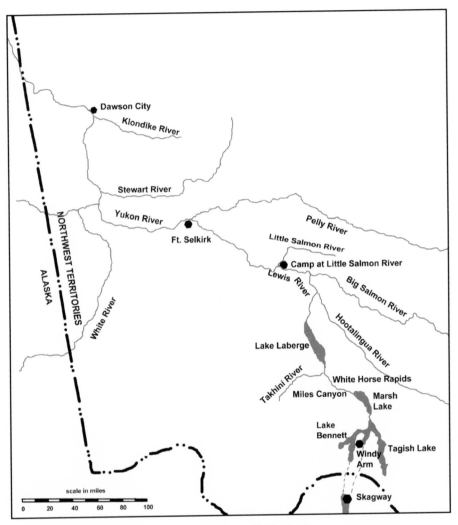

The Yukon River, Skagway to Dawson. *Catherine Holder Spude*

Chapter Five

WINDY ARM TO LITTLE SALMON RIVER
MAY 30–JUNE 6, 1898

╬══╬

T HE WOODIN PARTY RAPIDLY SETTLED into a routine once they embarked on the river phase of their trip. Will's second of the three diaries from 1898 covered the period from May 29–August 25. Unfortunately, it is missing entirely. Therefore, the only account of the river trip is his memoir, and a short story that he wrote years later that recounted the drowning of George Sherwood. This event apparently affected Will greatly, and he believed it served as a metaphor for the dangers of the trip. He called the story "The Toll of the Yukon."

George Sherwood appears to have been a nephew of Woodin party member William H. Wells. Wells' brother-in-law, who was also named George Sherwood, died in Michigan in 1892. His namesake son was probably only seventeen or eighteen years old.[1] It is curious that Will never mentioned Sherwood's relationship to Wells, and it is possible that he did not know of it. On May 15, at Windy Arm, when Wells first approached the Woodin party about becoming a member, he stated that he was traveling alone. Later, on May 19, he admitted that he had had trouble with his previous traveling partners and chose to leave their company. Will once implied that Wells was an unpleasant person (see May 15) and it is possible that he and his young nephew had parted company upon reaching Windy Arm.

More is known about Sherwood's childhood friend, George Milham (whom Will misidentified as George Melheim). He was a blue-eyed, light-haired, slender-built man who was born in 1882, making him only seventeen years old when he went to the Klondike. On June 10, Will states that it was William F. "Ed" Green who introduced the two Georges to the Woodin party. One of Green's colleagues in Seattle was Samuel Francis Milham, George's father. The two older men were featured in a 1909 Seattle newspaper article about the city's prosperous express men. Samuel, who was born in England, had come to Seattle from Wisconsin in 1879, three years before George was born. He operated an express business in Seattle from 1882 to at least 1905.[2]

This leg of the journey appeared to be the most dangerous, and men who were unaccustomed to boats were especially vulnerable to the cold river's hazards. Will often noted wrecked boats and graves lining the river banks; he must have keenly felt the dangers that he and his party faced.

I have included both Will's memoir account of the drowning and his short story, as the two complement one another. It was not really possible to integrate the two accounts, so the short story is here included as an insert opposite the memoir account. I deleted his description of Milham's reaction to Sherwood's death as told in the memoir, as it was shorter, not so well written, and duplicative of his version in the short story.

During this leg of the trip, the Woodin party encountered the first of several groups of First Nations people. While the words "squaw" and "buck" are now considered derogatory, their use was common at the time of his writing. Will's condescending attitude toward the native people of British Columbia and the Yukon Territory was characteristic of most Euro-Americans at the time. While I wrestled with the idea of making his language more acceptable to modern readers, I ultimately decided that it was better to reveal the prejudices of the time.

In a final note, Will often refers to the Lewis River in this portion of the float downstream. In 1898, the Yukon River was called the Lewis above its intersection with the Pelly River. Today, it is called the Yukon River all the way upstream to Marsh Lake.

We now rejoin Will and his party as they begin their voyage on the lakes that will take them to the Yukon River.

+=+=+

Authentic reports had been received during the day [May 29] that the ice had gone out of Lake Tagish, and was then fast disappearing down the river from Lake Marsh [the next lake downstream in the chain that led to the Yukon River]. This condition, if true, was such that a start down the lakes could be made at once, and it was therefore decided to leave on the morrow [May 30], instead of June 1 as first planned. We were awakened in the morning from the commotion caused by a number of neighboring parties razing their camps and preparing to embark on the long voyage. It was a busy scene that was presented to us as we emerged from our tent, having slept a little later this morning than we had intended doing.

About two score of parties were busily engaged in pulling up stakes and otherwise preparing for an immediate departure, and it did not take us long in following suit. It was not long thereafter that they began taking their leave. Some left singly, while others would form a party of two or three boats, keeping as close as possible during the day and camping and cooking their meals together at night. This latter rule was adopted by us, and I do not remember of one instance, although being separated all day, that when night came on, the entire party was not complete.

After eating a quickly prepared breakfast, we made all haste in moving the camp equipage to the boat, after which the tent was removed from its frame. Soon after, all was in readiness to begin the voyage we had so long looked forward to. It was at 8:30 that the command "all aboard" was given and was promptly obeyed. The boats were shoved clear of the moorage, the large square sails hoisted, and with the strong, favorable breeze blowing, filled immediately. The wind soon gave us good headway, and in thirty minutes, we had rounded Two Mile Point, shutting out from view the ever to be remembered camp at Windy Arm.

The day was gloriously beautiful and bid fair to continue so throughout. The cold mountain breeze was tempered by the bright sunlight, the effect of which was exhilarating and grand. It was so thoroughly enjoyed that I am quite sure our real mission was forgotten for a time. As we neared the main portion of Lake Tagish, a glance backward brought to our notice the magnificence and grandeur of the receding scenery, which in my estimation would be difficult to duplicate in any part of the world. Standing out bold above the distant foreground, the snow-covered sentinels of the far away coast range could be plainly seen, glimmering in bright sunlight. In our immediate vicinity, the stately hills, their bases lapped by the gentle surf of the lake, rose to a great height, now entirely devoid of its winter mantle of snow. Before us could be seen a portion of beautiful Lake Tagish with its surface ruffled by the breeze, adding a charm to the beautiful scene.

After we had rounded Two Mile Point, the already stiff breeze increased in strength, until it threatened to carry away the mast, and despite the heavily loaded boat, we gained a rate of speed that surprised all. It was about twelve o'clock that we spied a low, shelving beach on the right hand shore, an admirable spot to eat our lunch. We therefore turned the prow of our boat toward shore, and were soon on terra firma, thoroughly enjoying a cold lunch, our appetites having been whetted by the invigorating sail of the forenoon. The spot where we had landed was located directly opposite Caribou Crossing, the wide and sluggish river-like passage that connects Lake Bennett with Lake Tagish. It derives its name from the fact that during certain times of the year, the northern animal bearing that name crosses in herds of unaccountable numbers.

The body of water that Will called Caribou Crossing was actually the east-northeast trending Nares Lake, which connects the main body of Tagish Lake to Lake Bennett. Caribou Crossing proper was actually a narrow spit of land where Nares and Bennett Lakes meet. The Woodin party lunched near the confluence of Nares and Tagish lakes, located about 7.4 miles east-southeast of the present town of Carcross.

We were anxious to reach Tagish House [a post of the North-West Mounted Police] before night set in, so little time was spared for lunch, and in thirty minutes we were ready to hoist the sail once more. We were soon under way with a good stiff breeze still coming from the south that bid fair to assist us in reaching our given point. But alas, at about two o'clock, soon after entering Lake Tagish and leaving the influence of Windy Arm, the breeze subsided in a remarkably short space of time. It left us becalmed in the middle of the lake with no indication of a change during the remainder of the day. There seemed but one course for us to pursue, and that was to resort to the oars, which were at once brought into play, but with rather discouraging effect.

The sun was very hot, and now that the breeze had died out, it beat down on us without mercy. Even after discarding all clothing possible, we suffered intensely from the heat. The breeze did not freshen the remainder of the afternoon, so we applied ourselves to the oars until we put into camp for the night. Where we camped gave us a point of view of a greater portion of the lake, plainly showing where Windy Arm and Caribou Crossing [Nares Lake] entered, while for miles to the south the eye was able to follow the shore line of Taku Arm, the principle arm of Lake Tagish. The estimated length of this body of water is between fifty and sixty miles and up to this time little was known of the country bordering its shores being almost entirely unexplored by whites.

Some little time before going into camp and just as the sun was settling behind the mountains, bathing their crests and the western sky in a beautiful gold hue, we witnessed a sight that held our gaze in admiration: a sight the like that in all probability will never be looked upon again. Oh, what a subject for an artist's brush. As we rested on our oars and looked back, the mirror-like surface of the lake was bathed in a golden reflection of the beautiful sunset; it was thickly studded for miles with boats numbering between five and six hundred. Sails were set to catch any little puff of wind that might come along, and here and there among the vast assemblage could be seen at short intervals a quick flash of light as the dying sunlight struck the wet oars that were being plied in the absence of the wind. Now and then wafted over the still waters would come the melody of a popular air denoting that the occupants were in a happy mood, no doubt rejoicing in the thought that in but a few days the land of gold and fortune would be reached.

The exodus from Windy Arm and Lake Bennett during the day had been tremendous. One thousand would be a fair estimate without exaggerating the number of boats that entered Lake Tagish from those two points since daylight. Many of these had already passed out of the lake into the river, which connects Lake Tagish and Lake Marsh. Of course, those who had done so had spent the previous night in the vicinity of Caribou Crossing, and getting an early start, had reached the river before the breeze died out.

Soon after the sun sank behind the distant mountains, we turned the prow of our boat toward the left shore, preparatory to camping for the night. This shore afforded an easy landing at almost any point, but the pebbly, sandy beach was quite absent, a dark muddy soil instead being much in evidence where we camped. As the faint twilight gathered, the shore as far as the eye could see was lined with the travelers preparing their evening meals, as was evidenced by the many bonfires fed with a plentiful supply of brush and wood gathered nearby. After the evening meal was dispatched, we at once returned to the boats, after having constructed a temporary shelter thereon of one our small tents. Our fatigue was greater than we had felt for some days owing to our cramped quarters on the boat, and despite the millions of mosquitoes that surrounded us, we were soon fast asleep.

The morning [of May 31] at four o'clock found us astir. In spite of the early hour many boats had already shoved off and were now some distance from our camp making slow progress toward the outlet of Lake Tagish. The morning was clear and beautiful and so still that sound from the regular manipulated oars far down the lake came to our ears as plainly as though the boats were within a stone's throw of us. Little time was spent in preparing breakfast and little before five o'clock the word "all aboard" was shouted. Hoisting a sail was absolutely useless as not a breath of air was stirring, therefore compelling us to apply ourselves to the oars. As the day advanced, we suffered intensely from the hot rays of the sun.

As we neared the mouth of the river, the topography of the surrounding country took on a decided change. Instead of the immediate presence of the high mountainous hills, the country took on a comparatively level aspect, stretching out for miles, being finally interrupted by a range of towering foothills.

The river was reached at 10:30 that forenoon, and after a run of about one mile, we were forced to run in and tie up to the right hand bank. I say forced to tie up and in implying the word "forced" was quite consistent to the existing circumstance. It was here on the short narrow river about midway between Lakes Tagish and Marsh that the Canadian Government had established a custom house. Here they collected duties, thus making doubly sure that none other than their own subjects passed into the territory without paying the fee imposed. [As Will has previously related, customs were taken at the summit of White Pass. However, there was no similar presence on the Chilkoot Pass, so the North-West Mounted Police stopped all travelers as they funneled through this channel in order to check, and if necessary, assess the proper customs.] The offices were located down the river about one and one half miles from where we had run ashore. Owning to the great number of boats that had put in ahead of us, it was impossible to gain a closer proximity to the building, therefore we were compelled to walk the distance to and from many times before leaving.

The shore was lined with boats lying closely together, and in many cases, two and three abreast for at least two miles in length, their owners waiting only for their clearance papers before proceeding on their way

In this 1898 photograph by E. A. Hegg, the waterfront near the Tagish Post Custom House is lined with small sailboats, people, and tents. *Alaska State Library, P. E. Larss Photograph Collection, PCA-41-153.*

down the river. The number increased at a rapid rate, and each hour saw the line grow as the vast fleet of boats from the lake above came into the river, taking their place regularly in line. The vast number that was continually leaving seemed to make no impression on the multitude, and it was estimated at one time on the following day that the throng contained ten thousand souls.

Soon after landing and a lunch was eaten, Father, Green and myself proceeded with much anxiety toward the Custom headquarters. We had been informed soon after arriving that between four and five hundred persons were in line waiting for their turn in procuring clearance papers from the customs officials. At the rate they cleared people, it would require two days of constant waiting before our papers could be obtained. As we neared the mammoth log structure it became quite evident that what we had heard earlier in the day was not in the least exaggerated. As we came up to the line of humanity which extended, as it seemed, for one half mile, our hearts sank within us. Here men who stood or sat on logs, boxes and even the earth for hours, gradually moved by degrees toward their goals. Some of those in line were eating a lunch brought by a partner, for leaving the line meant a return to the rear. Some were visiting with his neighbor in front or in his rear, others were sitting silently, no doubt thinking of the wife or sweetheart at home far away. Possibly, their thoughts were of an optimistic turn, dwelling on the time that they would return to that wife or sweetheart with a plenty of the yellow metal.

I was, without loss of time, appointed by our party to take a place in the line, and will, while there, give a few descriptive lines to the locality. Up to the time of the discovery of the Klondike there had been two or three ramshackle log huts here used by hunters and trappers, many years ago, but which had long since been deserted. Besides these now stood three large roomy structures built expressly to house a large detachment of the North West Mounted Police and Custom officials necessary to cope with the tremendous influx of gold seekers. Located as it were on the narrow, shallow neck of water, a more admirable location for that which it was used would be difficult to find. Very few, if any at all, passed Tagish Post without first having their outfits inspected by one of the courteous police on duty here.

The entire afternoon was spent in the long, human line, and with the scorching hot sun beating down on our unprotected bodies, the hours dragged, seeming like so many days. When at last the doors of the Custom Office closed for the night, I felt an undeniable weariness and illness. Upon closing the office at the end of the day, a system had been inaugurated by the Custom officials whereby those in line at the time the office closed for the day did not lose their position after spending many valuable hours in line. At the closing hour, each person in line received a numbered ticket consistent with his relative position, which upon presenting on the following morning, he would be given his position of the day before. This plan was strictly adhered to, and prevented much ill feeling, and few if any comments against the plan were heard among the throng. My number when the doors closed that night read fifty-five, and a fair estimate of the number behind me was between five and six hundred, with the line growing at a rapid rate. As soon as the doors closed for the night, I returned to the boat, and at an early hour retired and was soon fast asleep.

Long before the opening hour on the following morning [June 1] found those in line of the day before holding their respective position, while at least two hundred new recruits had joined the ranks. Gradually, as the forenoon wore away, the number ahead of me grew less, and at eleven o'clock I was in possession of the long-sought-for papers. As I left the office and surveyed the long line which numbered, without a doubt, one thousand souls, I felt that I had been very fortunate in the fact that two and three days would expire before those in the rear would be able to procure their papers. Gratified with my success, I at once returned to the boat, and luckily little time was lost in securing an examining officer. With a long slender rod sharpened at one end, he pierced our sacks of flour and dried fruits to make sure that no whiskey, tobacco, nor other high dutiable articles were among our possessions. This was done to his satisfaction after a quick but thorough examination, and at 11:45 we were ready to resume our journey down the river.

Another Klondike diarist, Robert F. Graham, got to the Tagish Custom House a day later than the Woodin party, on June 2, 1898. He paid a four dollar bribe to the inspector and only had to wait three hours. Will had noted "tipping" a customs agent five dollars on the summit of White Pass on March 29, but apparently the party did not feel a similar bribe to be worth the time that would be saved at Tagish. Five dollars in 1898 was worth about $140 in today's currency.[3]

The day was hot and sultry, and as we left our moorings and gained the middle of the stream, the sluggish current bore us slowly toward Lake Marsh five miles below. A short time before leaving Tagish Post, we were informed that about twelve miles of ice still remained in Lake Marsh, obstructing traffic completely. The ice, however, was in an entirely broken state, and was rapidly disappearing down the Lewis

River. We immediately, upon receiving this information, decided to wait until morning before proceeding farther. After running down the river about three miles, we ran in on a beautiful sandy beach and set up camp for the night. We were now within one mile of the lake, and many miles out on its surface could be seen the shifting ice as it glittered in the sunlight. As night drew near, however, it had receded to such a distance that it became entirely invisible, and no doubt the following morning would see the lake entirely clear of ice. The night was very warm, and despite the low river bottom where we were camped, the mosquitoes gave us little trouble. We retired to our rude beds at an unusually early hour, and slept soundly until two thirty on the following morning.

We arose much refreshed, and as there was a brisk breeze coming from the south, we made all haste in preparing for an early start, so we might receive full benefit of the wind, and relieve us from much tedious labor at the oars. At four o'clock [June 2] we got under way, and in twenty minutes entered Lake Marsh. The wind caught our square sail with great force, sending the heavily loaded boat along at a good rate of speed.

Lake Marsh is a shallow body of water, twenty-eight miles long and varying from two to three miles in width, with few islands of any consequence appearing on its surface. However, there are many troublesome bars composed of a muddy, clayey composition dotting its surface at frequent intervals. In a majority of cases, they remain in a treacherous manner beneath the surface, and on several occasions while crossing the lake, I have reason to remember them. The lake was named after Professor O. W. Marsh, a well-known scientist, by Lieut. Frederick Schwatka, a noteworthy explorer of the Yukon Territories and Alaska, while on his trip down the Yukon River in the year 1883. During the rush to the Klondike in 1897, it was appropriately known and called by the gold-seekers Mud Lake from the fact that very few points on its shores could be reached without one being compelled to wade through the thick, glue-like muck for two or three hundred feet before reaching shore. It is nearly surrounded by marshy lowlands, and very few spots in its vicinity afford a suitable camping ground.

Beyond the low, marshy ground, a beautiful, level prairie country receded for miles, which no doubt in the summer-time affords a luxuriant grazing ground for the animals found in this section. Far away on either hand, the brown-hued foothills were to be seen forming a circular basin with the lake in the center.

After leaving the short river, the breeze increased continually until after the noon hour, and at one p.m., we entered the Lewis River. The wind had served us admirably, and even with considerable time spent relieving our boat from the treacherous mud bars, the entire length of the lake had been run in eight hours, causing much satisfaction, and congratulations were in order that we were not compelled to row that distance.

The river as it leaves Lake Marsh is between three and four hundred feet wide, I should judge, with little or no current for the first six to eight miles. The wind that had almost died out before leaving Lake Marsh freshened again, coming now from the northwest, and row as we might, little progress downstream could be made against the strong element.

Finally at a point about five miles from the lake we pulled into the shore to prepare a warm dinner, the need of which we felt very much after our long trip. Despite the gale that was blowing, the mosquitoes fairly surrounded us in clouds, and without further thought of our empty stomachs, we were glad to enter our boats again. Not until many feet separated us from the shore did the pests give up the fight. We had heard many times before what we thought exaggerated tales of the discomforts and suffering caused by the persistent little pests, but we did not come to a full realization of their combined powers until the descent of the great river was begun. The lay of the land adjacent to the river for about ten miles after leaving Lake Marsh is low, and in some places swampy, while all is covered with a heavy growth of stunted poplars and willows. This serves an admirable breeding place for the pestilent little insects, and at no point on the great river and its tributaries did we see them in greater numbers than here.

As we again gained midstream, we found that the strong headwind had not abated in the least. Giant strokes were required to make any headway, while to rest on the oars meant to be blown back upstream, as the sluggish current served great resistance.

During the afternoon, we came upon what appeared to be an old fort which might at one time have been used by the Hudson['s] Bay Co., but as to the authenticity of this, I am not able to say, and we were unable to find out.

As evening approached, the wind abated. The current of the river grew decidedly stronger, as could be seen as its waters rippled playfully around the sandbars that now appeared at frequent intervals. It required a more careful watch to be kept by the stern oarsman in dodging them. Our first realization of the dangers and perils we were to encounter in descending the great river were this afternoon fully demonstrated when one of the boats in our party ran fair and square astride a large flat rock barely submerged in midstream. The heavily loaded boat was carried with such force that but a small portion of the hull remained under water. After removing several hundred pounds of her cargo, we were able to release her, and it was found that little or no damage resulted from her mishap. But not so with all. Many boats have come to grief by its treacherous presence, the owners losing their entire outfits and barely escaping with their lives.

After reloading their outfit, we once more proceeded down the river in a more cautious manner. We were soon riding between high, white sand banks broken here and there by velvety green ravines and valleys, some with streams that tumbled carelessly over a rocky barrier into the mighty stream. With the setting of the sun behind the hills, our stomachs began to give evidence of the neglect during the day. We sought a camping place and found one on a sloping grassy bank at the entrance to one of the many ravines. Soon thereafter the smell of fried bacon and delicious coffee came to our notice, which did not at all diminish our ferocious appetites. After the meal was over, a ravishing bonfire was built around which the entire crowd gathered to discuss the probable results dependent upon the morrow. We expected that sometime during the next day the roughest waters on the Yukon River, namely Miles Canyon and White Horse Rapids, would be reached, causing excitement and anxiety to run high among the boys.

The next morning [June 3], all were ready to break camp at four o'clock. We entered our boats and proceeded with the assistance of a most favorable breeze, desiring as soon as possible to reach the angry rapids below. The beauty and grandeur of the passing scenery increased as we sped on our way, causing us to forget that we were on other than a pleasure jaunt. The rolling hills receded from the river now in a gentle slope, while again they would rise abruptly from the water's edge appearing not unlike a mammoth cheese freshly sliced. In places on the face of these high, abrupt sand banks, thousands of martins come great distances to hatch and rear their young. They had literally honeycombed the surface as they built their nests. There could be seen flocks of this feathered specie fluttering here and there before the openings, chirping and screaming as they did so.

At about nine o'clock it became quite evident that the water was rapidly increasing speed, plainly denoting the close proximity of the canyon and rapids. As we rounded the frequent bends in the river, a very sharp outlook was kept lest we should go too far and be unable to reach shore in the swift running water. We had previously been cautioned in this regard, as a number before had gone too far, and in their excitement had lost control. Their boats being unable to reach shore, they were carried onward by the swift, angry waters, and in a majority of cases landed safe and sound below the rapids. In our case, with our heavily loaded boats, we cared not to take this chance, much preferring to look over the situation before attempting it, even with the confidence that all felt.

As the noon hour drew near, a long straight stretch of river running between high picturesque hills was reached, which after running several miles, quickly swerves to the left and enters the Canyon six or seven hundred feet below. As we drew near the turn of the river, we could see that several hundred feet of the right hand bank was thickly clustered with boats. A man in the foremost, as we came near, began wildly gesturing for us to run for the shore. At this signal, we began with frantic efforts to reach the shore, succeeding finally after some difficulty, for here the water runs with the speed of a mill race. After fastening our boats securely, we prepared lunch, which due to the excitement, was barely touched. So leaving me in charge of the boats, the remainder of the combined party started out to inspect the perilous waterway from the start to finish.

Excitement was running high among the several hundred people temporarily located here. On most faces, anxiety was plainly written, for it was up to them to choose between three courses in passing this dangerous part of the route to their Mecca. There had gathered here from many parts of the world, men of lifelong experiences in lumbering and running boats in swift waters of this sort. To them, guiding a boat through Miles Canyon and White Horse Rapids was but an exhilarating pastime, and a source of great financial revenue to those so inclined. A pilot's price was from twenty-five to thirty and forty dollars [about $700 to $1,100 in today's currency] for running a boat safely through this dangerous stretch of water, his client paying for his service with easy grace and thanking goodness that men of his inclination was there to do it.

The voyager's second choice was to have his outfit and boat transported overland on tram cars operated by the White Horse Tramway Co., which also had built a large storage warehouse at this end. Their charges for moving an outfit around the rapids were far in excess of those asked by the expert pilot, but after all, the chance of loss of an

Barge with sweeps navigating Miles Canyon. *Yukon Archives, Anton Vogee Fonds, #143.*

entire outfit was reduced to a minimum. Few Argonauts of the ordinary class pursued this course, but the tram was generously patronized by the large outfitters shipping wholesale stores into Dawson City.[4]

Running one's own boat through the Canyon and Rapids by the inexperienced was usually done as a last resort. Long before reaching this point, many had expended every penny they possessed, and were therefore unable financially to hire the services of the expert pilot. But notwithstanding the fact of their inexperience, the rapids were run safely by ninety-nine percent of the vast number that made the attempt, and very few accidents of a serious nature occurred while we were there.

At about five o'clock, the boys returned to the boats. They had started at the canyon and made close observations at different points along the dangerous waterway until the foot of the rapids was revealed, after which trek, they had retraced their footsteps. At the canyon, as well as the rapids, they had viewed several boats ride safely through the gauntlet of savage waters. In mentioning the fact, their tone did not imply a whit of enthusiasm in following the example of those they had seen safely shoot the angry waters during the afternoon.

Shortly upon their return, my curiosity got the better of me, and now being at liberty, I started out on the sightseeing tour they had just finished. The Lewis River, before entering the Canyon, has a width of five or six hundred feet, but whereupon entering the canyon this width is reduced to less than one hundred feet, flowing between the high, perpendicular walls at a greatly increased rate of speed. The volume of water is so great, that as it enters the vastly reduced channel, the waters gradually rise from both walls and form a cone [actually, more like a ridge] in mid-stream, six to eight feet high. It was therefore absolutely necessary for a boat upon entering the canyon to ride the crest of this cone. Otherwise, serious results would surely follow, such as being dashed against the rocky walls, which meant certain destruction of the strongest boat or raft. As for the escape of a human being from the turmoil of angry water, it is impossible.

The canyon walls are of a basaltic formation, rising from fifty to one hundred feet its entire distance of three quarters of a mile in length. About midway there is a circular basin one hundred and fifty feet in diameter, the walls around which conform in formation and height to those of the canyon proper. In this circular basin, a portion of the swift water coming down the canyon is caught, causing a whirlpool that circles at a terrific rate. Woe be unto he who is drawn into its embrace, for hours, possibly days might elapse ere he would be caught by the onward current again. No accidents of this sort occurred while we were there, but a few were afterward recorded, where men had fortunately escaped with their lives.

As I took a position on the precipice giving me an unobstructed view of the yawning chasm with the swift moving water many feet below, a sense of bewildered excitement took possession of me. As a boat rounded the bend and mounted the cone on its mad onward course, I was held as one in a trance. It is a sight that I will ever remember, and a more thrilling scene would be difficult to find. After viewing several more boats, their occupants with white but firm, set faces fly past, I made my way down the shore line toward White Rapids.

After emerging from Miles Canyon, the succeeding link in the chain of turbulent waters in a stretch of water one and one half miles long is called Squaw Rapids. Aside from the swift current, this stretch is quite free from danger if the main channel is kept. After leaving the canyon, the river has a width equal to or a trifle wider than it was above the canyon. Far out from the right hand shore, it appears shallow, and is full of large rocks and boulders, and would be entirely unsafe for navigation.

Squaw Rapids are closely followed by White Horse Rapids, the most dangerous and most dreaded piece of water on the great Yukon River. The rapids are about one half mile in length and the entire distance is filled with treacherous rocks concealed below the surface. If struck by a boat, these rocks would surely mean destruction to all aboard. The rapids have a width of six to eight hundred feet, until the final plunge is reached. Here the low rocky shores close in to between seventy-five and one hundred feet, through which the leaping, seething water passes at a tremendous rate. This final plunge is no doubt the most critical point in the series of angry waters. The drop is considerable, and a boat and occupants, in passing through, are for a few seconds lost to view in the hopping waves and spray. Upon passing safely through, she glides into an eddy, and a landing is easily made.

Just previous to our arrival, two men had lost their lives in the angry waters of the rapids. Their boat came in contact with one of the many rocks in midstream, stoving it and sinking it immediately. The bodies had not yet been recovered, there being little chance that they ever would be. Scores of boats had been wrecked and thousands of dollars worth of outfits ruined. Fortunately, the owners had reached shore in safety, though many a narrow escape had been noted.

After viewing a number of boats shoot the rapids safely, I started on my return trip, my mind fully occupied with the thrilling sights of my afternoon tour. I will say that upon nearing camp, I had not as yet fully made up my mind that I should or should not accompany our boat over the treacherous stretch of rapids on the morrow.

The several parties included in our crowd had finally concluded, earlier in the day, to trust the piloting of the several boats to a young man from Seattle, a friend of one of the party, but owing to the many previous arrangements he had made, it would be two days before he could serve us. This unnecessary loss of time was not satisfactory to many, so Cal Johnson [see Biographies] of the party, a man of iron nerve and great physical strength, volunteered a desire to accompany his young pilot friend on one of his trips over the rough water route. The request was readily granted, and upon his very next trip found Cal a passenger and an able assistant. The trip was made with such success that upon Cal's return a couple of hours later, he concluded that the services of a pilot would be unnecessary, as he could, with the aid of a couple of good oarsmen, accomplish the feat with as good results as his friend, besides saving much time and expense to all.

So with his mind fully made up, early on the following morning [June 4], before many of us were yet awake, Cal called for volunteers to assist him in descending the rapids on his initial trip. Chamberlain and Daugherty at once proclaimed their willingness to accompany him, and preparations were immediately taken in arranging everything shipshape on Green and Chamberlain's boat. This boat was given first choice on account of the size, and also, it was not so heavily loaded, which was thought advisable on first trial. Soon all was in readiness, and with a hearty "au revoir" from those ashore, the boat left her moorings. Upon reaching the current, it shot forward at the speed of an arrow, and was soon swallowed by the canyon's formidable entrance. Notwithstanding the confidence we all placed in Cal's ability to guide the boat safely through the dangerous waters, nevertheless we were a bit anxious as to their success. But regarding this, it was soon evident that our fears were groundless, for in less than two hours, the trio, with smiling faces, put in an appearance. Unusual success had attended them on the trip, and although they fully realized the danger, they had more confidence in repeating it.

Another boat was soon gotten ready, as the former shared their good fortune. Their success caused much elation to be shown among the boys in our party, who showered praises upon the brave trio for their splendid work. After arriving at the canyon and noting conditions, it was feared that our boat was too heavily loaded to safely chance the treacherous waters. However, a lone party with a comparatively empty boat proposed to Father that he, for a nominal sum, would take on some of our goods to Dawson. After coming to a satisfactory agreement, the approximate weight was therefore quickly transferred to his boat. The owner then engaged a pilot, and soon after was safely tied up to the bank below the rapids to wait for us until the following morning, where he would accompany the fleet the remainder of the trip to Dawson. The reduced weight was plainly evident and our anxiety in this respect was allayed to some extent. The boat was still lower in the water than any in the party, but this condition conveyed no horror to Cal and his followers. Shortly after sunset, the three, accompanied by Father and our malamute dog, Skookum, were ready to risk their lives aboard the heavily loaded boat.

After assisting in arranging the boat for the descent, I had, after considering the matter, concluded that "terra firma" was best suited for my nervous temperament. Acting upon my decision, I set off down the tramway in advance of the boat. I had little time to wait after reaching the rapids, and had only reached a ledge overlooking the swirling, seething water where old *Skookum* rounded the bend one half mile above. As she neared the gap, it was a grand sight to note how she labored with the turbulent waters, now wallowing in the embrace of mighty breakers, while the next moment the sharp prow would pierce one, throwing the water to either side in a beautiful white sheet of spray. Cal kept her true to the course and struck the opening as precisely as an adept. For a few seconds all disappeared as completely as though swallowed by a monster sea serpent. Then, with a mighty leap and bound, and with the occupants straining every nerve and ounce of strength at the oars, the boat emerged from the leaping waters and glided swiftly downstream. The men appeared overjoyed to escape the angry, watery jaws that only a misguidance would have meant instant destruction and loss of life.

After running downstream a quarter of a mile, Cal made an easy landing close to the other boats. Being now quite late, a hasty supper was prepared. After a day full of toil and excitement, sleep was quite in order. But before retiring, a scow of huge dimensions and heavily loaded with merchandise had, in its descent, struck the rocky walls of the narrow passage and stove a hole in her bottom. To add to the serious injury, the long sweep oar broke, leaving the huge craft unmanageable and at the mercy of the swift and treacherous current. In its sinking condition, it was quickly being carried to destruction. With their first cries for help, many willing hands went to the rescue, and through their combined efforts, a temporary landing on a sandbar was made about one mile below the rapids. It was found, after an examination was made, that much damage had been done to the scow and much perishable merchandise had been ruined. As a result, a number of days would elapse ere they could continue on their way. This was but one instance of many where reverses occurred to the Yukon voyager, and many were of a more serious character than the one we had witnessed.

I was awakened the next morning [June 5] by Father shouting to Cal, advising him where to make a landing for his own boat. He had arisen early and had cleared the rapids with the last boat of our party. The landing was easily made, and after a hasty breakfast was eaten, preparations were begun to continue on our journey. However, due to a disappointing delay, night was nearly upon us before a start was made. The party who had, without solicitation from us, bargained to take the ton of merchandise to Dawson, informed us in the early morning that it would be impossible for him to take them farther, he giving no excuse other than he could not be bothered with the extra weight. Continuing firm in his wishes, there was but one alternative for us: the forenoon was nearly spent before the goods were reloaded and placed in their former places aboard our boat.

All now happy that White Horse Rapids was left behind, we gave a glad adieu, and were soon once more gliding swiftly down the great river. But our happy frame of mind was at once changed to one of disappointment and surprise in the fact that less than a mile below the rapids, a treacherous sand bar lay in wait. Row as we might, we could not avoid the sandy obstruction. The consequence was that one and one half tons of goods were moved to the rescue boats ere she was dislodged from her stranded position. When the goods were again reloaded, it was time to land for the night, which we did two miles below the rapids, where now stands the little city of White Horse.

The following morning [June 7] an unusually early start was made, it being but 3:00 a.m. when we shoved off into the stream. We planned that before a landing was made at night that all records in distances for former days would be exceeded by many miles, unless handicapped by some unseen delay or accident. It was now the seventh of June, and with the many bothersome, unavoidable delays, seven whole days had been consumed since our departure from Windy Arm. We had covered less than one hundred miles in that time. Much concern was beginning to be shown among the party over the delay, and every effort was to be exercised in the future to make up some of the time lost by travelling late into the night. As we afterward heard, many of the gold seekers with light boats and loads accordingly had made the entire distance in the time we had already consumed. Of course, no delays or mishaps had been encountered as in our case.

About seven o'clock we passed a good-sized river flowing in from the northwest, which we afterward learned was the Takhini River. It is about two hundred feet wide at its mouth and discharges a light brown muddy water, which can be traced in the larger river for miles. Many years before this river was navigated by the coast Indians in reaching the interior, but upon the white man's introduction into the country, it has long since been abandoned. Instead, the two well-known passes and upper chain of lakes are now being used by them.

As we neared Lake Le Barge [Laberge] shortly before the noon hour, the current became swifter, and, with the assistance of the sail, it carried us at a good gait. Shortly after the river widened to what we safely considered one mile in width, the current slackened to the extent that an onward motion was barely discernible. The entire width, as it seemed, reeked with the bothersome sand bars, which we barely avoided stranding on several occasions. But, luck smiled upon us once again, and soon after we were upon the most beautiful sheet of water imaginable, named Lake Le Barge.

This beautiful lake is the largest one in the series, being thirty-one miles long and varying in width from two to five miles. The lake derived its name after a Canadian by the name of Mike Le Barge, who was engaged by the Western Union Telegraph Co. to explore the river and adjacent country for the purpose of connecting Europe and America by telegraph through British Columbia and Alaska, and across Bering Strait to Asia, then on to Europe. The exploration took place in the year 1867, and the lake has carried the name since. The laying of the Atlantic cable in 1866, which, as we all know, proved a success, put a stop to

Prospectors and scows spread out across Lake Laberge (often spelled LeBarge). Several boats have their sails up. *Alaska State Library, P. E. Larss Photograph Collection, PCA-41-026.*

Le Barge's project, and he was recalled as soon as he was located in the wild and unexplored region.

About the middle of the lake, the watery surface is studded with an island. I should judge it is three miles long and a half to three quarters of a mile wide. It adds much to the beauty of the picture, with its majestic pose of rocky cliffs of a peculiar reddish color, rising to a hundred feet or more. On the adjacent mainland shores could be seen, in places, this same peculiar rock. Principally, the formation is of cut clay banks, while farther from the shore, singular mound-shaped hills rise to lofty heights, completing the picturesqueness of the scene.

With all of its beauty, it has the reputation of being the most treacherous and windy lake in the system. Due to its length and the river-side valley leading to and leaving it, a strong wind is almost constantly present. We had heard and were cautioned in regard to above conditions, but as we sailed out upon its surface, the sheet of water that met our gaze resembled more a huge mirror, so clear and calm was it. The weather conditions were so evident, that we at once fell to the oars. We continued thusly until 5:00 p.m., when as if by magic, a strong wind from the south relieved us from further toil, and but a very few minutes later our heavily-loaded boat was plowing the white-capped waves at a rapid pace. We continued so until the wind blew a hurricane, which caused us to seek a sheltered cove on the mainland opposite the lower end of the island, where we pitched our camp for the night. After the above experience, we doubted not the prophecy and advice advanced a few days previous, and from all accounts, very few who cross this lake are compelled to row its entire length. During the day, we had covered about forty miles, thus exceeding any previous day's run. We, nevertheless, considered this distance a very unsatisfactory run.

A start at four o'clock on the following morning [June 8], with a strong and favorable breeze, bid fair to put the lake behind us before the noon hour arrived. In this hope, we were disappointed, for at 10:30 the wind died out as quickly as it had arisen on the day before, and remained calm until we left the lake. The oars were unwillingly brought into play again, and we rowed as hard and steady as we could. Thirty Mile River was not reached until 3:00 p.m.

The Lewis River as it leaves Lake Le Barge is about one hundred yards wide and varies very little from this width until the Hootalinqua River is reached. The distance from the lake to the mouth of the latter river is about thirty miles and is called, not officially, but by the prospectors, Thirty Mile River. No other portion of the great river, for such a distance, attains the swiftness that is encountered between these two points. In the spring of the year, the many streams fed by the melting snows add greatly to its volume. Upon our introduction, it was at its glorious height, rushing madly onward between its low, tortuous banks, its speed being reduced only when being combined by the large Hootalinqua.

Before reaching this point, no intuition of the dangerous character of the stream had been suggested. Therefore we were caught unawares when a warning appeared. The stream, upon entering, has an easy current of four or five miles an hour, and after we had traversed what I should judge four or five miles, a danger signal floating from a pole on the right bank attracted our attention. This warning was strongly verified a moment later by a hail from the same side of the river. The Canadian government had established here a station and officers for the purpose of warning the unsuspecting prospector of the dangers of this stretch of swift water. By so doing, it prevented many fatalities and losses to outfits, and for which the government cannot be commended too highly.

After exchanging a few questions and advice from the uniformed officer, we sped on our way. Each moment denoted a visible increase of speed in the current for about a mile, whereupon, making a sharp turn to the right, the cause of the warning from the officer was apparent. As far as the stream was visible, the water was rushing madly on over log heaps piled high against a rocky or other obstruction. Here and there, large boulders in midstream lay in wait for the unwary or inexperienced navigator, the water seething and foaming as it met the obstruction. Resisting this current was out of the question, and a watchful eye was necessary to avoid these rocks, the responsibility resting almost entirely on the steering oarsman.

It was upon one of these rocks that, for a moment, destruction seemed inevitable for us, and our escape was afterward considered remarkable.

We were speeding on at a rapid pace that we considered seven or eight miles an hour, when, upon turning sharply to the right, we could see directly in our course, a mammoth rock standing out from the bank about ten to twenty feet. Father, hatless, and with a stern and firm-set countenance, was at the stern oar. As soon as the danger was noted, he gave orders to Daugherty and myself to row for our lives, which as near as I could afterward remember, we did. In an instant we flew past. The oar on that side, striking the rock, was almost wrested from my grasp.

Little time was spent on congratulations over our narrow escape, however, as danger appeared at every turn. That others had been less fortunate was shown by the splintered and wrecked boats appearing at close intervals, piled high and dry upon the drift wood, or detained by the rocks in midstream. The owners lost all, and in several instances, their lives. A few days before, a small steamer built at Lake Bennett had run on a rock. As we passed her, we saw the bow was entirely submerged, and the hull listed to one side, appearing almost a total wreck.

Steamer *Kalamazoo* wrecked on the Thirty Mile River, 1898. This is probably the sunken steamer that Will saw on June 8, 1898. *Alaska State Library, John Kill Photograph Collection, P147-21.*

About fifteen of the thirty miles of swift river was run before we landed for the night. With the exertion and anxiety of the long day, we all were much wearied, and sought our blankets early. Despite the singing of the mosquitoes, mingled with the sound of the swift-flowing river, we soon fell asleep.

When morning [June 9] came, we were much refreshed. On this morning, it was at once decided that to insure future safety, a vanguard should be sent downstream in the small boats to explore the lower portion of the thirty miles of swift water, even at the cost of several hours' time. This plan was readily adopted, and those going returned at 3:00 p.m. They advised that, as far as they had gone, the river appeared less dangerous, as the current gradually lost its swiftness as the confluence of the Hootalinqua was approached.

We soon after broke camp and pulled out, making about an hour's run before we ran in and made camp for the night. We caught enough fish during the evening to supply all with two splendid meals, which were much appreciated and enjoyed after our long monotonous bill of fare of beans and salt meats. The fish were not unlike the grayling in appearance, but differed to some extent in not being so palatable, the flesh being soft and infirm. Many were caught in a short time, the bait being greedily taken as soon as striking the surface. Not being a gamey fish, they were landed without effort and afforded very little sport. From here down the river, they were caught at our desire, but in no place did we find them as plentiful as in this locality.

On the afternoon previous, we had noticed, on the right hand bank back some little distance from the river, newly hewn boards set in the ground perpendicular. They appeared at irregular intervals, one or two together, while some distance would separate a single. We were curious to investigate their meaning, but due to the swift current, we were unable to when the object appeared. This afternoon, however, we were afforded the opportunity as one hove in sight. With difficulty, we ran the boat into shore and proceeded to investigate.

The terrible meaning was only too plainly shown, as we reached the mound of freshly turned soil. Upon the roughly hewn slab, an unfortunate gold-seeker's name was boldly scrawled in pencil. Beneath the name was inscribed "Came to his death from drowning in Thirty Mile River." The date of the disaster read but a few days previous to our arrival, and as we stood viewing the plot set alone in this lonesome locality, a feeling of awe and heartsickness took possession of our souls. For might not a wife, sweetheart, mother or other kin at home watch and wait until their dying day for some message or the homecoming of him, who without friends or ceremony was laid in eternal rest at our feet? Loving letters of cheer and encouragement might now be waiting in Dawson City for him whose life had paid the penalty to the lure of gold. As we recalled the many primitive headboards we had passed along this tortuous, turbulent stream, a true realization of its many dangers were pressed upon us two-fold and served little consolation to our already anxious minds. But the lure of our purpose outweighed all else, and we were soon battling with the swift current of the great river again.

Our exploring squad had today repeated their performance of yesterday and had preceded the main party in the small boats. They had the confluence of the Hootalinqua in view before returning, which they did by land. We met them at the mounted police station located ten miles above the mouth of the latter river, whither we landed to make inquires and eat lunch. They were much fatigued after their ten mile jaunt over the rough, irregular land, but were satisfied with the result of their mission, and believed that the greater dangers of the mighty river were behind us.

Soon after landing and while our lunch was being enjoyed, a band of interior Indians took us by storm. They approached our camp without hesitation, except the little fellows, some of which hung back timidly. They eyed us curiously from a distance, while others peeped from behind their parents in a wondrous stare. Their mission was at once made apparent by their gestures and a few words of broken English. They had come to trade, and they produced several specimens of tanned moose hides, also beautiful artistic moccasins patterned after the style so characteristic of the North American Indian. The squaws had strings of beads of many sizes and hues, while deftly-woven baskets of many shapes and sizes colored to high degree gave intimation of their principal occupation while in camp.

After viewing with interest and admiration the beautiful designs of aboriginal workmanship, several of the boys showed an inclination to barter with them. Some difficulty was experienced in coming to a satisfactory understanding as the price of trade. One of the boys intimated a desire that they make a pair of moccasins from a hide that he fancied. An old buck at once set himself about the task, completing them in a surprisingly short space of time. He received in payment a jackknife and small mirror, which his sharp eyes feasted longingly upon when presented for trade. Their desires and fancies in this respect differed little from Indians found in other localities of North America, it being evident that to satisfy those desires their most valuable pieces of handiwork would be sacrificed for some valueless trinket. However, some of them did show interest in our grocer line.

These were the first interior Indians we met, and they belonged to a tribe called Tagish or Sticks. They differ to some extent from the coast Indian, appearing not so robust or healthful, but are tall, slender and as straight as a reed, with some having a most graceful carriage. They depend and subsist almost entirely upon wild game and dried salmon found not too abundant in the Yukon country. They seldom venture beyond the range of mountains to the coast, where there seems to be a most pronounced hatred and fear of the coast tribes. They appeared bright and intelligent, but beyond a few guttural words, English is spoken little, nor is it understood by them.

After trading for a time, we began preparations to continue our voyage. They collected their effects and sauntered lazily off down the path leading to the camp some little distance down the river bank.

After a run of perhaps two and one half hours, we passed the confluence of the beautiful Teslin or Hootalinqua River, and went into camp about one mile below, where the small boats had been left earlier in the day. The Teslin, so named in 1887 by the eminent Canadian explorer Dr. George M. Dawson, but more commonly known as the Hootalinqua, is one of the principal feeders to the great Yukon. It flows in a northwestern direction, having its source among a chain of lakes and tributaries several hundred miles to the southeast. As one notes the width of this river at the confluence, it gives him the impression that a most serious geographical error has been made in deciding the main stream to be the one we had just traversed. It appears that the Yukon has a width much less than the Hootalinqua. In this, however, the observer is misled, as was satisfactorily proven by Dr. Dawson in his official reports to the Canadian Government. He says owing to the current of the Lewis being just double that of the Teslin, the discharge of the Lewis is 18,644 feet, while that of the Teslin is but 11,436 feet, thus proving beyond a doubt that the Lewis is the main stream.

After the entrance of the Teslin is passed, the Lewis takes on a decided increase in width, measuring perhaps seven or eight hundred feet wide. This widening reduces the current to four or five miles an hour, the difference being noticed almost immediately. In the almost clear blue waters of the Lewis can be traced for miles the dark brown waters of the Teslin as it sweeps onward in a uniform streak, finally disappearing, as it blends with the waters of the mother stream.

It was with much satisfaction and relief that we sought our blankets this night. Even in our tired, worn condition, little or no sleep was gotten, due to the intense heat. In addition, the black clouds of mosquitoes had, from the onset, given us a thoroughly warm reception, their real tenacity not having been realized until upon this occasion. Long before morning, we came to the conclusion that all the little pests in the North West Territories, nay the whole world, had lain in ambush for us, pent upon preventing us encroaching upon their forbidden territory. Smudges were brought into use with little or no effect on the pestilent little insect, for it seemed they had prepared for just such an emergency, and their onslaught was unchecked. The smoke from the smudges drove us nearly frantic, choking us, as the strong fumes entered our lungs, while our eyes smarted and burned beyond description. They were swollen nearly shut as daylight [June 10] once more appeared. Those of us who had shown the pluck combined with our weariness to stick it out, arose from our blankets with a feeling of lassitude and disgust. With all haste a strong cup of coffee was prepared and drunk, after which we eagerly embarked. We were soon rid of our little tormentors, who never venture beyond their stronghold, the low, swampy banks.

The Big Salmon River was reached at 11:05 in the forenoon, where our breakfast was finally finished. We then proceeded to the police station to procure our clearance receipt. Since leaving Tagish House, this custom had been compulsory at all police stations, showing plainly the small chance of evading the duty required of the Canadian government, even if the Custom officers at the summit had been safely avoided. These stations had been established at intervals of twenty to thirty miles apart between Lake Bennett and Ft. Cudahy at the far western boundary of Canadian territory. Besides serving as a loyal agent to their government, the keepers of these stations have shared their comfortable quarters with many a weary, hapless traveler, particularly in the stormy winter season when the danger of travel over the long, desolate white trail is greatest. More will be said in a following chapter of the North West Mounted Police stations and their keepers, as circumstances threw me much in their company and good graces.

The Big Salmon River has a width of about three hundred feet as it enters the Lewis, flowing from the southeast through a wide valley flanked on either side with high wooded hills. Beyond, far in the distance, mountains could be seen, their peaks clad in a mantle of snowy whiteness even at this time of the year. Little or no current is apparent as far as could be seen, the sluggishness no doubt caused by the high waters of the Lewis backing up into the smaller stream. One's first impression of the importance of the stream is misleading. We were informed upon inquiry that it was navigable for craft other than row boats, but a few miles from its mouth, notwithstanding its enormous length of more than two hundred miles.

The stream had many years previous been prospected, but without any notable success. However, in 1877, rich diggings had been discovered on the benches of the Lewis a short distance above the Big Salmon. These finds strengthened an idea that, if the benches of the latter river contained gold, it would have been found. It appears from all records that this section was thoroughly prospected in the late eighties with more or less success. We were led to believe that this region had long ago been abandoned for the richer strikes made below on the Yukon.

This report did not appear true as we appeared on the scene, for it was here that we were introduced to our first gold excitement on the Yukon River. It had been due to a party of miners who had, the autumn before, endeavored to reach Dawson before the winter froze them in, but who had been unsuccessful. During the winter, they bided their time here in prospecting, which effort had been not altogether unsuccessful. Their presence had been noted as the deluge of gold-seekers floated down in the spring, and the camp had grown from day to day. By the time we arrived, it contained three score or more tents, while here and there could be seen a substantial log hut of the miner of long ago. After inquiries by our party were made, we were satisfied that it would be useless for us to waste time in stopping here, so we decided to push on down the river. It was well that we did, for in less than a month hence, the camp became deserted of all living beings, except the mounted police located there.

We had seated ourselves preparatory to shoving our boat into the stream, when there came to our ears a cry of distress some little distance below us on the river. Shifting our oars and turning in the direction from whence the cry had come, we saw enacted in the next few minutes a tragedy so pitiful that to my dying day the memory recalled will haunt me. George Sherwood and George Milham, both hailing from Seattle, had set out together to share alike in the spoils obtained in the Yukon gold fields, and had been unusually fortunate on their voyage until this point was reached. The latter was of an easy-going disposition, taking whatever came in a matter of fact sort of way, being all in all a very congenial companion. Sherwood, a German by birth, was a giant in stature, strong as a bull, but a most nervous utterable [sic] temperament, which, without a doubt, was responsible for his tragic end. Green of our party had known both in Seattle, and after they had left Lake Bennett, coming up with us at Tagish House, this acquaintance tie had been responsible for their close association with our party. As a result, we had all become well acquainted. They had this morning arrived some little time after we had, Milham going ashore to attend the necessary business, while Sherwood had been left to attend the boat.

George Milham was a man of medium stature, with a well proportioned body, that in his prime evidence the height of healthy, vigorous manhood. Intelligence and good humor shone from his big brown eyes, and that he was shrewd and analytic in a professional sense, was at all times evidenced by his ever ready logic and foresightedness.

The other, George Sherwood, was a large, obese individual, with a full, ruddy face, from which a pair of smiling blue eyes peered forth beneath heavy blonde brows. Sherwood's was a face possessing a great strength of character. It was an aristocratic face, resplendent with intelligence and dignity, while a wide, heavy chin indicated a strong determination, and stubborn nature. With his well groomed body, and his pompous bearing, he at all times appeared to me to be incongruous to the situation, inharmonious with his surroundings, so to speak. Yet, like all fat men, he was jolly and gay, and always prepared to relate a funny story, or listen to one with delighted interest. That his corpulent, well-kept body was clumsy and lazy, one could see at a glance, and several times during our stay at Windy Arm camp, Milham secretly confided to us that he wondered, with Sherwood's scant assistance, how he and his partner had ever managed to move their heavy outfit thus far in the time they had.

"Why, he would stumble over a snowball, or slip up on an icicle, as if he were a clown in a circus, doing his stunt to amuse the kids," Milham would relate over and over again, and each time he would burst into hearty laughter. "It did not seem so funny then, though," he would add seriously, when his laugh had subsided, "and several times I got so blamed discouraged that I came near chucking the whole darn thing, and once or twice I thought of returning home."

In spite of his partner's imperfections, Milham loved Sherwood as dearly as one man can love another, and their inseparable companionship and affection for one another came to be an everyday topic among the gold seekers at Tagish camp. Not many days later, those same people, in a manner not thought of by them then, were made to realize the strength and sincerity of the friendship that existed between those two men.

We had hesitated in pulling out so that a clumsily constructed log raft should pass, thus probably avoiding a collision, but which after safely passing us, had run amuck on a sandbar in midstream. Sherwood had become absorbed in watching the owners in their efforts to remove the weirdly craft from its awkward position, not noticing that the moorings of his boat had become unloosened from its anchorage until it was some feet from shore. When we heard the warning cry, the boat was far in the stream gliding swiftly onward with the current, while Sherwood was standing erect in the stern and gesturing like a wild Indian. A little presence of mind or caution would have avoided the catastrophe that was imminent, but it appeared that self-reliance had been thrust upon him so suddenly, and knowing that he could not swim a stroke, his mental faculties seemed to have left him. Cries of encouragement from shore, others advising him to sit down, were given, but were not heeded, while by this time, a number of boats had put out from shore, going swiftly to his rescue. He was now far in advance of his closest pursuer and drifting swiftly toward the raft of logs stranded on the sand bar.

If he had retained any presence of mind at all, he would have jumped to safety when he came up with this obstruction, but instead he remained as one in a trance. In a moment more the boat struck the raft broadside, it was overturned and all aboard was lost to view for a moment below the surface of the angry river. Rising to the surface, he made frantic efforts to grapple with something to sustain his weight, but failed, and the poor fellow went from our view once more. By this time his outfit could be seen floating thickly about him, and when he again came to the surface, he was seen to seize with both arms entwined, a sack of flour which he held in a death grip.

It became evident to his pursuers that his great strength had been spent from his two immersions. Little time would elapse before, in his exhausted condition, he would relax his hold and sink from view for the last time. It was as he was rounding the bend in the river below the station many yards in advance of his closest rescuer, that he was seen to relax his hold, his head slipped below the surface and was not seen to rise again. Thus another life had been sacrificed for the greed of gold.

[See the end of this chapter for "The Toll of the Yukon," Will's story based on this event.]

[June 11] After leaving Big Salmon, the Lewis widens considerably. In fact, the complete character of the river changes and begins to indicate the great river it is. In places it widens to what I should judge a mile or more, continuing so for miles where it will return to its former width between low, clean cut banks. The surface in the wide sections is dotted here and there with many little picturesque islets, which were covered with a luxuriant growth of poplar and willow thickets coming down to the white sandy shore that encircles them. These little islands were the source of considerable annoyance to us, separating the wide stream into many channels, making it very difficult at first to decide which to choose as the main channel. A decided current flows between each, but the depth is to be taken into consideration. If by chance a false course is taken, it is quite safe to say that before it is run, your boat will have become stranded in the shallow channel, necessitating worming it through to deep water. This was our experience on a few occasions, having been drawn by the influence of the strong current that exists. No great inconvenience resulted from any of these predicaments. However, they were very vexing and many cuss words were proclaimed.

We had become aware, since leaving the Teslin, of a peculiar sizzling sound coming from the bottom of our boat. It was not unlike the familiar sound of frying meat over a hot fire, and grew in volume as we proceeded. At first we were at a loss to know the cause, but finally, the solution was solved. After some investigation, it was found that a powerful undercurrent exists that is not visible on the surface. It flows swiftly on in a rolling motion, gathering the sand and small pebbles from the river bottom, swirling them over and over again. Thousands of the little particles strike the sides and bottom of the boat, and beat a faint but merry tattoo thereto. The peculiar sound was rather annoying at first, but we soon became accustomed to it, and came to know that as long as it was heard, we were in safe and deep waters.

After leaving Big Salmon, the adjacent country is wild and beautiful. On one side the high, clean-cut sandy banks with their light brown surfaces, mutilated by the sparrows, extend for miles. While on the other, rising gently from the water's edge, great arid plains recede for miles and miles to the far-off mountain range. These scenes change as we drift on, and we come up to and pass low level, grassy, meadow-like plains, to be replaced further on by thickets of poplar. Away from the river, the primeval country appears extinct of human life.

The afternoon was run without incident. As the current was now strong and steady, the oars were rarely used, and then only in avoiding cross currents and sand bars, and it afforded us the first real pleasure we had enjoyed on the great river. Little Salmon River was reached at six o'clock that evening [June 11], having made a run of seventy miles during the day, which was gratifying in the extreme.[5] A tent village of surprising proportions greeted us as we came into view, and a short time thereafter we were seeking a landing among the scores of boats anchored along the low and uniform shore line.

Will's Short Story

Will Woodin wrote his short story about the drowning of George Sherwood at least fifteen years after he penned his memoir, and possibly when he was in his fifties. His typed manuscript (complete with cross-outs and strike-overs) carries his address at 6335 51st Avenue South in Seattle. He and his second wife, Jean, moved to that address about 1925, and he lived there for the rest of his life. While he had his memoir to draw upon, his diary had probably been destroyed during the trip or shortly thereafter.

In order to protect the identity of the principal characters, he changed their names and some of the pertinent facts about them. He gave George Milham the name George Coleman, and Sherwood he called Frank Hanley. He made them lawyers from Denver, Colorado, rather than working-class boys from Seattle. For the ease of the reader, I have substituted the real names. Will used the first names "George" and "Frank" throughout his short story; I have replaced those aliases with "Milham" and "Sherwood" (respectively) to avoid confusion between the two Georges.

In addition, Will began the story at Lake Tagish and provided a summary of the trip down the Yukon as background information. As the account in the short story summarized and duplicated the more informative version in his memoir, I have deleted that part of the story. I take it up when they all arrived at the Big Salmon River. Finally, I have moved two of the paragraphs that he included in the short story to the narrative in his memoir. They describe in some detail the personality and appearance of the two Georges, and fit quite well into the account as he wrote it when he was in his thirties.

Other than these major changes to Will's original story, I have taken a very light hand in my editing of it. For instance, his use of paragraph breaks was much more sophisticated than in the memoir. Unlike in his draft memoir and diaries, his grammar, spelling, and sentence construction is polished and quite delightful.

+≻═⊰+

The Toll of the Yukon

A Short Story by William J. Woodin

After father and I visited the camp at Big Salmon, we were just on the point of shoving our boat from the shore, when lo and behold, who should we see coming from upstream, but Milham and Sherwood, apparently unscathed from their perilous ride at Miles Canyon and Thirty Mile River. When finally they had made a landing and had joined us on the shore, it would have been difficult for an onlooker to decide whose pleasure was the keenest, our friends' or ourselves'. Milham was most demonstrative in his open, sincere manner of greeting, while Sherwood, although no less pleased, still maintained his natural, dignified pose. He appeared as if he had just stepped from a band-box, for his expensive khakis were spotlessly clean, and his well-fitting puttees shone like a mirror.

"How on earth did you two get through White Horse Rapids and Thirty Mile River with your lives?" Father and I inquired simultaneously, when greetings were over.

"Oh, we run them like a top!" Milham assured with unconcealed pride and elation. "We hit the snarling old mill-race before we knew it, and as we did not then fancy swimming ashore, we stuck to the ship, and came through without a scratch."

At that astonishing information, father and I gazed at each other in blank amazement, while our friends stood by and enjoyed our bewilderment.

"Thirty Mile River gave us more genuine concern that either Miles Canyon or White Horse Rapids did, but even there, I fancy due to a kind Providence, we were spared the disastrous punishment that some of those poor devils suffered," Sherwood said in his precise manner of speaking.

"Yes, with George's efficient assistance, and God's kindness, we weathered the dangerous gauntlet in fine shape," Milham remarked, giving us a sly wink, and his partner an affectionate smile.

"Tut, tut, George. You confer on me more credit than I rightly deserve, although, ugh, I will admit that I felt called upon to exert myself as I never have been before," Sherwood advised in such a ludicrous way that we all laughed heartily. Milham assured cheerfully, "Well, George, at any rate, I dare say we have left the worst of the river behind us."

"Yes, from what I have learned, little danger lies in the remainder of our journey to Dawson City," Sherwood returned with a sigh of relief.

Milham evidenced a desire to make the rounds of the tent city, and invited father and I to accompany them. To this we readily agreed, and at once set out, but Sherwood, for some unaccountable reason, declined, declaring as an excuse that he would return to the boat and wait for us. We did not urge him, and leaving him, we proceeded on our way. As we were returning from our explorations among the colony of tents, we became suddenly aware of a great commotion in the vicinity of the river.

"A man in a boat is adrift!" someone shouted, while another cried, "He has lost his oars!" and yet another cried in a lusty voice, "He has lost his head, too!" then the same voice added, "Set down you fool, you'll upset your boat!"

For an instant, we stood spellbound, staring at each other dazedly, then we started on the run for the river bend. As we reached the shore, we could see a boat floating swiftly down the stream, in which there stood a man gesticulating wildly. As soon as we were capable of comprehending the situation, Milham looked for Sherwood and his boat. It was gone, and as the terrible truth dawned on him, Milham cried out in frantic terror. "My God, it is George!" Flinging his hat to the ground, he tore his hair in his agony, while he ran up and down the river bank. "God Jesus, he must not perish, not after what we have gone through. Save him, men, and everything that I possess shall be yours!" Milham shouted beseechingly, his voice shaking with emotion.

Already, several boats had set out in pursuit, but in spite of their heroic efforts, they gained but little on the run-away craft. They persisted in their chase, however, shouting to Sherwood to sit down until they should rescue him.

Frightened beyond all sense of judgment and presence of mind, Sherwood refused to obey their warnings and persisted to stand erect in the boat. The tragic result of his disobedience was soon apparent when his boat was swung sidewise in a swirling eddy and capsized, leaving Sherwood to struggle for his life in the treacherous, merciless river.

From where we stood terror stricken by the terrible scene, we could see him battling frantically in the swift waters. Then, as a sack of flour from his outfit floated near, he grabbed it tenaciously and kept swiftly on down the stream. Noting his action, a faint hope possessed us that the flour might sustain his weigh until he should float ashore. We were grievously disappointed a moment later, when suddenly, Sherwood disappeared below the surface of the turbulent river, never to rise again with life in his robust body. The flour had become water soaked, and sank with its human burden. Thus again, the mighty Yukon had exacted its toll, and as it gurgled and swashed the low banks, it seemed to laugh at its fiendish accomplishment.

When the tragic moment had passed, Milham sank dejectedly upon a nearby log, where he succumbed to his grief in a pitiable manner. With his face in his hands, he gave way to violent sobs that shook his great body, while at the same time, he muttered little phrases, extolling the many virtues of his beloved partner.

"I have known him since childhood," he said brokenly. "We were school mates together, and all through life we have shared each other's joys and adversities. Now he is gone, and I feel alone in the world."

Great, strong men, their minds calloused and hardened with years of life, turned heads away to hide a tear, or to swallow hard, a lump that persisted to rise in their itching throats. On every hand, kind hearted sympathizers offered their services for the stricken man's comfort, but with sincere acknowledgement of his appreciation, he refused their kindly aid.

"I want to get as far away from this terrible river as possible. Every noise I hear coming from its rushing waters haunts me. I imagine that it is George's voice calling to me for help." He advised, in his utter dejection.

The North West Mounted Police took him in charge that evening, where they advised he should remain until they had recovered Sherwood's body, if such fortune proved to be theirs.

For the purpose of administering cheer to our saddened friend, we remained at Big Salmon Post that night. Early the following morning we bid farewell to Milham, but not to the Milham we had known at Windy Arm. His usually jolly good natured face was haggard and drawn, giving him the appearance of a man twenty years older than he really was. With a dispirited word of farewell, he turned away as we shoved our boat from the bank, evidencing no further show of interest in our future welfare, and so we left him, a broken-hearted man.

Four weeks later in Dawson City, we learned from a recent arrival that Sherwood's body, with his arms tightly clasped around the sack of flour, had been recovered from the river several miles below the Big Salmon.

Chapter Six

LITTLE SALMON RIVER CAMP TO DAWSON
JUNE 11–JULY 17, 1898

+━━◆━━◆━━+

WILL'S ACCOUNT OF HIS STAY at the Little Salmon River differs markedly from those of the travel over the trail, the stay at Windy Arm, and the river voyage. It is during this leg of the trip that he explains how the men divided chores. The older, more experienced men built boats and rafts, while the younger, less skilled members packed and hauled supplies. Will initially started out with the group that went to explore the Pelly River, but upon returning for more supplies, the men at the Little Salmon camp voted to have him guard the group's caches. It is possible that he was the youngest man at the camp, and so therefore drew the most boring and onerous detail; alternatively, he may have complained about the conditions during his trek up the Little Salmon and the others believed he would be better off at the main camp. Despite his efforts to find ways to divert himself while serving time as camp guard, it is obvious that Will felt left out of all of the excitement.

In fact, this enforced exile may well account for the disappearance of the second of the three log books that Will filled with diary entries during his journey to and from Dawson in 1898. Those entries in the first and third books suggest that the young man used his diary to vent his frustrations, especially about his loneliness. It was in his private musings that he often grumbled about his concern for the other members of his party, and his homesickness and idleness when left in camp for even one or two days (see, for example, his entries for March 19 and May 20). He endured an entire month at the mouth of the Little Salmon River without any of his friends and only a few strangers with whom to socialize. It seems likely that he spent much of that time pouring his misery into his diary. Once he was reunited with the party, Will may well have destroyed the diary for fear his father would find it and read of his discontent. Alternatively, it is possible that his father did find it during Will's illness in September (see Chapter 8), and destroyed it for fear other family members at home would read it and believe Will had been mistreated by being left to guard the camp.

Evidence exists that Will did not have the diary as a reference when he wrote his memoir between 1910 and 1914, and his short story in the late 1920s. In addition to omitting the relationships between the young Georges, "Ed" Green, and William Wells, Will confuses the name of the man who was initially elected to guard the Little Salmon camp. On June 12, he says that an older man named "Cris" was selected to stay in the camp on the Lewis. But on June 19, when he returns to the camp for more supplies, he calls the guard Charlie Lund, a younger man whom he mentioned on April 24 at Windy Arm (see Biographies).

A third bit of evidence suggests Will no longer had the diary for reference in the writing of his memoir and short story. Sometime between June 29 and July 2, he and a young man from Seattle took a hike to a nearby mountain. Will neglected to give the name of his companion, nor does he mention the same person again, something he surely would have recorded in his diary. However, it might have been difficult to remember the man's name a decade later when he wrote his memoir.

To minimize the effect that loneliness preyed on his mind, even in memory, Will focused his writing on the environment and visitors to the camp. He took exploratory hikes and rhapsodized on the beauty of the scenery. For the first time, he mentions his regret at not bringing a camera or having the skill to draw or paint the views. But his verbal descriptions, especially of the First Nations people that camped nearby, are detailed for someone recounting events a decade after they occurred.

At the Little Salmon camp, Will had more opportunity to observe the people who inhabited the river corridor. About June 21, a group of "interior Indians" camped nearby, which caused Will a great deal of concern. Afraid these people would invade their cache, he refused to leave the camp, wary of, in his words "the crafty nature of this specie of human kind." They proved his caution to be unnecessary, as they made no attempt to come near the camp of the miners. In fact, Will welcomed their return a week later when they appeared with fresh moose meat to sell to the stampeders. On July 5, a large group of native people camped across the Little Salmon River from Will's camp. The men visited the stampeders' camp in the evening, and despite a mutual lack of knowledge of each other's language, the miners and the native men entertained one another with music and shows of physical prowess. While Will noted the "grunts" and "jabbering" of the native speakers, he also noted the great deal of pleasure that both groups of men took in the impromptu party. These sorts of encounters appear typical of the interaction between the people native to the Yukon and the intruding miners. We now join Will at the confluence of the Yukon and Little Salmon Rivers.

Before leaving our camp of the spring, rumor was rife that fabulous finds of gold had been made on the headwaters of the Pelly River. The most practical and shortest route to the district would be to follow the Little Salmon River Valley to its head, striking then across the range of mountains to the head of the former river [Pelly] a distance from the Yukon or Lewis of about one hundred and twenty five miles. The evidence showed plainly that many had heeded the wildcat rumor, as it afterward proved to be. Many had already struck the trail a week before and word had been heard from them since. Several in our crowd had, before leaving Windy Arm, contemplated making the trip, and even after being apprised of the uncertainly of enterprise, were loath to pass without giving it a trial. Now, as we appeared on this scene of activity, their enthusiasm knew no bounds. They were doubly anxious to give it a trial, dreaming that their fortunes were already assured.

As to our individual party, little or no serious thought had been given the matter, as we knew much was to be gained us by reaching Dawson as soon as the current could take us. Regardless of the entreaties voiced by our loyal companions to stop and try our luck, we had turned a deaf ear. Now as we looked upon the scene, an entirely different color of the proposition presented itself to us. We decided that the night would be spent here gaining whatever information we could, and if not favorable, it would not be lost in a last night spent with our good hearted and congenial companions. So, making everything snug for the night we mingled with the first comers, or rather he who had been left in charge of the boats while his comrades had taken to the trail. Little information of a responsible nature was gained, but all were confident of success in the undertaking.

During the long pleasant evening, it seemed that few boats coming from up-river passed this point. Party after party cast anchor along the immediate shore to spend the night and investigate as well the cause of the excitement, so much in evidence. The morrow would find many gone on their way downstream, but a few would remain and become victims to the stampede, for such it might be termed. As the slowly gathering twilight began to make itself known, a rousing bonfire was built, dispelling the cool evening air. Our entire party gathered around its cheerful glow to discuss the long and tedious undertaking so close at hand. A full detail of plans for the long tramp were inaugurated with great enthusiasm. Now and then, an optimist would translate into speech the air castles that rose from his imagination, vividly picturing wealth and comfort that was already in their grasp. Little was mentioned of the toil and hardships there were to undergo in the miles and miles of travel through a wild and unexplored region before reaching their goal. Thus it was found to be and will not be forgotten soon by those who took part. The discussion held forth until the midnight hour grew nigh, and Father, pestered with their entreaties to join them, felt almost inclined to do so. With a promise of decision on the morrow, we drew our blankets snug around us and were soon lost in peaceful slumber.

Due to the long and exciting day previous, we slept late on the following morning [June 12], and as we awoke, the rising sun was bathing the surrounding mountain tops in its warm, mellow rays. Not far distant could be heard the musical sound of the great river as it swiftly sped past on its way to the sea miles and miles away. It was a beautiful, spring morning, and a Sunday. All were in a happy mood, thanking their Maker that they existed to breathe the fresh, fragrant air and drink in the beautiful scenery. Songs and laughter burst forth as the boys busied themselves about camp.

Fate plays queer pranks, a conclusion I am justified in arriving at, I believe, when I say that I am unable to state whether or not Father had lain awake to discuss in his own mind the advisability of remaining and sharing his chance with the others. But when he arose this morning, he seemed have come to an understanding with himself, and showed as much zest toward the enterprise as any present. This was glad news to me, as the fever had been growing. I had the night before evinced a desire to accompany the boys, which no doubt had no little weight in his decision.

Everything being settled and the morning meal dispatched, active preparations were begun for the trip to the interior. Much was to be done, as a start was to be made early on the morrow. Regardless of God's day of rest, we worked unceasingly all day and half the night. First the boats were towed up the Lewis to the mouth of the Little Salmon, thence up that stream about two hundred yards, where they were securely anchored along the low banks. Not far away was built a large, substantial scaffold constructed wholly of logs drawn from the nearby wood, and was to serve as a cache or receptacle for storing our outfits. When finished, all perishable merchandise was removed from the boats and hoisted aloft. When all was removed, it made one mammoth pile of provisions, fully protected from all sorts of weather, and quite secure from all prowling animals that might be in the vicinity. This was a long and tedious task, and when finished, night was upon us. Provisions and necessary articles for the journey were selected from the different out-fits, after which they were securely fastened with the pack straps already for the packers in the morning. Our watches showed the midnight hour when we sought our blankets and after the long hard day's work, we were not long in getting asleep.

But not for long. Three a.m. found the whole camp astir again. In the twilight, one could see the many camp stoves going, over which bent men preparing the morning meal, while the remainder of the party were putting the finishing touches on their packs. The camp was to be left in charge of one man and fell to Cris [probably actually Charles Lund], a witty little Irishman, one of a party of locomotive firemen and engineers hailing from Spokane and Seattle, which had joined us at Tagish House. The task was to be one of monotony and lonesomeness in our absence, and was not sought after by any, but when it fell to him, it was taken as matter of loyal duty. Without a word of protest he accepted.

At five o'clock, all was in readiness. Each burdened with a pack rang-ing from fifty to seventy five pounds, we broke camp and started briskly up the trail that led to the interior. At eleven o'clock, after a jaunt of what we considered twelve miles had been made, a halt was called for lunch. I will truthfully say that, long before that hour had elapsed, our brisk movement had entirely disappeared, and each was glad to cast aside his heavy burden to rest his tired body. The sun had risen bright and warm and as the noon hour approached, its scorching rays beat down upon us unmercifully. The heat added materially to our misery and fatigue, and now, when my memory takes me back to that day's march, I am tempted to say that, before or after, I never suffered more from the heat. Our clothing was saturated with perspiration, our bodies ached, and our feet were sore.

After a quickly prepared lunch was dispatched, all hands stretched themselves on a grassy plot beneath a grove of pines. Some fell asleep, while others rested and planned what use they would put their riches to when they returned from the Pelly. At four o'clock, all much refreshed after the rest, the march was resumed. At six o'clock, we went into camp for the night.

I will now return to our starting point and give a description of the trail traversed during the day. As we leave the level valley of the Lewis, a climb of some extent is met with. A level stretch of some few miles is traversed, before the trail assumes a very disagreeable aspect to the weary traveler. It then went downhill into a narrow, swampy valley, fairly alive with mosquitoes that accelerated our tired, lagging footsteps, escaping their vicious onslaught. We reached the crest of another ridge, the disagreeable task would again and again be repeated over the rough, uneven trail.

Thus ended our first day's tramp to the Pelly [June 13], which bid fair to continue in a like manner, and which held forth anything but an enjoyable holiday outing. Nevertheless, aside from an extreme weariness, all were in good cheer when camp was made for the night. It was estimated that only fifteen miles had been traversed during the day, although it seemed double that distance. In a clump of spruce, the camp for the night was made, and as we lay on our blankets, we had only the clear blue heavens above us. No tents had been taken on account of their weight. We found they would have added much to our burdens, and aside from a slight protection from mosquitoes, they were absolutely unnecessary, as the nights had become comfortable and warm out-of-doors. Sleep was attempted, but proved an utter failure, with the clouds of mosquitoes hovering around our heads, singing their blood-thirsty songs. I remember in order to escape their viciousness, we would draw the blankets completely over our heads until our lungs required fresh air. Then, as quick as possible, we would uncover and inhale a fresh supply. We kept repeating the process until, through weariness and fatigue, some fell asleep, only to awaken in the morning with a feeling of unrest.

Due to the uncomfortably warm day, it was deemed advisable, and was consented to by all, that we do the major portion of our travelling at night, after it became cool. It was thought also that in this manner, mosquitoes would be avoided to some extent, allowing during the day some sleep and rest to be gotten. So acting upon this plan, we arose at midnight, shouldered our heavy loads, and continued our tedious journey over the rough unbroken trail. All through the remainder of the night, we trudged on, stopping now and then for water or a short rest. At 7:30 [June 14], we went into camp with the sun scorching hot at this early hour.

Added to the already disagreeable features of the trail, we encountered burning forests during the night, and it was necessary for us to pass through them. They had been set by the careless, unthinking people who had preceded us. As no attempt or interest in checking the fire was shown, it was devastating all growth in its path, and would continue to do so until checked by the rains in the fall.

The day was spent much as the one before, but more sleep and rest was obtained, and when three o'clock in the afternoon came, the march was resumed in a more cheerful frame of mind.

At about eight o'clock that evening, we came upon an extensive swampy lowland, dotted here and there as far as we were able to see with small lakes. Here the travelled trail was lost by our leaders. When we all came up with them, the vexing predicament was discussed, which resulted in a number going in different directions in search of it. It had been agreed that a signal should be given by he who happened upon it, when we would reunite, and push forward from that point. Our situation proved more serious than we had at first thought, and after the minutes dragged into hours of waiting, we almost gave up hope of finding the trail until morning and daylight came. Finally, about eleven o'clock, the sign came faint from out of the darkness far to our right. With repeated calls from the fortunate ones, we directed our footsteps thither, and soon after were with them. After a roll call signified all present, we again were on our way.

Due to the shadowy mantle of the Yukon night and aided by the timbered growth, it was with difficulty that the soft mushy path was followed, but fortunately we did not lose it again, and about one and one half hours after midnight, we came upon the low banks of a shallow stream about eighty or one hundred feet in width. This stream, as we afterward learned, was the north fork of the Little Salmon, which united with the main stream a few miles to our right. To keep on our course, it was plain to see that the river must be forded before we continued on our way. We therefore removed our shoes, and rolling our trousers high, we proceeded. As the first of the number reached and entered the ice-cold mountain stream, an exclamation of surprise and discomfort was heard, and a backward movement was very much in evidence. But only for a moment, and soon all were floundering in an awkward fashion in midstream, each having about all he could attend to in keeping upon his feet in the swift current.

Some, in tucking their trousers, had not correctly estimated the depth of the stream, and upon reaching the other shore, found that article of apparel soaked, making it very disagreeable to sleep in. It was found that a wide, receding, pebbly beach formed the shore, and it was shortly decided to camp here for the rest of the night. A rousing bonfire was made and those with wet clothes dried them as best they could, while the remainder arranged the camps. But three hours was spent in sleep, and 5:30 the next morning [June 15] found us again on our way traveling under conditions similar to former days.

As the noon hour approached, lo and behold a large body of water came into view. As we neared its shores, we could see a lake of considerable size stretching for miles and miles among the foothills. We afterward discovered that this lake was the headwaters of the Little Salmon River. No information of the existence of this lake had been gained by our party, and our surprise was complete. It became evident that our original plan must be altered to cope with this new state of affairs. After our lunch was eaten, a council of war was to be called to decide our future course.

> Little Salmon Lake is about thirty-five miles, by trail, northeast of the junction of the Little Salmon River and the Yukon River. It is approximately twenty-three miles long and a mile and a half wide. At the point where the Woodin party camped on its shores, it is possible to see about five miles down its length before the lake curves to the east.

It was during the meal that one of our number, after gazing intently for a moment out over the surface of the placid lake, called our attention to a moving object slowly coming our way. It was so far away (at least five miles) that we were at a loss to decide just what it was. As the object slowly drew near, we made out a raft upon which were seven men vigorously propelling their reed craft towards our camp. As they came up to us, we could plainly see discouragement and failure marked upon each woebegone countenance. After greeting us pleasantly, their language bore out their tell-tale faces as they disembarked. We invited them to share lunch with us, which they accepted with no second bidding. While eating, they gave an account of the experience they had undergone since leaving the Lewis ten days before. They concluded with the remark, "No boys, we gave it a fair trial and have figured it all out, and say it is impossible to reach the Pelly River with fifty pounds of provision to the man. We are disgusted with the whole affair and are going to return to our boats and proceed to Dawson City."

This was not very encouraging to us. For a time it seemed that our expedition to the Pelly was sure to be abandoned right then and there, and a return to our boats be ordered at once. But some of the party were not to be daunted, stating that as we had successfully reached this point, an effort should be made to reach our goal, regardless of the discouraging reports of our visitors, who had failed. A conference was at once called, with Cal Johnson in the chair, and the situation was thoroughly gone over. The discussion ended unanimously in favor of pushing forward at all events. The returning party looked on with indifference, but wished us success in our fixed purpose.

During the afternoon, a second party of five men drifted into camp. In giving their views, they were consistent with those coming earlier in the day. This, however, had little or no effect on our persistent leaders, who began at once to put their plans in effect, which was this. Six men would remain at the lake and build three rafts, while the remaining fourteen men would return to our camp on the Lewis for another load of provisions, and whipsaw, as it was thought a small boat would be handy, if not necessary, for exploring purposes. Father, Green, Cal Johnson and three of the other party were chosen to remain at the lake, for the fact that they were experienced in the work. On the other hand, the younger men of the party thought it their place to do the heavy packing and long tramps. So it was arranged, but before starting out on the long jaunt, it was thought advisable to remain at the lake for the night, and get a much needed rest, better fitting us for the arduous task before us.

It was now the sixteenth of June and, considering the short northern summer, and no knowledge of the remainder of our course, little time was to be lost. Consequently, a record breaking trip to camp and back was to be made. We all fell to and made a rude but comfortable camp for the boys to occupy while we were gone. Then, as the scorching sun set itself behind the foot hills, we gathered wood and built a cheerful campfire, around which we gathered some to smoke our pipes and chat. Others lay prone resting their weary bodies, thinking and planning of the outcome of our venture. Now and then someone would start off a popular song (for there were some splendid voices in the crowd), and all would join in the chorus. In this way, many lonesome hours were whiled away that otherwise would have been spent in a longing for home and family. I will say a more congenial and jolly crowd of men taken in all would be difficult to get together.

As the gathering shadows of the northern night drew closer about us, we became attracted by approaching footsteps coming from the north. Soon after there appeared in the spreading light of our campfire seven men, hollow-eyed and unkempt looking creatures showing only too plainly the exposure and hardships undergone by them. They told us they were returning to the Lewis from an attempt to gain the Pelly, cursing their ill luck the while. Instead of building a raft and taking advantage of the lake, they had skirted that body of water and followed its shores over an unbroken, rough trail nearly to its far end. There they became disheartened at the prospect of crossing the formidable range of mountains and had given up in disgust. Their advice to us in strong terms was to turn back, and although conscientiously tendered, was, of course, given a deaf ear. Not many days passed when, by experience, our crowd came to the conclusion they knew precisely what they were talking about.

An invitation was extended them to spend the night with us, which was readily accepted, as they were much fatigued after days of hard traveling and little sleep. After finishing a narrative of their experiences, Father hit upon a novel plan to lessen their burdens the remaining distance to the Lewis, and at the same time be profitable to us in the way of packing. Their packs, containing the usual prospector's assortment of flour, bacon, beans, etc., were still heavy. Father proposed that they leave all except that necessary to meet their needs until our camp was reached, where an equivalent amount would be given them. This proposal was at once heartily agreed to by them, after which we all turned in.

A start at five o'clock the next morning [June 17] was gotten, and at noon we estimated that half the distance to the Lewis had been covered. After a rest of eight hours during the scorching heat of the day, we again set out and made camp on the Lewis at five o'clock Saturday morning [June 18], walking the fifty miles in exactly fourteen hours. It was a strenuous jaunt, but the trip out had done much toward preparing us for any duty requiring endurance, and when we reached camp, we were little the worse for wear. We found the camp as we had left it, and Charlie [Lund], the man left in charge, was sleeping soundly. Awaking him, he prepared a light breakfast. Soon after we tumbled in to our blankets, and did not awaken until five o'clock in the afternoon feeling much refreshed.

Upon investigation, we noted the camp's increase of population while we were absent, there being now approximately five hundred people sharing in the wild rampage to the Pelly. The vanguard of discouraged prospectors returning from the interior had not reached camp, but an optimism of the venture still prevailed. As yet many of those coming down the Lewis River had run in to await developments. Upon our arrival, the news flew to all parts of camp. During the entire evening, we were besieged by throngs of men desiring the information of our trip, and many different times the account of our adventures was gone over. Our information was given in a manner neither to influence nor to encourage. But when informed that we were going to return with a full supply of provisions, tools etc., they were loath to think otherwise than that we were withholding some valuable information from them. After much talk, they were only half convinced that we were sincere, and an expression of doubt was evident on every face. But when the discouraged parties began to arrive and give their account of the hardships that were necessary to undergo in reaching the Pelly, a different light was thrown on the venture. Those not having companions on the trail at once pulled up stakes and pushed on down the Lewis.

The night was spent in a good long rest. The next day [June 19], we were occupied in preparing for the return trip. At eight o'clock that night, three men armed with saws, hammers, axes and other necessary tools left camp for a point on the North Fork of the Little Salmon where they would build the boat. From this point, they would load the provisions received from the packers, after which the boat would be poled up the river to the camp on the lake. This plan would save much labor in packing and also valuable time.

On the following evening [June 20] at eight o'clock, the remaining eleven boys, with heavy loads, left camp, only to return in the morning for another. The plan was to carry a double load, and establish relay caches at intervals of one day's tramp for the round trip. In this way, the monotony of the heavy packing seemed less, and I dare say the distance was accomplished in less time than a direct pack would have been.

Charlie Lund, the man who had been left in charge of the camp during our first absence, was not in favor of continuing any longer the lonely, monotonous vigil, and strongly urged they put some other one in charge, that he might join the prospectors on the trail. He, finally, after some arguing, had his way, and much to my displeasure, I was chosen his successor. During their absence, the future was to be looked forward to in any but a cheerful light. But, wishing to assist any way in the undertaking, I assented with some hesitancy, and at once took upon myself the duties required of me in that regard. Only those who have experienced an isolation among strangers in a strange, wild country can imagine my feelings, when upon the following evening [June 21] at eight o'clock, the boys left camp for the last time on a mission that no reliable time could be set for their return. As the long days dragged by, my waking hours grew almost unbearable.

My necessary duties were few, being confined to cooking my meals, washing my clothing and mending some. Due to inactive exercise, my appetite failed me. Food became detestable in taste and smell, and soon I was content with one good meal a day. My nights were either sleepless or restless, and when morning came, a sense of languor and morbidness possessed my entire body. Our camp had been made some little distance from the main body of tents, and for many days, no disposition was shown on either side to become acquainted with one another, which otherwise would have avoided many long lonely days for me. I felt my duty would not allow me to wander too far away. With only the companionship of my husky dog, Skookum, throughout the long days, the loneliness became unbearable, and I soon felt compelled to break the monotony.

It was about one week after the boys had left [June 28] that I hit upon a plan to occupy my mind and give some exercise to my now almost dormant muscles for a few days at least. This was to overhaul and take inventory of our huge outfit, checking from our way bills as I did so. This work occupied the major portion of the second week, and when completed gave me an idea of the draw mode on the commissary during our trip from Skagway. Also, in this way, I discovered that a few articles had either been stolen or overlooked, and left at one of our many caches. Not only did the work pass many hours that otherwise would have been spent in loneliness, but proved very valuable afterward.

One morning early, as I was busily engaged in my work, a mounted police officer from the post nearby accosted me pleasantly. Noting his inclination to visit, I ceased my work, and we sat talking for three hours, he telling me of the many thrilling experiences which had fallen to his lot as a police of the North West Territories. He told of the many long dreary winters spent in solitude, miles and miles from any white settlement. Aside from what wild game they were fortunate to bag, they lived upon the coarse monotony of food the government sanctioned, which was composed of no delicacies. Quite frequently his eye ran over our splendid stock of groceries, and I could see a longing desire in his hungry eye for such delicacies as canned pumpkin, canned roast turkey and chicken, plum pudding, canned maple syrup and many other articles that for months, yes, years pass without their having an opportunity of tasting. Before he left me, I gave him a can of oysters, and his appreciation was unable to be shown in words. As he left, he gave me an invitation to visit the post on the following evening and at any time afterward, which I did. I was one of his welcomed guests, and many a pleasant hour accompanied by my mandolin, I spent in their humble quarters.

There were two officers stationed here. Pat McKay, the officer who had visited me, and Mr. [Franklin H.] Thompson [see Biographies], a big stalwart fellow with a boyish, clean cut countenance, and a quite manly disposition. Pat was different in disposition, as one could see by the mischievous twinkle in his dark brown eyes, and also demonstrated by his actions. A story told by him was sure to bring an uproar of mirth from his interested listeners. He could sing splendidly as well as dance, and all who knew voted him an all around entertainer.

Father had given me orders before leaving to dispose of a limited amount of our large outfit, provided the prices offered were satisfactory. I informed McKay of this fact on the morning he visited me, and procured the means of selling many articles at fancy prices. Those traveling light would almost be sure to stop at the post, and would inquire if provisions could be procured in the camp. The officers would direct them to our camp, and each day during the week of checking [July 5] was ushered out with many good sales at stiff prices to my credit. Even those in camp, after becoming aware of our stock being on sale, would run over and purchase a delicacy they did not have. At the latter end of our stay, business petered out, as a few boats passed down river, and the camp contained but one fifth of its former population.

It was rather difficult for me to accustom myself to the long, light evenings, and many a night after my work was done, I sat in my tent until after the midnight hour, reading or writing without taxing my eyes in doing so. The longest days of the year were now present and between the midnight hour and two o'clock, a twilight would gather, giving the only evidence of the passing of a night.

The fore part of the week, a band of interior Indians coming from the hill had built their camps about two hundred feet back of me. This act gave me no little concern, and the two days during their stay, a close vigil was kept lest they help themselves to our easily approached caches. But throughout their stay, no sign of an attempt was shown toward pilfering, and upon the second morning after their arrival, I arose to find the spot where they had camped vacant. They went as quietly as they had come. However, their visit had put me on the defensive and the days that followed, I was on the alert, knowing only too well the crafty nature of this specie of human kind.

It was now the 26th of June, and already two weeks had been spent at Little Salmon. The stay would soon prove either a waste of time, or we would be rewarded by our persistency in proving a strike on the upper

Pelly. The days were long and beautiful with continual sunshine, which was not too hot, while the short nights were cool, requiring nearly at all times a couple of warm blankets for comfort. Rains were few and far between, and then only light showers would fall. Thunder storms and high winds are unknown in the interior.

The 26th fell on Sunday, and was really the first Sabbath that I had observed since leaving the States. Every day had seemed the same to me, and at times, a Sunday would pass before we were aware of the fact. Today, I eliminated all unnecessary labors, and surely would have gone to church if such a religious institution had been in the vicinity. Instead, I was honored by visitors from the nearby camps, and the day was whiled away in relating our adventures since leaving our homes, which were interesting in the fact that people from all parts of the earth went to make up the throng of gold-seekers.

The day was nearly done when Ed Hering, Charles Lund, and Ned Foster came stalking into camp, foot sore and hungry as bears, as was indicated as they ate ravenously of the substantial meal I had prepared for them. They had returned from the North Fork of the Little Salmon River, which they had left in the early hours of the morning, making the distance in record time. Due to the low marshy country they were traversing and the hordes of mosquitoes that invade such localities, it had become absolutely impossible for them to get a wink of sleep, day or night. Therefore, they were compelled to return for three tents for their protection. Before they had left, no word was received from the party at the lakes, but the boys at the North Fork were reported as having the boat nearly finished. It would be ready when the boys with the tents returned to push up the river to the lake, and join the party there.

Soon after the meal was over, the three, overcome by their long tramp turned in. Our watches indicated 10:30 when they arose on the following morning [June 27]. After a hearty breakfast, they at once began preparations to return that evening. They wanted to travel all night to avoid the heat which is felt more keenly in the interior than on the Yukon River basin. When night-fall came, they shouldered their heavy packs and were off on their long tramp once more.

They had not been gone many minutes, when a party of nine who had their camp next to ours, came from the trail in a dilapidated condition.

A more forlorn, discouraged lot of men would have been hard to find than they. They had arrived at Little Salmon about a week in advance of us, and had at once set out to reach the Pelly. They now claimed they had done so, and had found nothing to warrant their remaining. Becoming fearful that their grub would run out, they had made a bee line for the Yukon.

A party of thirty-two who had engaged the services of an Indian guide also returned during the day [June 27]. They reported absolutely no success in their undertaking, and at once made preparation to push on down the river. The return and discouraging report of these two large parties had a tendency to check further interest in the Pelly River stampede. All those from up-river, having run in to await developments, at once pulled up anchor, and again were on their way down the great river.

Upon the following morning [June 28], about thirty-five boats were ready to leave. After saying farewell to their newly-made friends, one by one, they shot out into the swift current of the mighty stream. They were lost sight of as they glided around a bend on their way, none of them knew where: their one and only thought was of gold, gold, gold. The exodus of the past two days had made a marked impression on the large settlement of tents. A few more days, or a week at the most, would see Little Salmon deserted of all except the N.W. Police station. Many times during the days to follow my gaze would wander to the trail expecting every moment to see our party returning to the camp. In this I was disappointed, and many days passed ere I saw their faces again.

During the day the band of Indians who a week ago, about June 21, installed themselves back of my camp, returned, bearing between them a large moose carcass. They peddled the meat from camp to camp, and it was interesting to see how rapidly those moose steaks and roasts vanished among the meat-hungry men who had not tasted fresh meat since leaving Skagway months before. Of course, it was possible of bagging this and other game in the course of travel, but it necessitated a tramp of many miles to the wooded foothills, which the prospective miner could not see, for he was after gold, and any loss of time other than in search of the precious dust was not to be considered for a moment. The Yukon Territory Indians are well aware of the value and denomination of Cheechako's money. But they were not at all particular, and if offered flour, beans or bacon in payment, they were accepted with alacrity. These articles of food that we had grown so tired of, were considered by them to be as great a delicacy as the fresh meat was to us. They had done well by their sales, and when I awoke the morning following [June 29], there was not an Indian in sight, indicating, as I supposed, they were off for another hunt and would return with another moose: but either I was

> "Cheechako" is Chinook jargon meaning "newcomer." In common usage by whites, the term was used in contrast to the "sourdough," who was a person experienced in the ways of the north. Will's use of the word at this point in this narrative is especially appropriate, as the native speakers would have considered all non-natives to be Cheechakos.

wrong in my supposition or the game was scarce. They did not return while we were at Little Salmon.

The remaining days of the week [June 29–July 2] were spent in various ways to pass the time. As I began to feel the effect of idleness and lack of bodily exercise, I would take a little jaunt each day to keep my now almost dormant blood in circulation. One of these little trips was one that I will never forget. After leaving the camp in care of one of my neighbors, a young fellow from Seattle and myself set out one morning early to climb a small mountain about one and one half miles to the north of our camp. The ascent required about one and one half hours, and when we reached the summit, we judged we had attained an elevation between two and three thousand feet above the Yukon River, from which it rose sheer.

From our lofty altitude, the sight we saw is never to be forgotten. Miles and miles to the south could be seen the mighty Yukon, shimmering in the morning sunlight, winding itself serpentine-like among the low foothills, and looking in the far distance not unlike a silken thread. To the east could be seen the course of the Little Salmon, almost to its source, with a chain of small lakes, beginning about ten miles distant. To the east and west, mountains rose to quite an altitude, but were now quite devoid of snow. Little to the north, on our future course (as it proved to be) could be seen on account of the obstructing, timbered hills.

As we sat and drank in the beautiful landscape, we were inspired, and, oh, how much we would have given to have had the ability to sketch what our creator had laid before us. It has always been a great disappointment, and one that I have felt keenly, that I did not possess a Kodak or camera on this trip. The pictures I could have made would now be a treasure that no price could claim. The superb scenery from Seattle to Skagway, actual pictures of life and happenings on the trail, scenes of narrow escapes on the great river, and Dawson, the Mecca of the gold-seeker, with its wonderful deposits of gold, would go to make up a set of views that no man would, in my opinion, part with.

After viewing the grand panorama spread before us while resting our tired limbs, we retraced our steps down the steep incline. We reached the level in much less time than it had taken us to ascend, and arrived in camp with an appetite for lunch such as we had not felt in many days. This little outing had set my blood in circulation again, and made me feel better for it. I declared that each day in the future, I would take a little jaunt, or I would suffer an illness. Little does one know, unless placed in my position, the effect that loneliness creates in a person. With no one to speak to except my husky, who after all was considerable comfort to me, my responsibility in caring for our outfits was no little item of worry. All taken together, it became each day a greater strain on my whole physical system, and at times I felt that I was very much in need of medical attention.

The days dragged along, and no word was received from the boys, indicating that they were to be game to the last. Each day, however, could see men coming to camp after their hard and fruitless search. As soon as preparation could be made, they would push on down the river, showing only too plainly that the Little Salmon rush would soon be a thing of history.

During the latter end of the week [about July 1], the steamer *Ora* ran into the police station for the mail on her way to White Horse, the source of navigation. This was the second steamer up river this season, and caused no little commotion among the stragglers left in camp. The upriver navigation is a slow process at this time of the year on account of the high waters, which create a swift current, and many days are required from Dawson to White Horse, a distance of five hundred miles.

A few days after the climb to the mountain top [first week in July], I got together my fishing rod and rifle. Accompanied by my husky, I left early for one of the lakes about four miles to the north of camp, to spend the day in fishing and hunting. A number of persons had visited the lake with good results, as I had learned, and also evidence to back them up. Pickerel and white fish were the species, and the lake seemed to abound with them. I found they were easy victims to the baited hook, and I landed several good specimens during the day. Nothing was seen in the game line, and as I learned, one would have to go to the foothills miles away to satisfy oneself in this sort of sport. To do so was impossible for me, but nevertheless there was a longing to go.

A few mornings later, I was awakened very early by the loud reports of firearms that made me hustle out of my blankets in a hurry to learn the cause. I thought for a moment that a band of uncivilized Indians had swooped down on us, and was about to take the camp and pilfer our outfits. But upon arising and peeping through the flap of my tent, it dawned on me that the firing was to remind us of the anniversary of the Declaration of Independence, of which I had not given a thought of the nearness. How well I remembered the celebrations, as my thoughts went back to my boyhood, yes, until I was a young man, how my brothers and I looked forward to the day. We saved our pennies for weeks previous to Fourth of July with its firecrackers, and then took a trip to the little country town to spend the day in the glorious celebration. And here I had entirely forgotten such a day was on the calendar. It seems that all is forgotten except that concerning our mission, gold, which we must have.

After July 4th, rains became frequent, and seldom a day passed that we did not have a shower. Now and then a heavy rain lashed nearly the entire day, making it cool in the daytime, while at night, the heavy blankets were quite welcome. For all that, the days were long and beautiful, not unlike spring in Washington. The air, tempered by the showers, was refreshing and healthful, and vegetation flourished in its rich coloring of green. The nights had not yet appeared to lengthen, and I had not yet used artificial light at Little Salmon.

Late one afternoon soon after the Fourth [July 5], I had taken a stroll down to the Yukon to satisfy my curiosity as to the congregation there of about half of the camp's population. They were looking up the stream, and seemed to be very much excited as they gestured with one another. As I came up to them and followed their gaze, I could see in the distance six large rafts coming down the river, each raft thronged with Indians. The steersmen of each one pulled on their oars for dear life, to make a landing in our vicinity. They were adepts with the oars, and soon the great, clumsy crafts were out of the swift current of the Yukon, headed up the Little Salmon, and about 300 feet from its mouth they tied up on the bank opposite us.

Immediately after landing, the entire party got busy unloading their camp equipage, after which fires were built and tents erected, which we considered meant a long stay. There must have been in the party sixty to one hundred men, women and children. As we afterward learned, their mission was to fish for salmon, which, in the fall of the year, battle with the swift stream from the ocean to spawn in the smaller streams eighteen hundred miles from its mouth. Coming this great distance upstream (or even as far as Dawson), the fish coming in contact with particles of sand and pebbles always swirling in the strong undercurrent, changes the appearance of the salmon to a bright salmon color. In some cases I have seen where they were lacerated by the sharp pebbles. The meat seemed uninjured, however, by their long journey.[1]

It was as the dusk of the Yukon summer night began to gather, showing the vivid lights of the many camp fires reflecting on the dusky faces, that we saw a couple of rafts leave the shore, loaded to their capacity with our new neighbors. For a moment we thought they were going to pull out down river, but soon changed our minds as we saw them propelling directly across to where my camp lay. As they struck our bank, two stalwart fellows leaped ashore and made their rafts fast, by tying with a rope to a clump of bushes. They all disembarked and came up the bank to where several of my neighbors and I had built a large bonfire. As they did so, we bid them the time of day, but all the answer we received was a grunt or shake of the head, indicating that they did not understand what we had said, or did not want to.

Some of the bucks were great stalwart fellows standing six feet or more, and had not at all bad features to look upon. None of the squaws or children had accompanied them, presumably having been left to look after the camps, where they could be seen busily engaged in washing dishes at the river and caring for the smaller children.

As they gathered around our bonfire for no other reason than curiosity, some of the boys spoke about having some music as a means of entertainment to our uninvited guests. So I got out my mandolin, which I had not touched in days, and along with a guitar and zither player in camp, we made a fairly good combination, such as it was. They seemed delighted as the strains of "At a Georgia Campering" [sic], "The Irish Washerwoman," and other syncopated numbers were given. The boys in a humor to make things lively began to dance, whereupon several of the young and bolder of the tribe followed suit with much gusto, keeping perfect time with the music the while. It was great sport for them, and even after the boys in camp tired of the dance, they kept it up until we tired also and ceased to play.

They were out for a night of it, as they gave us to understand. After a conversation among themselves in their own tongue, they were anxious to give us an exhibition in athletics. For the next two hours, they wrestled among themselves, jumped, turned handsprings, kicked the hat, and numerous other feats, which they did exceedingly well, commending their specie. By this time, the whole camp had turned out to see the fun, and fun it was. We thought they would never weary, but finally they did. At a grunt from he who we presumed was their chief, they motioned us a good-night, and clamored aboard their rafts, shoved off and were soon on the other side. We could hear them jabbering and laughing, no doubt over what they had shown the white man they could do. Looking at our watches, we discovered it was 12:30 a.m. and the whole party at once dispersed.

The day following [July 6] the male portion of the tribe canvassed the now almost deserted camp with moose meat and cured hides in trade for almost anything they could get in the line of provisions. After returning to the opposite side to their camp, they were soon engaged in breaking camp, an activity that came as a surprise to us. One of the boys, through signs, asked them why they were going so soon, and by their gestures, we took it that it was too early for the salmon this distance up the river, and they would go farther down. This reason was proven some days later on our journey downstream, for at intervals along the banks, we could see string after string of salmon drying on horizontal poles under the rays of the hot sun. They subsist almost entirely on a fish diet during the long winter months, and in the season bend their efforts so far as their lazy habits will permit to lay in a good supply. The day was drawing to a close when they poled out of the smaller river into the Yukon. There, the swift current soon caught their rude crafts and away they went, the oarsmen working like Trojans, while the remainder, with hands and hats flying, bid us a hearty farewell, and soon after were out of our range of view.

I was awakened early on July 7 by an unusual downpour of rain that seemed for a while would flood me out of my tent. I arose and moved my stove inside before I could cook breakfast, the rain was coming down so hard. I had hardly finished breakfast when three fellows coming from the trail hailed me, asking me if my crowd had gotten in yet. When I informed them to the contrary, they told me they had come direct from our party. Father told them to call and tell me to have everything in readiness to leave Little Salmon in a day or so after their arrival, which would be the following day, no doubt.

This news did not create any surprise with me, for I had long since been expecting it from the discouraging reports coming from prospectors arriving every day from the Pelly stampede. However, I was very much disappointed about sacrificing one whole month, when the season was so short, not to mention the severe toil and hardships undergone. There was nothing to show for it but defeat. If only we had made a direct run to Dawson City instead of bothering with a wild goose chase, such as we had done, what now would have been the result? These were my innermost thoughts. Now it must be too late for us doing anything in the mining city, with its overrun population of ten or twelve thousand souls, who had arrived one month in advance of us. But we had played our cards, and had lost, so would have to make the best of it.

About forty people left for Dawson this morning [July 7]. After bidding them goodbye, I set about cooking and baking a supply for the hungry boys who I would expect to arrive in camp between now and the following morning. This information was substantiated, for about six o'clock a party coming in over the river trail had seen the boys about fifteen miles back. They had built two large rafts at the lake, which with the boat they had also built, carried the larger portion of the party, while the remainder was coming overland. The boys giving the information were of the opinion that they would have a rough time of it before they arrived, as the stream is very treacherous. The stream is small in volume, but is tortuous, and at almost every turn, falls, cataracts, or rapids greets one. They say it will necessitate their laying up during darkness, it being very dangerous even to make the run in broad daylight. I went to bed early with the thought that on the morrow, I would again see dear old Dad, who I had not seen in three weeks. I had worried, for he had not felt very well when he left. It would also lift the spell of loneliness I had surely felt and monotony I had undergone.

The next day [July 8] broke clear and bright, and the early sun was just rising above the low eastern mountain tops, when I aroused myself from a sound, refreshing sleep. My first thought was of the return of the long absent boys. In the forenoon, I repeated my labors of the day before, and when midday, I considered I had enough pork and beans, potatoes, stewed prunes, pies, cakes, etc. on hand for a full regiment. As the afternoon began slipping by, I became anxious, and began to think something had happened, some accident to the river crews. This surmise, however, was soon allayed, for at four o'clock, Cris and Mr. Hopley, each bearing several white fish, came marching into camp. They told me upon inquiry, that the entire party would be upon us by six o'clock. They at once set about cleaning the fish to add to what I had already prepared for them.

About six o'clock the vanguard from the trail began to arrive, and ten minutes later the first raft made its appearance around a bend in the river commanded by Dad, who held the stern oar. Soon after, the second raft came into view, and finally Cal Johnson in the small boat brought up the rear. The party coming by land had all arrived, and after assisting the boys to land their awkward crafts, the whole party made a stampede for the supper table, where they certainly did justice to ample supplies of edibles.

Notwithstanding their safe return, with all well and healthy, it was a discouraged bunch of men who sat down for their meal, and many curses were vent on the Little Salmon venture. A month had been wasted by the unfounded rumor of some rattle-brained Cheechako, whose name we never heard. Crying, however, would not now help matters, but all possible haste would be indulged in reaching Dawson without another stop, aside from necessity.

Due to the long, hard day encountered, all turned in early and arose early the next morning [July 9]. They spent the day bathing and washing their clothing, both of which they were in dire need.

On July 10th, although it was Sunday, all arose before sunrise, and immediately began the task of loading their outfits on board the boats, preparatory to an early start on the morrow. By noon everything except the tents, bedding and cooking utensils were aboard. During the afternoon, Pat McKay from the Police station came over and invited the bunch down to the station that evening to a farewell gathering. The invitation was received with thanks from all and the evening was enjoyably spent by music, singing, dancing and story-telling until a late hour. At that time, we bid our amiable hosts good-bye and bent our way campward to sleep for the last time at Little Salmon River.

Sleep, however, was out of the question for me. I had, for nearly a week, been troubled with frequent spells of severe toothache. Having lost our medicine chest on the trail, I had no remedy for it. I realized that little could be done to allay the pain except extraction. Until today, this remedy seemed almost impossible in this wild section, unless I happened to run onto some dentist going into Dawson. During the day, while the tooth was nearly driving me wild with pain, I happened upon a young fellow from Seattle, who told me one of their party had included in his outfit a pair of forceps for just such an emergency. He said he had never heard of him using them in his life, but if I could muster up the nerve to let him practice on me, he thought he could relieve me. Although I had suffered untold pain for a whole week, I did not feel glorious over the prospect of letting an absolute novice in dentistry operate on my jaw. But mind you, I had the fellow on my thinking board all the time.

This night, after coming from the police station and trying to sleep, I arose and made for the tent where the man with the forceps lived. I was fortunate enough to find him at home, and I at once made my business known to him. After some hesitancy on his part, I told him that I would take all responsibility if he would begin operations at once. Thereupon, he began preparations as if he were a professional. Did you ever have a jumping toothache that, after trying every possible means to quiet, but upon entering a dentist parlor and gazing upon a pair of cold forceps, that you did not immediately get relief? It was so in my case. In the absence of a modern chair, he placed me on the sod floor of the tent and examined my jaw, thereby locating the troublesome tooth with the aid of a candle. He placed the candle on a box and brought the forceps into view, which made me shiver. Placing his knee upon my thighs, he grabbed the tooth, and after getting a good grip, gave the instrument a quick twist and a pull that seemed to raise me from the ground. When I came back to terra firma, he was holding a large double molar tooth in the instrument.

It was done so quickly that I hardly realized any pain in the extraction. The relief from the torturing pain was instant, and after giving him one pound of smoking tobacco in pay for the extraction, I went back to the tent and to bed to sleep as I had not done for several nights.

> The going rate to have a tooth pulled in 1898 was about 25 cents. At the same time, a pound of tobacco was worth anywhere from 15 to 55 cents a pound, depending on its quality. Therefore, it appears that Will paid the man with the forceps a fair price for the service he rendered. Twenty-five cents in 1898 would be worth the equivalent of about seven dollars in 2014.[2]

The morning of July 11th found us astir at an early hour. After a hasty breakfast was prepared and eaten, the work of breaking camp was begun, and at 7:30 a.m. all were in readiness to shove their boats into the stream. Before I go further, I will state that due to the overloaded condition of our boat, which caused considerable trouble on our previous voyage, we engaged a single party leaving with us, who was travelling light, to take about a ton of our outfit to Dawson. This arrangement saved the sort of time and anxiety that we encountered on the upper river, while the extra load served as a comfortable ballast to his boat.

Some of the boats had already left the landing, and we were about to do so when McKay came running from the station with the mail for Dawson and intermediate points. After bidding him another farewell, we pushed off and were soon floating easily on the surface of the swift-running Yukon. Our fleet numbered ten boats now, and when we left, the number of tents remaining at Little Salmon could be counted on the fingers of one hand. A couple of days more at the most would see the once thriving camp entirely deserted, with the exception of the police.

Upon leaving Little Salmon, the Yukon or Lewis makes a long, steady turn bearing to the northwest, until within a few miles of Five Finger Rapids, where it bears almost due east. The adjoining banks of our day's run are low, occasionally studded with a sandy cliff of small proportions. The valley reaches far to the foothills, being almost entirely level and appearing to be clothed with a luxuriant growth of redtop or timothy. Little or nothing of note happened during the day, and when we pulled in for the night, Five Finger Rapids were but four or five miles distant, having covered between sixty and seventy miles during the day.

We got an early start the next morning [July 12], and not a little excitement was shown generally in anticipation of the run of Five Finger Rapids, so close at hand. We had been under way perhaps forty minutes, when upon a sharp turn in the river, we saw about a mile ahead of us five large masses of rock raising themselves from the surface of the river to a height ranging from forty to sixty feet. They extend from shore to shore in irregular positions, with several feet of swift water intervening between each. Each one is thickly studded with stunted pines on their summits, while on all sides, they rise perpendicular, presenting a very beautiful sight. Their appearance leads one to believe that at one time, they formed an obstruction in the mighty stream, making a dam over which the water poured. In time, the river had worn the several channels. This is my surmise, and one I think quite probable.

We had previously been cautioned about this obstruction, and had been instructed to keep to the right hand channel, it being deeper and appearing to be the main channel, although much narrower. As we made the sharp turn, we could notice the increased speed, and not many minutes thereafter, we were going at a terrific rate between the towering walls of two of the fingers. As in Miles Canyon, a cone is formed by the tremendous volume of water passing through the reduced space, and woe unto him who varies from its crest. With the exception of one of our party, all went through like a top. This party happened to be the one who we had bargained to assist us in our overloaded outfit. When a hundred

Watercolor painting of Five Fingers Rapids found in the papers of William J. Woodin. Given as a gift from a friend, "Maimie L." Artist unknown. *Sandra Dunn Collection.*

yards from the channel, his boat swung sideways with the current, and every effort of his to bring her head on proved of no avail. He came through in that position, barely missing the right hand rock. Our hearts stood still for a moment, for we knew if he came in contact with that solid formation, absolute destruction would be his. Shouts of gladness rang from the several boats as he swung clear from the massive walls and righted his boat not far behind us.

The current, after passing Five Finger Rapids, is very swift. At 9:30, we were in the embrace of Rink Rapids, the last and least treacherous stretch of water from Windy Arm to the Bering Sea, fifteen hundred miles from here. These rapids are perfectly safe if the right hand channel is kept. The left channel, if it can be so called, is absolutely impassible for a boat drawing more than six inches of water at this time of the year, and is very dangerous at any time. Thousands of large, jagged rocks form the river bottom. They extend two thirds of the stream's width, and about one half mile in length. Very few of these rocks are visible above water, even at the lowest stage, but it was noticeable that they were not far beneath the surface. Over the countless rocks the swift waters rush, lashing its entire surface into snow-white foam, which is carried a great distance downstream before dissolving. To me it was a beautiful sight to see the dancing waters, but I was glad to say good-bye to the last dangerous water on our voyage.

Up to the rush of the gold-seekers in the summer of 1897, no steamer had attempted to brave these rapids for no other reason than an impression that they were impossible to ascend. But since 1898, many boats of the river style have plied the great stream from St. Michaels to White Horse Rapids at an open season of the year. This fact was demonstrated to us a few miles below when we met the mail steamer *Willie Irwin* laboring against the swift current on its way to White Horse, and loaded with passengers for the outside, who exchanged shouts and waves of handkerchiefs.

The old Dalton Trail starting from Haines Mission, Alaska, makes its appearance on the left shores of Rink Rapids, and we could see a pack train resting as we passed. For miles, this section is thickly wooded with a healthy growth of pine, especially on the north shore. About ten miles below Rink Rapids, we came to a small stream coming from the east by the name of Tatshun River. About the mouth of the stream, a number of tents had been erected, indicating that another touch of gold fever had taken root. As it was nearing lunch time, we decided to run in and investigate the cause of the apparent excitement. Upon landing, we learned that a Chicago newspaper had financed a party of prospectors to search for gold, and they had chosen this section for their operations. They had gone to a great expense in building sluice boxes and drawing the stream for an ample supply of water, all of which appeared that the gold was there in inexhaustible amount. After looking over the ground for some time, we could not see any gold. We concluded that it was a wild-cat boom proposition, and pulled out down the river. We camped for the night within six hours run from Ft. Selkirk.

Soon after our start the following morning [July 13], we ran hard onto a sand bar located in the middle of the stream, which after several minutes of tugging on the oars, we were unable to remove. We were therefore compelled to call for help from our companions, who came up and relieved us of one thousand pounds of goods before the boat would budge. After leaving Rink Rapids, little trouble in navigation is encountered, except the sand bars, which are impossible to avoid in the wide stream, and many a one we have cursed.

Our run during the forenoon, aside from the troublesome sandbar, was without mishap, and we enjoyed the beautiful summer day tempered by the cool moving waters and gorgeous scenery on both sides of us. As we advanced, civilization was much more in evidence. Here and there we could see a camp of prospectors' tents, usually at the mouth of a stream which sluggishly emptied its muddy waters into the Lewis. Indian villages were seen more frequently, and now and then we could see an Indian grave surmounted high and dry on four stakes a short way back from the shore.

At three o'clock we tied up at Fort Selkirk, the old Hudson Bay trading post, which for years was inhabited by the only white men in all of the great North West Territories. The old Fort was burned by Indians in the year [1852] but was rebuilt [in 1892],[3] and at this time was occupied by fifteen Northwest mounted police who patrol this section. They were housed in several well-built log buildings surrounded by well-attended gardens of early, small vegetables and large patches of thriving potatoes that were good to look at. To us, this was the first evidence that such truck could be produced in the frozen north.

Directly opposite Fort Selkirk, the Pelly River, comparing nearly in size with the Lewis, empties itself into the latter, and from here the two rivers form the great Yukon proper. The Pelly was discovered and named in 1840 by Robert Campbell, who descended it in 1843, and who five years later established Fort Selkirk for the Hudson Bay Company. From the Fort, the mouth of the Pelly cannot be seen on account of several heavily wooded islands, which form at all large tributaries of both the Lewis and Yukon. The Pelly is navigable for many miles, but due to the absence of gold on its bars and tributaries, navigation has not as yet been attempted.

After looking over the ruins of the old fort, of which little can be seen except a solitary stone chimney standing as it has for years, we stopped at the Post. There we mailed several letters, which we were told would go overland by carrier via the Dalton Trail. The trail terminates here and was extensively used in packing supplies to the Hudson Bay Post, in order to avoid the many rapids in the upper river.

Having several hours before sunset, we left the fort, and were soon gliding swiftly down the great Yukon, where it soon widens to nearly twice the width of the Lewis above. Hundreds of little wooded islands are to be seen from the Pelly down, making it rather difficult at times to pick the main channel. If the wrong course is taken, an ugly sandbar is almost sure to present itself, and is master of the situation. These little wooded islets set irregularly on the wide expanse of the great river present a very beautiful sight, which is not excelled by the Thousand Islands of the St. Lawrence River.

To add to the beauty of this section, the Upper Ramparts begin at the mouth of the Pelly and extend along the north shore of the Yukon for fifteen or sixteen miles. These are solid walls of picturesque rocks, ranging in height from fifty to sixty feet, and upon close observation are as smooth as polished marble. The rock itself compares favorably with the Alaska diamonds found along the shores of Windy Arm, which we gathered while there. The formation is grand and resembles old castles' towers of every description.

After leaving Fort Selkirk, we made a run of twelve miles, and ran in for the night not far from an Indian village of large proportion. They told us the fishing season had begun at this point, but the fish had just arrived, and they were making preparations to care for them. The next morning [July 14] when we left the landing, we were minus several of our party who had remained behind to prospect a small stream that looked promising to them. The remainder of the party could not see it, however, and, as they shouted that they would catch up to us before night, we left them.

The run during the day [July 14] was much the same as the day previous, with the exception of a little mishap that might have proven serious. We had run into shore at twelve o'clock for lunch, after which we had fairly got a start again, and for some reason unknown had taken the wrong channel between two small islands. We were taking it easy on our full stomachs, when all of a sudden our huge boat gave a fearful lurch, at the same time emitting a scraping, tearing sound. The next we knew, we were raised six inches out of water astride a mammoth flat rock, which, combined with the motion of the stream, meant to capsize us at any second. However, after some minutes of rocking, we swung clear, and upon a thorough examination of the boat, found the strain had in no way opened our caulks. We proceeded on our way until night, where we camped upon one of the pretty little islets in midstream.

Broke camp early the following morning, July 15th, and made White River at 3:00 p.m. It was a beautiful run among the wooded islets, which all day have dotted the Yukon, now widened to a mile or more. Out of curiosity, we ran into the settlement at White River, after a hard pull across the Yukon. Here we found several parties prospecting the bars of the large stream and many of its nearby tributaries, but as to their success in finding gold in paying quantities, we were unable to learn. The White River is one of the larger of the Yukon tributaries, and enters the latter river from the west. However, its true course is northeast until within a few miles of the Yukon, where it takes a sharp turn due east. Its headwaters are in Alaska directly opposite the watershed of a tributary of the Copper River. At the time I write, the White River is the most feasible route to the Suschanna [Chisana] district, one of the latest discoveries of gold in the northern country. The river is about one hundred and seventy miles long and about six hundred feet wide at the mouth, and is navigable for small steamers for a number of miles. It derives its name from the light grayish waters that, after entering the Yukon, can be traced for at least one hundred miles, the coloring no doubt coming from the clay banks on either side.[4]

After a rest of half an hour, we got underway again. At seven o'clock, we tied up for the night at the mouth of the Stewart River, another large tributary of the Yukon. Here we found the largest camp of gold-seekers seen since leaving Windy Arm, and it presented the first real live gold camp it had been my lot to see. On both sides of the wide tributary and back from the Yukon as far as the heavy timber would permit, could be seen tents of all shapes and sizes and erected in such a manner that would indicate a long stay. Hundreds of boats made fast could be seen a great distance up and down the banks. Many had, after leaving one of the party to look after the camp, gone up the river prospecting, but as yet none had returned with any success to anyone's knowledge. However, as long ago as 1885, gold was found on its bars and tributaries in paying quantities. Since that time, many small fortunes have been wrung from its sands by a few who dared to brave the hardships and absolute loneliness of the isolated district in the early days.

The Stewart is a long, wide stream navigable by small steamers for many miles. It has its source in the mountains dividing its watershed with that of the great McKenzie River, which flows northward into the Arctic Ocean. The Stewart has many tributaries, among which Henderson Creek is the best known, on account of the richness discovered in the early eighties. That is now nearly exhausted, at least with primitive means of extraction. I think it would be safe to say that the evening we landed there, everything for miles had been staked, with more arriving every hour to join in the stampede for an undisputed claim. At the time I write, no gold worthy of mention has been taken from this district since the Klondike was discovered, although a thorough and perfect prospect has been given it.

Due to the local excitement and mosquitoes, which came in clouds, we were unable to close our eyes in sleep until 2:30 a.m. We were reawakened three hours later [July 16] by the same disturbances. We had, at no time after our arrival, been fired by the prevailing excitement to decide for a moment to remain and join in the chances of the thousands already here. Therefore, we made early preparations to continue on down the Yukon. Dawson was now but seventy miles distant, which destination we hoped to make before sunset of the day before us. So after making a few sales

---

The Wildcat Strike on the Stewart River, Summer 1898

+———+

Another traveler of that summer, Frederick Stephen Wombwell, wrote in an unpublished account that he ascended the Stewart River between June 25 and August 13, 1898. He and his party were forced to build smaller boats to negotiate the river as it was clogged with flood debris, and they spent more time portaging over sandbars and river blockages than they did poling their boats upstream. When they finally arrived at the head of the Stewart, in early August, they discovered prospectors who had taken out twenty ounces of gold over several weeks, an amount that they deemed not worth the effort. Wombwell's party did not arrive in Dawson until August 14, and he was not able to stake a claim in the Klondike district.[5]

of our outfit, such as cornmeal at $7.50 per sack, bacon $1.50 per lb., beans $.45 per lb., etc., we bid goodbye to Stewart River, and were soon floating with the six mile current.

Due to the troublesome sandbars, our run for the day had not come up to our expectations of the morning, and when night came, we were yet twenty-three miles from Dawson City. Early in the afternoon, we had passed Sixty Mile Post and Ogilvie Post, opposite one another. We camped for the night two miles below Indian River, a small stream of no particular importance.

According to an advertisement by the Seattle Clothing Company, which outfitted individuals going to the Klondike in 1898, a twenty-five pound bag of cornmeal cost $.44 in Seattle, bacon went for $.125 a pound, and beans were $.03 a pound. It appears that the Woodins sold these supplies for ten to seventeen times what they paid. Will and his father realized substantial profits on their sales.[6]

All were astir at an early hour on the following morning, Sunday, July 17 in anticipation of the last day's run on the Yukon before reaching our objective point, Dawson. Although we had enjoyed the trip, I can't say that a one of us were sorry that the end was near. Much activity on the river between Sixty Mile Post and Dawson was to be seen, which, at first, we wondered at, but we soon learned the cause. Timber is very scarce at Dawson, and hundreds were coming up river in search of cabin material and fire wood. Many men were employed by the two or three saw mills on the Klondike that were running night and day to supply the tremendous demand made upon them for building material. For miles above the city, the timber on both sides of the river is cut swath-like for perhaps a couple hundred feet inland. This peculiarity, we learned, was on account of the handling of the logs. There were no horses or donkey engines to do this work, such as used in modern Washington logging camps. Therefore, the work had to be done by human strength. As the hauling distance to the river was taken into consideration, the timber more than two hundred feet from shore was left for the horse and engine at a later period.

As the morning slipped away and ten o'clock came, we knew by the little groups of tents here and there on either shore that our destination was not far distant. At 11:30, upon rounding a turn in the river, a cry went up from the first boat. Looking downstream, we saw about two miles distant, hundreds of tents shining in the bright sunlight. As we drew nearer, we saw many log buildings of an unusual size, while along the waterfront several river steamers were anchored.

Chapter Seven

DAWSON

JULY 17–SEPTEMBER 1, 1898

$+\!\!\Longleftarrow\!\!+$

U PON ARRIVAL AT THEIR DESTINATION, the Woodin party set about fulfilling their mission in coming north. They connected with people they knew from Seattle and with friends they had met along the way. They set up a household, explored the countryside, made a token attempt to file claims, and concentrated on selling the extra supplies they had labored so hard to bring north.

They did not arrive in Dawson without some preparation. Hiram Ulysses Woodin (see Biographies) had originally accompanied his older brother Jay to Skagway in the fall of 1897. At that time, Jay decided the trails were too difficult to travel in the depths of winter, so he packed for others for several weeks before returning to Seattle to plan for a more ambitious endeavor starting in March. Hiram went on to Dawson that fall in order to develop the critical connections the party would need upon its arrival the following summer.

It is curious that Will does not mention Ed Green, Bill Chamberlain, or William Wells after their arrival in Dawson. It seems likely they did not get that far, and with the absence of his diary, Will could not remember when they parted company. Will mentioned Green on June 2 at Miles Canyon and again on June 15 on the trek up the Little Salmon. His last mention of William Wells, who had joined with Green and Bill Chamberlain at Windy Arm, was on May 29, when "the Green, Chamberlain and Wells Co." embarked on the river. The final notation for Bill Chamberlain was on June 3 at Whitehorse Rapids. It is possible that Green, Chamberlain, and Wells all turned back after the drowning of George Sherwood at the Big Salmon River, as both Green and Wells had known the young man before coming north.

Will does account for Jim Daugherty, the man Jay Woodin grubstaked for the trip. On July 25, a week after arriving in Dawson, Daugherty found a paying job with a mining company in Forty Mile, a community below Dawson on the Yukon River, in Alaska, and he left the Woodins' company. This break-up of partnerships either during the journey or on arrival in Dawson was fairly typical.

Besides Hiram Woodin, another person who would become important to Jay and Will was Abraham Kiger (see Biographies), a neighbor from Seattle who had been in Dawson for several months upon their arrival. Kiger had a productive claim on Lovatt Gulch, a small tributary of Bonanza Creek, the first stream to have been staked in August 1896. Kiger was also Cal Johnson's father-in-law. Johnson had been extremely helpful to the Woodin party since the camp at Windy Arm, and it is likely that the friendship with Johnson proved useful in locating their claims.

It was during their stay in Dawson, on August 23, that Will began his third log book of the trip. A comparison between his memoir and his diary from that point on is instructive about the accuracy of memoirs in general. For instance, in his memoir account of August 28, Will described the fruitless wait to register his and his father's claims on Lovatt Creek. Despite the fact that the wait was important, and resulted in his failure to record their claims, he made no mention of the tedious task in his diary. In fact, his August 28–31 diary entries indicate he was more interested in disposing of his father's goods and watching the paddle-wheelers than in filing the claims or looking for a job.

It is obvious that the Woodins never seriously considered mining once they got to Dawson. They had gone north to sell their extra goods. Will ends his memoir by expressing disappointment in his adventure, which he called "a fruitless search for gold." However, his father realized profits of 400 to 500 percent on the goods he sold along the trail and in Dawson. While Will had already noted that "a few articles had either been stolen or overlooked, and left at one of [their] many caches," the loss seems to have been negligible. Jay's endeavor was, without a doubt, successful. Will provided enough information in the early portions of his memoir and diary to estimate their costs at around $3,000, or $84,000 in today's currency. Thanks to Will's detailed description of prices that they realized for goods they sold on the Yukon River and in Dawson, it is possible to estimate their earnings on their goods at about $7,800, or $218,000 in today's currency. While the project did not net Jay Woodin the fortune he wanted, he was certainly able to support his party and family back in Seattle for the length of the March–October 1898 expedition, as well as for a few months later while he reestablished his business (see Appendix C for a detailed accounting of costs and profits).

It is difficult to determine whether these profits paid all of their expenses. In addition to supporting a family back in Seattle, Jay paid the cost of the passage for himself, Will, Daugherty, all of the cargo, the two horses, the dog, and return passage back to Seattle. It was, perhaps, in the end, a very hard way to make a living, and not the fortune they had hoped for.

While they were in Dawson, Will and his father took a trip up Bonanza Creek, where the first and richest finds had been made, and this trip offers some interesting commentary on the potentials for the acquisition of wealth in the diggings. On August 19, Will described nuggets that miners had found worth between $50 and $578. The largest nugget that he reported weighed 30.45 ounces, and in May 2014, that nugget would have sold on the gold market for almost $40,000. Will noted pans of gold yielding as much as $200 per pan, or 10.54 ounces. Those pans would bring the modern miner almost $14,000.[1] Obviously, if a person obtained a good claim, he could make a fortune.

However, most people had much less luck with their claims. William Haskell wrote that the average miner panned out about seventy-five cents per pan. Tuck and Flick Flaharty, who went north about the same time as the Woodins, gave up their claims because they earned less than a dollar a pan (less than $70 worth of gold in May 2014).[2] It is little wonder that the Woodins chose not to record their claim; indeed, they did not even work it.

We now rejoin Will on the outskirts of Dawson.

+≻═━≺+

At twelve o'clock on July 17, we landed about one half mile from Klondike City, and made lunch, after which we climbed the mountain-like banks (the shoreline being impassable), and finally descended to the lower ground upon which Klondike City is located. Upon inquiry, we soon found Uncle Hiram at his real estate office. He had reached Dawson with the great rush of the previous fall, and being unable to locate a worthwhile claim, had been dabbling in real estate, which showed indication of valuable results. So he had rented a substantial log cabin at Klondike City and hung out his shingle. He had done well, and with the great influx pouring in each day, real estate looked good to him, as many were buying and already preparing for the long winter ahead of them.

With the greater portion of the afternoon before us, we had a desire to have a look at the great mining town. He at once accepted an invitation to accompany us, so we set out.

Dawson City is located on the north banks of the Yukon, on a flat circular basin receding back to high mountainous hills, their summits devoid of vegetation. On the north, the hill rises to a great elevation, and is called [Moosehide Mountain],[3] on which is located an observatory and lookout station, used for the purpose of locating steamers

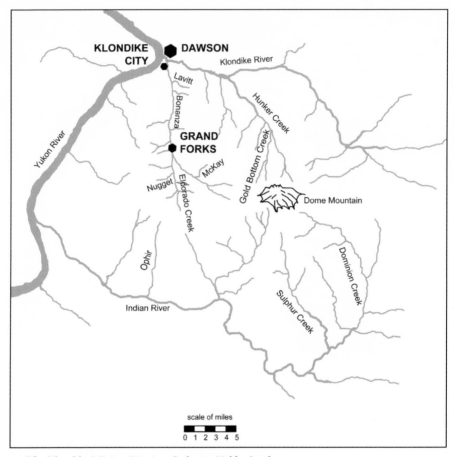

The Klondike Mining District. *Catherine Holder Spude*

coming up the river. From this point, the river is visible for miles, and steamers in the far distance appear not unlike crawling fleas on its shining surface. To the east, the hills are not so high and they slope down to the riverbanks. Hundreds of little cabins can be seen in terraces on this slope. They reach back a mile or more from the business portion of the mining city, and spread nearly to the summit. To the south of the town is the abrupt elevation we scaled in reaching Uncle's cabin.

Through this basin flows the Klondike River, from which branch the famous gold-producing creeks: Bonanza, Eldorado, Hunker, Gold Bottom, Bear, and many others well-known to the whole world. The

Panorama view of Klondike City (below the waterway) looking north to the larger city of Dawson, below Moosehide Mountain. *Yukon Archives, Anton Vogee fonds, #123.*

Klondike River is about seventy-five miles long, and as far as we ascended it, it had a width of about one hundred feet. At the time we arrived, it was very swift and shallow, the waters as cold as ice and as clear as crystal. As it enters the Yukon, a large island separates it into two channels, which reduces the depth to a degree that we had difficulty in crossing in our small tender.

The stream separates Klondike City (or Lousetown, as it is sometimes called by the sourdoughs), from Dawson City. Each channel was spanned by a wooden constructed foot bridge. Its builders and owners exacted a toll of fifty cents a head, man or dog (any other animal larger than a dog being excluded from crossing). This private thoroughfare proved a great inconvenience to the Dawson residents, for it was necessary in going to and from the creeks to either walk a distance of a half mile upstream to a cable ferry, or patronize the bridge owners. In either instance, a toll was charged. On the day of our arrival, we evaded the charges by using our small boat, though it was not altogether convenient to do so. We repeated this method many times during our stay in Dawson.

From the Dawson City end of the bridge, the main business street begins. We found it lined on either side for quite a distance with large tents, under which all sorts of mercantile business was carried on briskly. These tents were temporary, and would soon give way to log or frame structures, some of which were already under construction before the long Arctic winter set in. On going farther up the street to the older part of the city, the tents gave way to substantial log and frame buildings of large dimensions. The mammoth warehouses of the Alaska Commercial Company, Healy and Company, and several other large companies were located within a stone's throw of the Yukon at the extreme north end of town. There the heavily-laden river steamers from downstream run alongside a large wharf, and discharge their cargos, after which the merchandise was transferred to the respective company stores. At the time of year we had arrived, this part of the city was a busy scene at all times of the long day. A day hardly passed that a steamer from White Horse or St. Michaels did not arrive, loaded to the rails with foodstuffs for the long, hard winter. They reduced prices and played havoc with our anticipation of ridding ourselves of our large stock at stiff prices later on.

As you leave the warehouses, the street continues onto the base of [Moosehide Mountain], where it takes a gradual grade halfway to its summit. Here is located the Catholic Hospital. During the summer and fall of 1898, it was crowded to overflowing with patients suffering from typhoid fever and dysentery caused from the unsanitary conditions that prevailed, and with which the city government was unable to cope, so great was the tremendous influx and growth of the city.

The afternoon, so full of interest, passed quickly and 'ere we reached camp, the night's shadows began to gather. Thoroughly tired after our long tramp, we soon sought our beds.

The following forenoon [July 18], we ran our boats down to Klondike City, landing opposite Uncle's office until such a time should arrive that we could secure, or if necessary, build a cabin for storing our goods and to house us for the winter. This was now our first thought, to get settled for the winter. We lost little time in trying to rent a cabin, but found little chance of doing so at this time of the season. Few were renting, and those selling were asking exorbitant prices, which we could not pay. For a time, we were of a mind to begin building at once. This plan we postponed, and finally were rewarded in doing so by renting a small cabin in Klondike City, not far from where we had landed. We traded our large boat for two month's rent of same, a price we considered of $75.00 per month.

This happened on Monday, a week after we had arrived [July 25]. At once, we transferred our goods to the little cabin, it taking us almost the entire day to do so. There was little room left when we had finished stacking boxes and sacks of merchandise snugly to the ceiling. With our bed, stove, table and a couple boxes for chairs, it was much crowded. During the week, little of any consequence happened except securing the cabin and moving the goods. Nothing was done toward disposing of a single article.

However, we were busy all that week [July 18-25] making three trips up the Bonanza. Father and I staked two claims each on two tributaries of that creek. The first staking was adjoining a property Uncle staked after his arrival the previous autumn. In the early spring, he had let two lays on the claim to two strong, young fellows who were now developing it by sinking a shaft to bedrock. The day we arrived at the claim, they had reached a depth of fifty feet. It was very unusual to dig this deep before reaching the rocky strata holding the gold. But they were cheerful, and it appeared that time alone was responsible for the uncovering of untold riches, and that time would soon come—possibly on the morrow, almost any time now.

> The "letting of lays" involved finding men who would be willing to work a claim in return for a portion of the gold they retrieved. This practice allowed men such as Hiram Woodin, who had other interests in Dawson, to own a claim, garner some percentage of the gold found there, yet not have to invest any personal labor in the effort. This practice also allowed those men who came in the summer of 1898 to dig on the richer claims when they were unable to locate claims of their own.

We were much interested in seeing this, our first staked claim in the great Klondike. On the morrow [July 19] we returned to watch the progress of development. We had not been on the property more than an hour, when a shout from the bottom of the shaft reached our ears. Later, we were informed that bedrock had been reached, and the shout was for the man above to quickly examine the dirt taken therefrom. With shaking hands, he removed a portion of the precious earth to his gold pan, adding sufficient water, while we stood around in an expectancy of the results. Not one color showed itself in the pan when the necessary maneuvering had been completed in removing all except the heavy black sand. Not satisfied with the result of the first bucket, several more were hoisted and given the same treatment with the same results. Enough was enough. Three months had been spent, long days of the most arduous labor in sinking this hole, goaded on and on by dreams of riches that lay secreted in mother earth. A more broken-spirited pair of young men would have been difficult to find in the diggings than these two were, so confident had they been of success. With a curse, they at once collected their scant camp equipage and tools together, and with our assistance, accompanied us to Dawson, undecided what next they would do. It was all a gamble, as was plainly told by the abandoned worthless shafts that honeycombed this particular section of the Bonanza. This example was but one of thousands revealed to us.

The rich claims had been discovered farther up the creek, although some spotted claims had been developed with paying results within five miles of Dawson. During the influx of the previous autumn, everything on the creek had been staked. Below No. __,[4] however, few were being developed when we arrived, having been deserted and leaving them open for those who desired to take a chance.

Early one morning a few days after our return from the worthless shaft [July 21], we were awakened from our slumbers by several quick knocks on our cabin door. Upon arising, we found Mr. Kiger, an old friend of ours, at the door. He had come a distance of six or seven miles during the early morning to advise us to at once accompany him back and stake a claim apiece adjoining the one he and his son were working. Theirs was a lay which, he excitedly told us, was showing up very satisfactory. The old fellow was a typical German, small of stature, slightly stoop-shouldered from hard work, although well-preserved and as tough as an ox. He and his son had preceded us a few weeks, and upon their arrival at Dawson, had at once taken a lay and continued development on Discovery Claim of a little creek call Lovatt Gulch. The claim belonged to a friend who wished to visit the states after spending several years in the Territory. Where they had taken the lay, much development work had been done by their friend, who had realized little or nothing for his pains, and had little confidence in future results. However, his confidence was to be shaken ere another year rolled by.

This particular morning the old fellow was greatly excited, and it was some time before we were able to understand him, so thoroughly did he hash his broken English with the German language. We finally got the drift of his meaning after much amusement, and, although having little confidence in location, we set about preparing for the trip. He remained for breakfast with us, after which we all set out. We followed the trail along the Klondike River for two miles, at which point it turns to the right and enters the valley of the world famous Bonanza Creek. A tramp up this valley of three miles brought us to claim No. 91 [below Discovery], where we turned to the left, and followed a narrow valley that cuts through the high sloping hills on either side of Bonanza. This is the second tributary on the Bonanza after leaving the Klondike, and is called Lovatt Gulch. At the time I write, it was considered of little consequence by the prospector, and no development except of what I speak had been attempted. After proceeding about a mile, the valley terminates in a wide, sloping basin surrounded by high hills, which are almost barren of all vegetation. The formation is a glacial deposit appearing upon the surface much as all the richer country does in this section.

Their claim and camp for the winter was located at this juncture. Evidence showed that much work had been done by their friend, as a great deal of dirt had been moved from the creek bottom. The owner of the claim had built sluice boxes and other contrivances necessary in placer mining, and had erected a windlass. Here we met Kiger's son, who had remained in camp while his father came for us. He was busily engaged wielding a shovel as we arrived, and aside from a short but hearty welcome, he returned to his task with renewed energy.

After some explanations of the workings and progress on his claim, the old man directed us to claims open for filing in his vicinity. Since arriving, he had acquainted himself with the surrounding properties, which enabled him to select several for us to choose from, claims either abandoned or had never been located. From outward appearances, choosing a claim in the Yukon or Alaska regions is much like drawing a lottery ticket. Many the old California miner and prospector have been misled by the surface formation appearing so much like those experience has taught him to consider a valuable placer claim. To this day, the experienced placer miner cannot claim the distinction of locating and developing the richest claims. This merit is distributed among men of all professions, and not a few of the valuable properties were either forced upon, or taken as a last resort by their now affluent owners. After going over the entire gulch with the old German, we found we had a pick of six unlocated claims, all above Discovery. Upon the advice of the old fellow, I planted my stake on No. 2 above, and Father took his chance on No. 3 on the opposite rim.

This task had hardly been finished when two young fellows who had closely followed us from the city rushed by and staked the remaining four, where upon they returned the way they came, whether to the city to record, we could not say. We considered no immediate rush was necessary to record ours, and upon an invitation from the old fellow to remain all night, we did so.

Early in the morning [July 22] after bacon and flap jacks, we were on our way back to the city, where we arrived two hours later. After a lunch and rest, we crossed to Dawson City with the intention of recording our newly acquired placer mines, but were fairly stunned when we came in sight of the Commissioner's office. There lined up for a whole city block, were foot-weary men, who, upon inquiry, told us they had been in line for the greater portion of a week patiently waiting their turn to record their claims. At Lake Tagish, we had a similar experience with the Canadian Customs office, but the time required was nothing compared with the recording office at Dawson. A man would start at the foot end of the line, and at night (or rather office closing time), an officer would come down the line and hand a numbered ticket to each, whereupon they would disband until the following day (not very early, for the English are no early risers). Upon presentation of their ticket given them the night before, they would take their place in line for the day or until such a time he was fortunate in reaching the Commissioner's desk. The Canadian officers in charge, although polite and civil, were inclined to be slow in all of their official duties, regardless of public opinion, and the latter became to expect it as a matter of course.

When we came to realize the true state of affairs, we decided to postpone recording for a time at least, and attend to affairs that we thought more important. Here the reader can see plainly how much confidence we placed in claims we had staked. If we had known then what we do now, we would have remained in line a week through sunshine and showers, yea, blizzards of snow and sleet, in reaching our goal.

However, we did not do it, but set about immediately to find buyers for our large stock of saleable goods before the tremendous supplies came in on the last boats from St. Michaels. Little was accomplished this day [July 23] however, in ridding ourselves of the stock, as prices offered were very low, occasioned by the large exodus which had now set in from Dawson. Those leaving Dawson could not return with their outfit, so it was sold in a lump for almost any price offered by the thrifty merchant, who doubled and tripled on their purchase. Several friends of mine, who I can name, made snug little fortunes buying outfits of the disheartened gold-seekers and selling them at the prevailing Dawson prices.

But Father said "We will wait awhile until things settle a bit," so leaving him, I went to the post office for the mail from the steamer *Ora,* which had arrived from White Horse during the afternoon. Service not unlike the land office was in evidence here. I have stood three hours in boiling sun, waiting for my turn to call for mail. Then I was rewarded with the answer "No mail for you," when I knew there was, for the fact that the next time I called, I would receive four or five letters bearing post marks dated a week or ten days apart. These conditions, although disagreeable, were overlooked as unavoidable at times, and our hearts made glad when word from our loved ones were handed us.

The following day [July 24] was Sunday, and its observance is strictly enforced by the city officials. A strict vigil is kept on saloons and dance halls, and all stores, as well, are closed to trade. Father and I set out to

Recording Claims with the
"Department of Corruption"

James McRae, another diarist who was in Dawson about the same time as the Woodin party, experienced a frustration similar to Will's in trying to record his claim. He had heard that the Canadian mining commissioners hindered rather than helped the miners record their claims. On August 15, while at McQuestion, he wrote, "They say that the Government at Dawson is rotten." A couple of weeks later, after staking a claim on Gold Bottom Creek, he wrote on September 2: "We found out after we came home [Dawson] that the Government holds half of each unrepresented 500 feet claim, but they posted no notices to that effect before men went out to stake. It will be 1 chance in 1000 if we can get a claim recorded."

The next day, a Saturday, McRae continued his record of his party's frustrations. "I went down to the department of corruption this morning and stood in line 'til nearly 1 o'clock but I could not get in. The Office closes at 1 o'clock on Saturday to give the lads a chance to divide the spoils so they can go to Church on Sunday and pray for strength to help them rob the public during the following week."

On Monday, September 5, McRae wrote: "Tucker, Jack and I went down to the recording office at 7:30. There was a big crowd there. This office did not open till 9:30. We got in on our nerve. They took Jack's application, but they would not take Tucker's and mine. They said the claim was not run out. Tucker, Andrew and I went up Bonanza this afternoon to look at a claim where we can get a lay for the winter."

While Will Woodin does not express disgust over the procedure in the way that McRae did, it is obvious that the process of recording a claim was so daunting that many miners simply put the task off, or chose to work another man's claim for a share of the gold.[5]

spend the day in a quiet way, but our quietude was interrupted late in the afternoon by some exciting events that took place along the river-banks in Dawson. A heavy downpour or rain had set in soon after our return from the claims the day before, and had increased in volume until at noon today, when it came down in sheets, causing the river to rise rapidly. By noon, it had risen twenty-four feet, and those having camps along the water front began hurriedly moving their outfits to places of safety. Some, however, had neglected to heed the rising river until too late, and consequently suffered for their procrastination, by losing a portion of their camp equipage in the swift current of the mighty river.

It seemed the entire town turned out to assist in the rescue, and by nightfall, with helping hands, all had secured temporary shelter until the swelling river subsided. Old timers claimed such heavy rains at this time of the year were very unusual, and few remembered the river rising so rapidly as it did on this occasion.

The following morning [July 25], the sun came out warm and bright again, and a few days later, the stream took on its normal bounds. Our co-partner, Jim Daugherty, today secured an all winter position with a mining company at $15.00 per day with board and room. The company will use him on their Klondike property, when later they will send him to Forty Mile for the remainder of the winter. He was much elated over his good fortune and could scarcely eat, so excited was he.

Tuesday, July 26, saw the arrival of three steamers from White Horse, the *George A. Barr, Sovereign,* and *Willie Irwin,* each of which had only a few passengers aboard for Dawson, evidence that the season's rush to the gold field was at an end. The passengers aboard the *Willie Irwin,* the last to leave White Horse, gave us our first news of the victories gained by the United States Navy of the Spanish at Manila, which occurred several weeks previous.[6] The entire city went wild over the news, and immediately they set about arranging a celebration that very night in honor of the glad tidings. Evening had hardly set in when a parade was formed and marched up and down the main street, hundreds of men keeping step to the patriotic songs they sang. In the street in front of the Alaska Commercial Company's stores, a large platform had been built, and around and around this they marched, until a speaker arose and gave the news in details that brought a deafening roar from the thousands present. Many eloquent speeches were made by Americans, and to cap the climax, a vaudeville house donated their orchestra and stage talent to add to the inspiring event and was appreciated very much. At the finish, I thought the crowd would go mad, when two vaudeville actresses wrapped in American flags and accompanied by the Orchestra sang the "Star Spangled Banner." Although the larger portion of Dawson's population was made up of people from the States, our British neighbors shared our enthusiasm in quite as much zest as we ourselves did. This is an event that time cannot blot from my memory, and as I now look back upon the scene, I am proud to have been one of that mass of our nation's patriotic citizens.

That week that followed [July 27-August 3] ushered in nothing of especial interest. Many steamers arrived with loads of provisions and a few passengers, only to return loaded to the rails with the latter on their way out. Father spent the entire week prospecting his claim on Lovatt Gulch, while I remained in the city in charge of the goods. Made some very good sales at good stiff prices, such as one hundred pounds of ham at sixty cents per pound, bacon the same price, and all staple articles sold in proportion.[7] Many new cabins were being built, and as we had a very good line of hardware, I made very good sales in that line. It necessitated a house-to-house canvass, which took much time, and much patience.

It was on Tuesday, August 2 that Father returned to the city, having been taken the evening before with severe pain in his bowels, followed with a bad case of dysentery. When he reached our cabin, he was so weak and exhausted after his long walk, that I became anxious over his condition. I put him to bed and did what I could for him, with the simple remedies at hand, which seemed to ease him for a time.

During the preceding week, I had covered the greater portion of Dawson in my soliciting tours. It gave the opportunity to call at the homes and camps of many of the residents, and I was astonished and fairly frightened at the many cases of dysentery, malaria and typhoid fever that existed and was cared for outside the hospital. I was told that scores had died of typhoid fever, while not a few had succumbed to dysentery or malaria fever, all no doubt caused from drinking without boiling the river water, and chiefly the sanitary condition existing through the entire city.

Father's illness now reminded me of the pitiful cases I had seen in several patients, and I became anxious in regard to his condition. The following day [August 3], he was no better, and it was necessary for me to be constantly in attendance. For five days and nights, he suffered the ravages of the disease. On Sunday morning [August 7] he awoke, feeling much better, but very weak and sore. He improved rapidly, and few days later, was as well as before.

But almost a week had slipped by and nothing accomplished by either of us. We had decided during his illness to dispose of our stock as soon as he was able to be about, and as the next day was Monday [August 8], I started out with my hardware. Before night, I had disposed of nearly all of it at good prices. Each day large sales were made, and toward the end of the week, we saw a decided rise in the price of all provisions due to the non-arrival of steamers from St. Michaels. A week had passed without a single boat arrival from down river, which proved no little concern to the large commercial companies. They were not concerned that their stocks were running low in their warehouses, but rather for the possible accidents which might have befallen the boats on the lower river. The companies' officials, however, were not the only anxious ones, but four or five hundred out-going passengers had purchased tickets for St. Michaels, a great many as long as a week before. Since disposing of their outfits, they had been compelled to pay enormous hotel and restaurant rates until going aboard their steamer. Anxiety was quelled, however, when on the next day [August 9], the steamers *P. B. Weare* and *Susie* came to anchor, loaded to the rails with provisions for the large commercial companies' stores and only a few passengers for Dawson. The number of passengers they will make up on their downward trip.

Leaving Father in charge of the cabin, Uncle and I left early the morning of August 10th for Discovery on Hunker Creek, a good stiff walk of twenty-five miles. We carried blankets and food, each weighing thirty pounds or more, and you can take it from me that they weighed one hundred and thirty pounds when we cached in that night. We had made it to No. 47 Hunker, a distance of twenty-one miles during the day.

Uncle was in search of a location for a road house, or in other words, a way hotel, and in his opinion, this section was the most likely place to establish one. His prospective point was the mouth of a tributary of Hunker Creek called Gold Bottom. On a former visit to this locality, he had observed that no road house existed within five miles and none after leaving No. 3 Hunker.

Night was upon us when we reached No. 47, and finding a deserted cabin containing two "bunks" filled with straw on the claim, we remained for the night. The next morning [August 11], leaving our packs at the cabin, we walked up to the mouth of Gold Bottom. There, to our disappointment, we found a large road house nearing completion.

Our mission had been useless, so we retraced our steps to the cabin where we had left our packs and turned in for the night. Early the next morning [August 12], we started for Dawson. We took our return trip more leisurely and were able to observe the richness of this wonderful creek. From No. 5 below Discovery to No. 40 above, the creek abounds in riches, and the spring clean-up saw thousands of dollars taken from its dumps. This process was practically over for this season, although some who had water were doing summer sluicing.

We arrived in Dawson at 7:15 p.m., footsore and weary, having taken another trail in returning. For a great distance, it proved to be wet and swampy and covered with moss, and we would sink nearly to our knees in walking. Father was in fairly good health and was glad to see us back. During our absence, Daugherty, our boat mate, had gone down to Forty Mile, and Father bid farewell to several of the boys who we had become acquainted with at Windy Arm on their way to Seattle via White Horse or St. Michaels. This news, I can truthfully say, caused me to feel my first homesickness since leaving Seattle.

The next morning [August 13], we did not rise at the usual early hour. When I did crawl out, I found my legs and shoulders so stiff and lame, I could hardly move from the effects of the long, tedious jaunt of the three days previous. I did finally get courage toward noon to go to the post office, but nearly lost it again when I saw five hundred men lined up waiting for the doors of the office to open. I stood one and one half hours in line before I saw the inside of the office. Due to standing so long in the scorching sun, I left there with a bursting headache, which lasted throughout the afternoon and entire night. If I had then known the true character of the terrible symptoms menacing my health, we would have taken the next steamer leaving Dawson for the outside.

The next day was Sunday [August 14], and after a sleepless night, I arose tired and haggard, my head still aching to the point of splitting, so it seemed. During the day, I did my baking to last a week. It was while at this task that, through Uncle, Father and I made the acquaintance of Major Strong and wife, who had taken a cabin next to ours the day before. Little did we think then that the major would someday be governor of Alaska Territory, but such is his honor at the date I write.[8] During our stay in Dawson, we found the major and his wife mighty congenial neighbors, and I got to know them quite well. They had no more prospects in view than we did ourselves, but were in the race like thousands of others. They finally went to Nome upon the discovery of gold there and until he was appointed by President Wilson to the Governorship of Alaska, he was editor of the *Nome Nugget,* the leading press of that thriving mining camp to this day.

I arose Monday morning [August 15], after another sleepless night from the terrible headache, which never for a moment seemed to cease. Upon advice from Father, I went over to town and purchased some medicine, which after taking, gave me relief. However, I felt weak and nauseous and had little ambition to do anything in the line of work. But work we must. So we set about getting a line on our stock, preparatory to closing it out any time we deemed necessary, or to our advantage financially.

Since Father's illness, he seemed to have lost courage, and ventured a remark now and then, that if prospects did not show brighter aspect before the last boats should leave, he would return home to remain until spring. I could remain with Uncle in Dawson to be on hand if anything should turn up. This arrangement suited me, in the fact that I did not fancy, after so much time, labor and expense, the idea of returning empty-handed. Therefore, I spent each day thereafter looking for a position for the winter. A portion of the week passed, and each day decided Father more definitely on returning home on one of the last boats to leave Dawson, so we set out each day soliciting a sale of our large outfit.

Prices had advanced steadily on all staples until word was brought that the steamer *Louisa*, within a day's travel, was towing two large barges loaded with provisions, while others were closely following in her wake. The next day [August 17] the *Louisa* steamed in with her two barges alongside, loaded with thirteen hundred tons of flour, sugar, beans, potatoes, etc. Her arrival, and news of other steamers to arrive soon, relieved all minds that Dawson would ever again suffer a famine such as was experienced the previous winter. This news had a tendency to reduce prices, but not at the companies' stores. The disheartened gold-seeker was the individual to reduce his outfit in sales to the small retail merchant in order that he might realize enough money to pay his fare to Seattle. This new state of affairs caused us to hesitate again in an attempt to dispose of our stock for awhile at least. The following day, the steamer *T. C. Power* came to anchor of the N.A.T. Company's wharf,[9] loaded to the rails with provisions. The weather continued warm and beautiful through the now shortening days, but at night there was to be plainly felt the chill of the approaching winter.

On August 18th, Uncle and I left early for a trip up Bonanza and Eldorado creeks to a claim on Eldorado that he had staked and recorded the previous autumn. He had done very little at this claim, in fact just enough work necessary to hold it. His mission was now to let a lay to a party who was to meet us at the claim. Together, they would look the property over, and then decide one way or the other about the lay. Instead of taking the trail along the Klondike to Bonanza, we scaled the hill south of Klondike City, and cut across country to Bonanza, coming out at the roadhouse at No. 66 below Discovery. We had taken this trail because of its dryness underfoot, but we were sick of our bargain before we had gone one mile, on account of the terrible climb.

At No. 66, we took the well-worn trail up the Bonanza to No. 30, where we threw aside our packs for a lunch and rest. No. 30 was being worked by a friend of Uncle's by the name of Henderson,[10] who gave us the use of his stove and cooking utensils in preparing our lunch. We remained here a couple of hours, and then pushed on up the creek again. As we proceeded, the evidence of placer mining became more prominent, and now and then it became necessary to climb over sluice boxes and high cones of tailings that blocked our path. Below Discovery on Bonanza proved of little value, when compared with claims above, but many were paying their owners a neat daily wage at that.

By the middle of the afternoon, we arrived at Discovery, where in 1897, George Carmacks and his Indian brother-in-law, Skookum Jim, discovered the first gold in the Klondike. Here on all sides, the earth surface appeared not unlike the work of an ant colony on a mammoth scale. The light-colored tailings from the many sluice boxes rose high, some sloping to a height of several feet, while in the center stood a mammoth water wheel, appearing not unlike a miniature Ferris wheel. The clean-up for the season had long since been made, therefore was deserted until operation began in the winter.

As we reached No. 6 above Discovery on Bonanza, I was treated to a surprise in the fact that a settlement of some proportion met my gaze. Scores of neatly constructed log cabins, large and small in dimensions, conformed to regular streets. They housed firms catering to all needs of the miners from the shoe shop to the saloon (which were proportionately in the majority). Here the Eldorado, a tributary of the Bonanza, joined the latter stream at this point. Therefore, the settlement was called Grand Forks, or better known to the miners as "The Forks." It is a distributing point of the section, and did a tremendous business with the miners for miles around, saving them a long, tedious pack from Dawson City.

We remained here for a few moments' rest, and then pushed on up the world-famous Eldorado Creek toward our destination. Late in the afternoon, we overtook the party who Uncle was to show his claim, a Mr. Whitlow by name, and together we proceeded to No. 42 above. There we secured an empty cabin in which to spend the night, and I assure you we lost little time in hitting our blankets, so tired were we. We arose late the next morning [August 19] to find Mr. Whitlow quite ill with dysentery and unable to get around. Uncle and I made a tour of the surrounding territory to pass the time away.

Although thoroughly prospected during the previous summer and winter, no claims above No. 37 paid their owners for their trouble. In fact, the majority of owners lost heavily on their ventures. Nevertheless, for miles around or within our scope of travel for the day, everything was taken, and no doubt, all had been recorded. Now, however, they all were apparently deserted until the winter set in.

At night, when we returned to the cabin, we found Mr. Whitlow much better, and the next day [August 20] we all went to Uncle's claim. The claim proved to be a bench or hill claim, i.e., a claim adjoining the boundaries of creek or gulch claim. These types of claims extended uphill, not to exceed one thousand feet, with a length of two hundred and fifty feet, measured in the general direction of the river. The property, upon the face of it, appeared as promising as any of the rich properties we had visited. The great drawback was that it lay in a section that had not yet proven of any value, and it had not been prospected. However, Mr. Whitlow was highly pleased with the property, and although he did not say he would take the lay, he told Uncle he would consider it.

On the following morning [August 21], our real mission fulfilled, we began our return to the city, but at a more leisurely gait than which we had come. I will here mention a few of the wonders seen on our way. At No. 37, a large crew of miners was already at work, shoveling the gold-laden dirt into the long, trough-like sluice boxes. There the swiftly running water would force the dirt down the inclined surface, and the gold lodged against the riffles, as it became dissolved from the dirt. Stiles and McDonald were the owners of No. 37 and the adjoining claim No. 38. Mr. Stiles was foreman of the crew, and as Uncle knew him quite well, he invited us to come down and watch the procedures of placer mining, an invitation we quickly accepted. I had seen virgin gold in sluice boxes before, but not in yellow chunks like those that lay before our eyes here. Notwithstanding the early morning, the upper riffles had collected a number of beautiful yellow nuggets, which Mr. Stiles said were small compared to those found at the end of the day's clean-up. He also called our attention to the richness of the ground where the men were at work, and as they shoveled along the bedrock, we could plainly see the particles of coarse gold in the black soil.

Claim 37 had turned out famously rich, and was known in the region as the Nugget Claim, deriving the name from the fact that numerous nuggets of immense value had been taken therefrom. Mr. Stiles told us the largest tipped the scales at $578.00, while another weighed $480.00, another $400.00, and several $50.00 to $200.00, and as high as $700.00

had been washed from a single pan of earth. It was a wonderful and fascinating sight and was worth our long tramp to witness. Although several other claims in the section were more wonderfully rich that this one, it was not our good fortune to see them. Between No. 37 and "The Forks" lay claims of several famous Klondike Gold Kings, such as Alex McDonald's claim No. [30], Stanley's No. [unknown], Berry Bros. No. [5], Lippy's No. [16], Wilson and "Swiftwater Bill's No. 16 [actually, No. 13][11] and many others, where millions of dollars have since been taken out in virgin gold.

Opposite No. 17 Eldorado, French Creek comes in from the west. Although it is a short creek, it has turned out very rich on its bench or hill claims, and proved a wonder in the annals of placer mining. At a height of perhaps 300 feet from the creek bottom, coarse gold was found in large quantities and at the time we were there, they were rocking out in a primitive rocker $200.00 per day in a single rocker. These mines are known as the French Hill properties. Their discovery prompted gold-seekers to stake and record claims located at the very summits of all the adjacent hills in the Klondike region. But no others, to my knowledge, became producers of the precious metal like these.

Due to sightseeing during the day, little progress was made toward Dawson, and upon reaching No. 17 opposite these wonderful mines, we took advantage of an empty cabin for the night, although the day was not yet gone. Early next morning [August 22] we were again on our way. Until "the Forks" were reached, Uncle was kept busy pointing out the famous claims which lay between these points, giving the claim owner's name and amount of treasure taken from each the previous spring.

At "the Forks," a good view up Bonanza is had, as it inclines gradually toward the "Dome" ridge, which attains an altitude of about 4,000 feet, and is the watershed of all the gold-bearing creeks in the district. Bonanza and Hunker flow north into the Klondike, while Sulphur, Dominion, Quartz and Ophir flow south into the Indian River. At the eastern extremity of this ridge, there rises above the rest a large dome-shaped mountain, which is responsible for the name of the hills. It is spoken of by the miners as the mother lode, or source of gold found in the region. Little credence can be given this theory, as no gold has been found in the mountainous hills, although much prospecting has been done. Since reaching Dawson, I had heard much of this interesting landmark, and a desire had taken possession of me to cross it to Sulphur and Dominion Creeks, now that we were so near. But our time was limited, so I gave up the notion until such a time that the trip would not interfere with business.

At the left, opposite Discovery on Bonanza, Uncle pointed out where Big Skookum Creek came in, while at No. 4, Little Skookum made its appearance on the same side. These two creeks, although short, were very rich as also was Adams Creek, coming in at No. 6. From here down to the Klondike, though, very little can be said in that respect.

Aside from a stop for lunch at No. 30, we lost no time and at 5:00 p.m., we threw off our packs at the cabin in Klondike City, feeling not at all the worse for our long walk of the day. We found Father in fair health, but ill at ease from the fact that several boats had arrived since our departure, each loaded with provisions. The next day [August 23] saw the *Yukoner, Rock Island,* and *Domville* added to the steamer fleet at the companies' wharves. A few days later, a new river steamer of huge capacity came in from St. Michaels with 5,000 tons of provisions consigned to a recently organized company called the Alaska Exploration Company, which had, during the summer, built a mammoth warehouse in the north end of the city. The arrival of this steamer put a rumor to the effect that a big cut in the provisions of all kinds would be the result when they began competing with the two old, established companies, and the logic of the rumor gave us no little concern.

That night, Father and I sat up late going over our lists, and reviewing the state of affairs that now existed and which was daily growing worse. Before retiring, we had fully decided upon selling all as soon as possible, after which he would go to Seattle and I would remain.

August 23, Klondike City, Northwest Territory. I start this Book No. 3 of my trip to and through the North West Territories this day Aug 23, 1898. Where will one year from today find me? In one year from today I will be very careful to refer to this page. Have been in Dawson City five weeks last Sunday. Today Father and I took a load of provisions over to Chars. Jones amounting to over $200.00. It is beginning to tell on the pile of goods we at first had and could sell all the rest in one day's time if we should see fit.

One boat arrived from St. Michaels today at noon. The "Canada," also the "Willie Irving" [Irwin] *from White Horse Rapids with papers of the 8th of this month.*

The next week was a busy one for us, and at its end all that remained of the large outfit could easily be disposed of in one day's time. We sold at fairly good prices, some of which I will give: butter, $1.00 per pound, evaporated potatoes, 50 cents per pound, flour $8.00 per sack, raisins, 50 cents per pound, syrups, $4.00 per gallon, onions 50 cents per pound, cheese $1.00 per pound, tobacco, $1.50 to $2.50 per pound, ham 60 to 75 cents per pound; but the old Alaska menu, bacon and beans went for 25 cents and 10 cents per pound respectively, a price ridiculously low. Clothing and hardware were almost unsalable at any price, but having very little of the former articles to dispose of, we did not suffer a great deal financially from that source. [See Appendix C for a comparison of prices paid with those received.]

August 25. Did not leave the Cabin all day today. A batch of yeast bread kept me at home, but finally got it baked by dark. It gets dark now at 9 p.m. and the nights are beginning to get rather chilly, too. Some frost already. One month or less will end this season of warm weather, then comes the long and tedious cold Winter. Nothing but snow for six months, the daylight lasting only six hours. Can I stand a winter in this country? Not unless I have something to reward me. No. Have not got anything of any description yet.

At the latter end of the week [August 27], Father took a run up to the claims on Lovatt Gulch, but returned the same day. He found it impossible to sink a shaft on account of the caving earth, which in order to avoid, a cribbing of small poles will be necessary. Our neighbor, Mr. Kiger, he found as enthusiastic over the future riches of the gulch. He was at a loss to see why so little interest was taken by us in our claims. Father took little stock in the properties, but upon his return that evening, he advised me on the morrow to take a place in the human line leading to the recorder's office. In the event of a possible strike by them during the winter, we would be on the safe side, at little expense to us in doing so.

Nine o'clock that morning [August 28] found me in the rear ranks of an army of men in line, numbering perhaps ninety or one hundred, some no doubt in another year would leave with a snug little fortune from their now prospective claims. When the doors closed for the day, forty-seven gold seekers had secured privileges to mine their claims under the laws of the Canadian government, but more than that number during the day had taken their place, thus placing me near the center of the line. Disposing of applicants at this rate, I figured it would take me until the forenoon of the third day, but fate had planned it differently, for I never returned to the line.

That evening [August 27 in the diary, August 28 in the memoir], upon hearing the news that ex-Mayor Wood[12] of Seattle had arrived on his new steamer, *Seattle the III,* from St. Michaels, I took a walk over to Dawson to see it and get the news from the outside. I had not been feeling well all day, but lay it to the hard work we had done during the week. On my way back to the cabin, I was taken with chills and a feeling in my limbs and body not unlike a severe attack of La Grippe. When I reached the cabin, I at once retired, and was soon burning with fever, while at the same time, I was shaking with chills. With snatches of restless sleep, the night finally wore away. In the morning [August 29], although the chills had left me, the fever still continued. Adding to misery, a severe headache had set in that nearly drove me wild.

August 28. Another lonely Sunday nearly spent. It is now evening and a beautiful evening, too. We did not rise until very late this morning. Have done nothing all day but kill time. Went over town this afternoon to see the "Rock Island" sail for St. Michaels, but her date of sailing has been changed until tomorrow, but instead the "Linda" sailed with a great many passengers on board. The rates are cut down to $60 now, so many are taking advantage of the opportunity and going now. Must finish a letter to my little wife tonight.

August 29. This is Monday, the busiest day of the whole week and Father and I have been rustling all day. I made some pretty good sales today and we also sold an outfit of dried fruits. Three new co's goods have arrived and a big cut in prices are expected every day now.

August 30. We have done not much of anything today worth recording or nothing new to mention, but have not struck anything as yet.

August 31. We awake this morning and found that a nasty disagreeable rain was falling and kept it all day nearly. We went over town this afternoon and found that 4 new boats were in, two from St. Michaels and 2 from Bennett, the "Willie Irving" [Irwin] *and the "Ora" from above and the "Hannah" a magnificent steamer of the A.C. Co's and also one for the A.E. Co., do not know the name. The "Rideout" left at 6 p.m. today for St. Michaels with 120 passengers for the outside.*

Up to this date, Wednesday, August 31st, the weather had been fine with hardly a touch of frost in the night air. This morning, a cold rain had set in, which the "sourdoughs" said was a conclusive forerunner of the approach of the Arctic winter. During the rest of my stay in Dawson, weather mattered little to me, but I speak of this day as my last recollection of the Yukon interior and habits God had given it. The three weeks that followed are almost entirely a blank on my memory, except the pain and suffering I underwent, and I wonder now that I am alive to write these lines.

Chapter Eight

DAWSON TO SEATTLE
SEPTEMBER 1–OCTOBER 2, 1898

✦──✦──✦

W ILL BEGINS THE NEXT EPISODE IN HIS MEMOIR with the following: "The lines that follow are taken from notes written after my arrival and recovery at Seattle, given to me as they occurred by Father." He did not keep a diary between September 1 and October 8, almost a week after he arrived home. He was quite ill for the first three weeks of this period, so his inability to write during that time makes sense. It is curious that he did not resume what was a lifelong habit until after reaching home. It seems likely that he was disheartened by his perceived failure in the north, compounded by his extreme illness.

The account that he wrote immediately upon his return is fresh and frank. The version he wrote in 1914 de-emphasized the discomforts and his emotional toils, but expanded on details that stood out in his memory. In the account that follows, I have integrated the two versions, supplementing his memoir (in plain type) with details from the writing he did in October 1898 (shown in italics).

Will states that he was diagnosed with typhoid malaria; however, modern doctors distinguish between typhoid fever and malaria. During the Civil War, the two diseases were often confused, but by the turn of the century, most physicians had concluded they were distinct and caused by different agencies. Typhoid fever (which is probably what Will had contracted) was not well understood until after the Spanish-American War, during which the disease killed far more soldiers than did the firearms of the enemy. It is caused by bacteria transmitted through human feces, and is common wherever sanitary conditions were not kept under control. The bacteria causes prolonged fever, diarrhea, abdominal pain, skin rash, prostration, and delirium. The disease takes one to two weeks to incubate once a patient has been infected, and three weeks to run its course.[1] Will may have contracted typhoid fever while visiting Bonanza Creek with his Uncle Hiram. Indeed, Hiram came down with a similar illness, although not so severe, at much the same time that Will fell ill.

Will's observations on the changes in Skagway are of interest. Upon reaching the port in late September, Will noticed the saloons and gambling resorts "a-plenty." Legends of Skagway's iniquity made much of these types of places during the spring of 1898. Although Will commented on their presence in Wrangell the previous March, he neglected to mention any when he first got to Skagway. Will's failure to mention the legendary Soapy Smith contrasts sharply with memoirs written much later, in which writers inevitably say they saw the notorious con man. Apparently Smith was not known to every stampeder who went through Skagway.

Following is Will's account of the last phase of his adventure.

+≻═≺+

The lines that follow are taken from notes written after my arrival and recovery at Seattle, given to me as they occurred by Father. During the first day of my illness [September 1], an aggravating dysentery set in that caused me no little inconvenience. At night my fever had increased to such a degree that I became delirious, and only force exercised by Uncle and Father kept me in my bed. The following day [September 2], Father became alarmed and went in search of a physician, which he finally found and who made a call that evening. He at once diagnosed my case as a severe one of typhoid malaria. He left medicines and instructions that if we could not check the fever in a few days, it would be advisable to leave with me for the outside immediately, this course being the only left in saving my life. His attendance, however, gave me no help, and after the elapse of a couple of days, he repeated his former advice, and Father at once began preparations to depart as soon as possible.

Things have changed somewhat in the month with me, both in appearances and location, sixteen hundred miles separate the distance. I will be very brief in giving the accounts of the last month. On Sept. 2nd went over town at Dawson to see Bert Eastman about a position in Condahy Sky Co's Wholesale House which he had promised to help me to get. I did not feel much like walking over today for my whole body ached every symptom of La Grippe, so after seeing Bert, I came home and felt worse as time passed. So began doctoring with quinine and physic that night before I went to bed.

Did not sleep good all night and piled out at 6:30 feeling much worse than the night before, and before the day [September 3] was over, the dysentery had set in and had a terrible chill, and then fever, and could not eat a mouthful of food, but at this time I did not know how serious my case was to be, and what changes it would make in my life and surroundings. I had weighed myself a few days before and tipped the scales at 145 pounds, the highest it ever went in my life.

The second night [September 4] *nervousness set in, and for three whole weeks I did not get a night's sleep. Some nights without closing my eyes, so sleeping powders were given me by the doctor, which Father had got now to see to my case. I would get up and prowl and roll around the Cabin like a lunatic, as I was flighty nearly all the time, and lots of incidents I cannot record on this account. My strength after the second day began to fail me and in a week I could hardly stand alone and did not care what became of me, did not expect to see my dear old home again, and did not think of it much, either. But my dear little Wife, how could I leave her without being with her first?*

As the days went by, I became weaker from the ravages of the disease that seemed to be burning my body by inches through the long days and nights. As the disease advanced, my delirium became more pronounced, and during my conscious moments, I cared little for the circumstances that surrounded me, nor the future outcome of the disease. Father was almost always at my side, thereby causing himself much inconvenience in disposing of the remainder of our goods and arranging for our departure. Uncle was of little use, for he was taken ill soon after I was. His illness kept him in bed for nearly a week with symptoms of the fever I was suffering from, but which he broke, and was fully recovered when we left.

Uncle Hi was taken down with symptoms of Typhoid Fever which lasted about five days, and he broke it up before the week was up. The Doctor advised Father to get me on my way Home if he did not want to bury me in Dawson. So Father began making the necessary preparations in a hurry as I was growing lower and weaker. So on the 13th of Sept. everything was in readiness to leave (all the goods disposed of and Skookum dog sold. We sold him for $75.00).

About a week after I was taken to my bed, Father had everything in readiness to depart, even to the passage on the steamer secured. This, he had secured on the steamer *Canada* for White Horse, which route he was advised would land us in Seattle many days in advance of a steamer leaving via St. Michaels.

So on September 13th, I was half carried and half wheeled aboard the steamer, more dead than alive and caring little which. The *Canada* was one of the very best-equipped passenger steamers on the run between

Dawson and White Horse. It had a limited number of first class cabins on her upper deck, while on the lower deck were built clean, comfortable bunks, one above the other in a crosswise of the boat, leaving a large space for a dining table that extended the full length of the deck between. This was for the use of the second class passengers, who ate their meals, read, played cards, or rambled up and down the large room in the day time, and slept at night. This arrangement was not very good surroundings for a man sick unto death, but to save time, it was the best Father could get under the circumstances. Weeks in advance, many of the rich claim owners had secured all the cabin accommodations on all late boats.

I was bundled aboard and into a bunk, and about three o'clock in the afternoon, the last whistle sounded out. After Father said farewells to Uncle and several friends who had come down to see us off, the steamer paddled out into midstream, and soon thereafter, was slowly forcing her way against the mighty current.

Before leaving Dawson, Father had secured the services of a doctor, who was going out on the same boat, and who charged $10.00 per day for attending to me. Dr. Simpson [see Biographies] was a young man who, affected with the gold craze, had ventured with his doctor friend, Lindsey, into the northern gold fields. They had found circumstances not as they expected, so were returning to their homes. He proved very attentive in my case, and did everything in his power to ease my suffering. However, before reaching White Horse, he himself was taken ill with typhoid fever, and the last I saw or heard of him was when he was borne from the steamer at Bennett City in a very serious condition. When he took to his bed, Dr. Lindsey attended us both. I dare say my case was greatly neglected in consequence of his loyalty to his friend.

It is unnecessary to give in detail the journey up the river to White Horse Rapids. I will state that it is very dangerous to navigate after darkness sets in due to the shallowness of the great river at this season of the year. Each night, therefore, the captain would run in to shore, and take on a supply of wood. He would remain there until the first light of the morning, when he would proceed on his way. The September days were shortening fast: only about thirteen out of the twenty-four hours were sufficiently light to avoid the treacherous rocks and sandbars that infested the wide stream. This slow progress, due to the Captain's caution and good judgment, required nine days in reaching White Horse, a distance of four hundred and fifty miles.

How long those nine days were, no one can realize unless placed in my shoes. They seemed like as many months instead. I lay in my bunk, hour after hour, in a semi-unconscious state, my body burning with the terrible fever that enveloped it. Now and then, day and night, I would be partially aroused from my stupor by the boisterous laughing and shouting of passengers engaged in gambling all about me. At times, I nearly suffocated from the fumes of tobacco smoke that filled the room. These conditions had a sad effect on my tired nerves, but it was impossible to curb the privileges of the passengers, and I doubt if any attempt was made to do so. Aside from the doctors and Father, none aboard realized how ill I really was, and probably none cared a great deal.

However, when we reached White Horse, I was still alive. When the steamer landed, Dr. Simpson and myself were borne ashore and placed, not very comfortably, aboard a tram car, which was used in transporting freight overland around the canyon and rapids. This tramway had been built and put into operation during the summer, and had already proven a great benefit to the public in moving their outfits around the dangerous strip of water. The cars were similar to the ordinary flat or coal car, but small in proportion and run on small steel rails placed on ties that were set in a rough uneven roadbed. The road was not built for passenger travel, which the doctor and I realized only too well before the journey of five miles was ended. When we were transferred to the little steamer in waiting, I had a feeling that every nerve in my body had been shaken up, while the doctor had suffered severely from the long, rough ride.

Aboard the steamer *Nora* that plied between White Horse and Bennett City, I was placed in one of the many comfortable bunks that extended the length of the cozy cabin on either side. Soon after, passengers from the *Canada* came straggling aboard in twos and threes. Finally the word "all aboard" was given, and the little steamer left her moorings and was on her way to Bennett City.

It was after nightfall [September 22] that the steamer, having run into shore to wait for the light of another day, that I felt a pleasant relaxation of the terrible fever that had burned so steadily for three weeks. As the passengers, men and a number of women, gathered in the cabin discussing their fortunes or misfortunes as the case happened to be, I listened with an interest of one who had been marooned on an uninhabited island for an indefinite period. I also felt a craving for food, which I had not tasted in over three weeks. In accordance with the physician's orders, I had subsisted on whiskey and condensed milk given at frequent intervals during each twenty four hours. Now that my appetite was returning, I detested the sight and smell of the potion, and it was due to an argument with Father that I swallowed even another ounce. Long before all the passengers retired, I fell into a sound, peaceful sleep, the first since I became ill. I was not awakened until the steamer's engines were started on the following morning [September 23]. My first desire upon awakening was food, which my appetite craved, but Dr. Lindsey forbid it in a tone that he meant just what he said. Father again doled out the nauseating whiskey and condensed milk.

Under ordinary summer conditions, the run from White Horse to Bennett City required ten hours time. Now, due to the shortening day, the same caution as below White Horse was taken, and twenty four hours elapsed ere we reached Bennett City [September 24]. Here, Father half carried me to a hotel close by. After securing quarters for the night, he ordered and brought to me a couple poached eggs and toast, which I hastily devoured. Neither before nor since have I tasted food that was so thoroughly enjoyed. I called for more, but this Father absolutely forbid, as he had already overstepped the doctor's orders in giving any solid food at all. With the bowels in the ulcerated condition of the convalescent typhoid patent, the giving of solid food for days after the fever subsides is allayed, with great danger of perforation therefrom. But Father has told me several times since that he "knew it would not hurt me, although the doctor said it would."

Sam Moore and "Sport" Smith [see Biographies] *put up at this Hotel tonight. Sam was going to Dawson to go into the Barber business and "Sport" has a position in the recording office at Circle City which place he was bound for.*

And he was right, for soon after I went to bed and to sleep, and in the morning [September 25] I felt much stronger and refreshed. Father was already up, had his breakfast and had gone to secure a horse for me to ride over the trail to Skagway. He had given the cook orders to prepare poached eggs and toast for me when I awoke, which I was enjoying when he came in. He told me he had secured for me a quiet horse to ride, and that we would start for Skagway as soon as I was ready. I was much surprised that he could feel that I was able to sit astride a horse over a trail such as we would be compelled to travel, so soon after my fever had subsided, and in my weak condition. But he was determined we should make a start, and if necessary, we would stop at a road house, [several of] which were located at close intervals along the trail.

So after I was bundled up to such an extent that it was laborious to carry—for the weather was very cold here—Father assisted me to the saddle, and taking the bridle rein, we started over the long, bleak, rocky trail leading to White Pass. The trail followed closely the portage between lakes Bennett and Linderman [Lindeman], to a point where the Dyea and Skagway trails fork. There the Dyea trail leads straight ahead along the shores of Lake Linderman, while the Skagway trail turns sharply to the right and leads over the barren waste to Log Cabin.

For two or three miles, a good trail and easy travel is encountered, then suddenly we find before us, leading upward, a mass of irregular boulders as far as the eye could see. My sure-footed little animal made her way over this rough, rocky expanse with a careful precision that was wonderful. At noon, when Log Cabin was reached, no mishap had befallen us. Here we ate our lunch and rested for an hour, and although my back felt as if it was at the breaking point, we continued on our way.

My back and legs paining me terrible, I was helped on my horse again and preceded on our way toward Skaguay for two miles, the trail was very good, but from there on to the Little Meadows, it was something Horrible and I hope will never have to make the trip again on a horse, sick or well. Thousands of feet above the level of Shallow and Middle lakes, among the rockiest of mountains, my sure-footed animal carried me safely all day. I every moment thinking it would be off with me for one misstep or slip on this trail would throw me to my death or serious injury, and nobody can tell how pleased I was when we reached the packers' camp that night.

From here we travelled over the old winter trail until Shallow Lake was reached. There we struck off to the right and began a climb up and up the steep, rocky trail that leads to the summit of the mountainous hills that surround the chain of small lakes that form the source of the great Yukon. I felt that I never could reach the summit, my back and limbs were in such pain, aggravated at each step my faithful little animal took.

Finally, late in the afternoon, the long rocky incline was behind us. As we turned and saw the tiny shimmering bodies of water thousands of feet below us, we all three were glad that the summit was reached. From here, although very rough and rocky, the trail was not bad. When the little meadows were reached, we struck out at a good gait and reached an extensive packers' camp a little before dark.

The Little Meadows, so called by the gold-seekers, is much like an oasis on the desert. Entirely surrounded by a rocky barren waste, there exists an extensive area of land covered with a luxuriant growth of a specie [sic] of bunch grass. Here the packers had wisely established their camp midway between their two starting points, Lake Bennett and White Pass, while the location also afforded a bountiful feed for their tired and hungry pack animals. The packing company in question had a number of pack trains (as several pack animals attended by a man in front and one in the rear are called) in operation between the two points mentioned above. Evenly divided, one section would leave White Pass; on the same morning, the other section was leaving Lake Bennett. By this arrangement, both pack trains, on alternate nights, were housed at the camp at the little meadows, and the evening we arrived happened to be the night that all were there.

This fact did not stand in the way of our securing shelter for the night. When Father requested accommodations of the boss, he immediately had our horse taken care of, and we were soon served an elaborate supper. I, of course, had broth and poached eggs, which tasted awfully good. In the day's travel, the boss told us we had covered eighteen miles, and the way I felt, I would have believed him if he had said fifty miles. My body ached from the tip of my toes to the top of my head. After going to bed, it was some minutes before I fell asleep, although I was extremely tired.

I awoke the next morning [September 26] terribly lame and sore, but feeling much refreshed and stronger. After eating a substantial breakfast of toast and eggs, I aroused enough courage to tell Father I was ready to continue our journey. We thanked the cook—for the packers had left early—and we were on our way. After leaving the meadows, we encountered as on the previous day, a rough and rocky trail that grew more difficult as we neared White Pass. It was only through harsh advice from Father that I remained on the horse's back, so impossible seemed some of the places necessary for the little animal to traverse.

I remained mounted until a mishap befell the patient little beast. We were halfway down a short, but steep and rocky incline when my pony's forefeet slipped on a large round boulder. Coming to her knees, her body careened to one side and pinioned my foot on that side between her body and a large sharp rock. The incident caused me more fright than injury, although it was painful and was responsible for my limping for several days afterward. This little mishap, due to my weak and nervous condition, unnerved me for the balance of my journey on horseback. Much to the disgust of Father, I refused to ride while descending from the summit of White Pass. Instead, I dismounted and began the descent afoot.

The weather was very cold, the air being filled with fine particles of snow driven by a high wind that made the face sting wherever they struck. The downward course was steep and slippery, but by a little caution assisted by brush that grew along the trail, I managed to reach the bottom without further mishap. Nearly exhausted from my exertions, I was glad to regain my mount, although I had long ago tired of my ride from a pleasure stand point.

Soon after our ascent, we arrived at the Ford Hotel, as the group of tents was called, and here I did an act that, to the majority of human beings, it would have caused instant death, or at least a relapse of the disease I was recovering from. Due to the long ride and breathing the invigorating crisp mountain air, I had developed the appetite of a cannibal. When Father ordered some delicious baked beans as his portion, I seconded the motion. At first he objected to me eating such heavy food, but I was persistent, and finally won out, although I knew I was taking a chance in doing so. I ate my fill, no food ever tasting as good, and I am in a position to say no ill effects resulted therefrom.

From the Ford, a ride of two and one half miles brought us to the temporary terminus of the White Pass and Skagway railroad. Here the faithful little animal was turned over to her owners, my everlasting blessing going out to her as we parted.

It was with much astonishment that we noted the radical changes the short time had wrought along the old winter trail on which we had labored so strenuously in the early spring. In the canyon at the base of the towering walls several substantial buildings had been erected. They served as quarters for the army of men employed in the construction of the White Pass Railroad, which was already completed to this point and was forging its way rapidly toward the summit. This construction was evidenced by the thundering roars coming from five hundred feet up the rocky wall of the cliff, as the blasting crews set off the heavy charges of dynamite. They were clearing a way for the iron steed, which in time would connect, commercially, the source of the great river with the Pacific Ocean. Regular passenger service had been established from Skagway to this point, one train making a round trip in the forenoon, and one late in the afternoon. As we waited for our train, a work train from Skagway loaded with heavy rails and ties for another section of the road farther up the canyon thundered past. There must have been a huge army of workmen employed, for it was wonderful considering the difficulties met in the rough, rocky survey to have covered this distance during the short summer.

The White Pass and Yukon Route, then known as the Pacific and Arctic Railway and Navigation Company, ran locomotive service between Skagway and Heney Station, above White Pass City. The railroad had completed surveys and grading all the way to White Pass Summit, but did not receive permits to construct into Canada until late September 1898. They began construction on Canadian soil on October 4, 1898, after Will and Jay left Skagway. The point where the Woodins caught the train was the northernmost station at the time.[2]

Near five o'clock, we began our ascent up the face of an almost perpendicular wall of rock to reach our train on its return to Skagway. Steps or notches had been hewn from the solid rock at such a distance apart to present an easy ascent to the little station located on a jutting ledge alongside the tracks. After many stops to rest, I finally reached the station, nearly exhausted from the terrible climb of five hundred feet, and I thought I would starve, my hunger was so great. It seemed that I could never get my fill of food, and one hour after eating a hearty meal, the pangs of hunger would again appear and continue until satisfied with a full stomach.

After a short wait, the locomotive and two ancient passenger coaches hove in sight around a curve in the road, and came to a stand opposite the improvised station. Along with quite a number of other passengers bound for Skagway, we boarded the forward coach. Soon after, amid a clanging of the bell and a shrill blast from the whistle, we were moving rapidly toward Skagway aboard a real passenger train.

Oh! What a difference from a horse's back. How good it seemed once more to be in civilization. The train left promptly on time and what a ride, too. How a person could enjoy it with good health, but with me I can say it was the first thing I really enjoyed since I was taken sick. An artist could spend a whole month sketching on this twelve miles of road.

The coaches were found to be very old style, uncomfortable affairs with hard, cushionless seats that made one conscious of every bump in the rough, uneven roadbed, and so cold that it is beyond me to know how the travelling public endured even the short ride in the extreme winter weather. This condition, however, was soon after changed, and in its place, new comfortable coaches were afforded the gold-seeker. Today [1914], the Alaskan traveler can leave Skagway and travel in luxury to any point on the great Yukon.

How different it was from transportation of the early spring. Then, even those who possessed means for the very best had either to choose a saddle horse or be dragged over the rough trail aboard a narrow sled, with every moment in danger of being thrown into a snow drift or a shallow puddle of cold, dirty water. When we left Skagway in the early spring, the railroad was merely a talked-of project. Many doubted it would ever be carried to completion, but in the surprisingly short space of time had proven differently.

After becoming as comfortable as possible, I forgot all else but the beautiful scenery we were afforded from the car window as we slowly made our way along the narrow ledge on the mountainside. Many hundreds of feet below, in the depths of the dark canyon, ran the Skagway River, winding its way hither and thither between its high rocky banks. Now and then it plunged over obstructing rocks, forming beautiful falls and cascades in its mad rush to the ocean. Majestic mountains rose from the walls of the narrow canyon. As we came opposite fissures opening into those in the foreground, we could see the towering, snow-covered sentinels of the coast range in the far distant west. They shone a golden splendor from the dying rays of the setting sun. As we rode slowly through this scenic valley, I thought how negligent we had been in noting nature's grandeur on our way to the interior. But then our thoughts were of gold, not of nature's beauty.

Our train descended slowly to the Skagway valley due to the many, sharp, dangerous turns on the narrow, mountain road. It was past six o'clock when the conductor sang out "Skagway, end of the line" having taken one hour to make the run of twelve miles. When we stepped from the train to a long platform, we were surprised to find it a part of a substantial up-to-date depot such as a city of considerable size afforded. I will venture to state that the city of Seattle was compelled to tolerate a much inferior structure at the same time.

The city of Skagway, as it now rightfully claimed to be called, presented a most phenomenal growth since we had left it in the early spring. As we came to the main street, we found ourselves on a thoroughfare ablaze with electric lights. For many blocks, brightly lighted stores of various trades, hotels, saloons and gambling resorts a-plenty lined either side. Two new wharves had been constructed, and railroad terminals had been built. Located as it is without opposition to the commerce of the Yukon gold fields, during the greater portion of the year, everything looked favorable in general for this new Alaskan city.

Our first move upon gaining the main street was toward a hotel Father planned on staying at, and which we had no difficulty in locating. It was a rude affair, temporary constructed as many of the first buildings were—with built-in bunks on either side of a long unheated room and lighted by night with candles or kerosene lamps. The proprietor and his wife were old acquaintances of Father's, therefore he selected this cheap hostelry for the time we were to spend in Skagway.

That to say we were made comfortable and well-fed, would be putting it mildly, for nothing was good enough for us. For myself, I will never forget the kindness Mrs. Lewis showered upon me. The good lady cooked special duty meals for me and at night I was given the spare guest room with a genuine bed with springs and mattress, upon which were woven blankets and snowy white sheets, the first I had seen since leaving home.

We arrived in Skagway at 6 p.m., just one hour coming the 12 miles. The train runs the full length of the main street of Skagway. We got off and went to the Rainier Hotel to stay while we were in Skaguay. Father was well acquainted with the landlord and his wife, Mr. and Mrs. Lewis [actually Lewis and Lucinda Lyman; see Biographies], *old Seattle residents, and Oh! How kind they were to me while* [we] *were there. Nothing was good enough. Mrs. Lewis especially, and now I began to eat like a pig and feel stronger in fact better all around.*

The next morning [September 27], I arose feeling much rested. With breakfast over, I got a much needed shave at a nearby barber shop, after which I took a walk along the main street. The morning was cold and invigorating, and as I walked, I seemed to gain strength at every step.

Two days later [September 29] we bid our kind friends goodbye, and left at noon for Seattle, having secured passage on the staunch little steamer *Dirego*. At nine o'clock that night, we arrived in Juneau, where Father and I left the steamer, and purchased oranges and apples, which were the first we had eaten since leaving home. Next morning [September 30], we were steaming smoothly through the beautiful, landlocked sea called Stephens Passage. Early in the forenoon, we had passed the short stretch of open sea called Frederick Sound, but aside from a few ground swells, we were not conscious of it.

Near noon, the steamer came to a standstill, and as the passengers ran forward to note the reason, I also followed. The cause was soon apparent in the shape of a miniature iceberg floating in the course of the steamer. The Captain was giving orders to a crew of sailors who were already lowering a boat. One carried the end of a cable, which the man at the wench was letting out slowly. When the boat struck the water, the crew rowed to the berg, and after some trouble, made the cable fast around the mass of ice, and orders were given to heave in. Slowly the berg was towed to the steamer's side, and a huge mass weighing at least a couple of tons was raised to the deck. This procedure, the Captain explained, was the manner in which they reimburse the ship's ice supply in their perfect cold storage system. The Captain said they could almost invariably depend upon their ice supply summer or winter in this region. The great glaciers to our left, on the mainland, were forcing huge masses of ice into the sea.

We arrived at Wrangell at 2:00 p.m., where we remained two hours, loading horses and mules for Seattle. Where they came from, nor why they were there, I am unable to say, but apparently they had been hard-worked.

The morning following [September 30], I was suddenly awakened by being tossed from one side of my berth to the other. As I came to my full senses, I barely saved myself being thrown to the floor, the ship was rolling so. I scrambled out of my berth and dressed as soon as possible and made my way to the deck where few passengers were to be seen. The latter's absence was explained by groans and moans emitting from the nearby state rooms, and as near as I could tell about three-fourths of the passengers were seasick. Upon inquiry, one of the officers told me we were crossing Dixon Entrance. Although the morning was clear and beautiful, he said there had been a storm at sea a day or two previous, and that only now we were getting the heavy swells from it.

The incessant heavy roll of the little steamer gave me no feeling of seasickness. On the contrary, the bracing morning air had given me a ham and egg appetite, with a stack of hot cakes thrown in. This sort of a breakfast in mind, I went below and to the dining room door, but the door is as far as I ventured. It was evident that other passengers had preceded me and more were seated as I looked in, but some had been there already, without a doubt. How many got away with food on their stomachs is more than I can say, but I venture to say but few, judging from the trails left in their hurried exit and to the rails of the vessel. I at once returned to the deck with a loss of appetite and a nauseous feeling in the pit of my stomach. However, it passed away after being in the cool, fresh breeze awhile.

In about two hours, we ran into smooth waters sheltered by the Queen Charlotte Islands. After a hearty meal at noon, all the passengers, having recovered from their seasickness, came on deck to enjoy the beautiful, warm sunshine, and the superb scenery on either side. We passed through narrow passages with retreating rocky banks, picturesquely wooded here and there, where soil afforded little groves of beautiful little green pines. The little steamer wound its way through other passages where perpendicular rocky walls devoid of all vegetation rose towering on either side. In crevices and narrow ledges along these rocky banks, thousands of sea gulls perched, seemingly waiting for the steamer to come that they might follow and feed upon the refuse thrown therefrom. We would come suddenly upon scores upon scores of wild ducks paddling about in sheltered coves, who, upon our approach, would rise and soar away to a more secluded spot to finish their interrupted meal amid a deafening flapping of wings.

The following morning [October 1], I was again awakened by the heavy roll of the vessel, which I afterward found was caused by the ground swells on that open arm of the sea, Queen Charlotte's Sound. The distance was shorter and the roll of the vessel less severe than the previous morning, therefore few were seasick. The weather continued beautiful, and the scenery even grander than the day before. All aboard were jubilant, talking and laughing together, expressing their joy at being so near home and loved ones.

At ten p.m., the steamer came to stand-still, and those who had not retired rushed to the deck to inquire the cause. The Captain explained that we were nearing Seymore Narrows, and that it would be unsafe to proceed further until the high tide diminished. He further explained that to proceed now would mean utter destruction, as the sea rushes through the treacherous narrows at a rate of thirty miles per hour. We lay here until one o'clock in the morning [October 2], after all had retired. I knew nothing until long after daylight came.

It was a beautiful autumn morning kissed by the ascending sunlight, the air invigorating and made cool by the momentum of the swift little steamer. And oh, what scenery we were passing. We were threading our way among the islands of Georgia Bay. The mainland of British Columbia was on one side, and Vancouver Island served a shelter from the mighty Pacific Ocean for one hundred miles on the other. I will venture to say that the grandeur of the scenery in this stretch of water extending south to include the San Juan Islands on Puget Sound, is unsurpassed in the whole world. There are hundreds of small islets or pillars of rock rising out of the sea, whose tops are surmounted with a thickly studded growth of tiny pines, while others are larger, but thickly wooded, and all had a picturesqueness that is beautiful to behold.

About two o'clock, we entered Victoria, B.C. harbor, and not many minutes thereafter, we safely anchored at the wharf. We were informed that we would remain here two hours, whereupon I went to the nearest telegraph office and sent a telegram to Mother, stating that Father would arrive in Seattle at or near midnight, but omitting the fact that I was accompanying him. Since my illness began, no word had been sent of the fact, and now Father thought it advisable to refrain from doing so to avoid shock or worry on her part.

We left Victoria at four o'clock and after a pleasant run across the straits of Juan de Fuca and up Puget Sound. At midnight [October 2], we arrived at the wharf in Seattle, where we met my brother, Claude, and cousin, Sean Smith. We bundled our luggage ashore, amid joyous greeting and quickly put questions and answers. We hurried to the terminus of the Madison Street cars in an attempt to catch the last one for the night, for at the time, all cars ceased running at midnight. We were, however, doomed to disappointment, for the last one was gliding over the hills on its way to Lake Washington.

Father suggested a conveyance for me, but I insisted upon walking, although our home was two miles distant, and our walk would lead up and down steep grades the entire distance. The night was warm and beautiful and the walk was a delight to me although I was pretty tired when the old home loomed up in the bright moonlight. Dear old mother was much surprised to see me, but nonetheless happy to see us both safely at home again, and it was a happy family reunion that lasted into the small hours of the morning. Thus ended seven months of strife, hardships, sickness and disappointments in a fruitless search for gold.

Epilogues

✛━━✛

Will Woodin's Epilogue

L ITTLE MORE REMAINS TO BE TOLD. I cannot refrain from adding that
one year almost to a day after our return, Mr. Kiger, the old German who had insisted upon us staking a claim apiece on Lavitt [Lovatt]
Gulch, arrived in Seattle accompanied by his son. They had returned to
stay, entirely satisfied with the snug little fortune they had taken from
the gulch claims. The amount, of course, they did not divulge, but the
evidence was visible later, when they built several neat bungalows for
renting purposes. Very soon after their return, the old gentleman called
on us, and imparted the sad information that soon after our departure
from Dawson City, our claims had been restaked, the new owners having developed them with good results the previous winter, and had,
before the Kigers left, sold the claims to a dredging concern for twenty-
five thousand dollars apiece. I took this information much to heart and
felt sorely responsible for our defeated purpose, but consoled in the
thought that fate had played another trick in my course of life.

A few words now of Seattle, with her ideal climate, the healthiest city
in the United States, and the coming supremacy of the Pacific Coast.
The gold from the Klondike and Alaska made our fair city what it is
today, and she will continue to reap from its vast treasure vaults long
after our children are dead and gone. Seattle and the Klondike and
Alaska are so closely associated that many people throughout the world
and even in the eastern United States are under the impression that Seattle is located in either the Klondike or Alaska. I know this to be a fact
for with my own eyes, I have seen letters, yes many of them addressed
to Seattle, Klondike, or Seattle, Alaska, which, of course always reached
the addressee at Seattle, Washington. Located as she is the most northwestern port of consequence in the United States, she is connected with
the world with her many steamship lines and three transcontinental

railroads.[1] She is without a single competitor in the vast, northern commerce, which is growing by leaps and bounds each year.

Seattle, when founded in 1854, was destined to be a great city without the aid of the northern gold fields, but which have only advanced her greatness beyond all expectations. In 1880, the government census gave her 8,000 inhabitants, 1890 it was given as 42,000 [actually, 43,837], 1900 she had 80,000 souls [80,671], almost doubled in the ten years, and I am safe in saying she gained them in the three years preceding the northern gold strike, while in 1910 she ranked eighteenth in population of the cities of the United States with a population of 237,000 [237,194], a phenomenal growth of 300 per cent in ten years. At the time I finish these pages, four years later, she has an estimated population of 313,000 and has a substantial prosperous growth that any successful Klondiker may feel sure of a safe investment.[2]

— The End —

Editor's Epilogue

WHEN WILL WOODIN AND HIS FATHER, Jay, returned to Seattle, they went back to their former jobs in the lumber industry. Son James helped them both obtain positions as box nailers at J. W. McDonnell Company, where he worked. The entire family continued to live in the very modest house that the women and children had occupied while Jay and Will were in the Klondike. By 1902, Will and James hired on with the Bennett Box Company, and Jay had once again become a freelance builder and contractor.[3]

In December 1900, Will married his "little wife," Blanche Graves. Only then did he move away from his parents. Two daughters and a son were born to the marriage: Madeline on January 9, 1902; Helen on April 29, 1903; and Harold on May 20, 1905. To Will's great sorrow, Blanche died on August 29, 1905, only three months after their son, Harold, was born. She was twenty-nine years old.[4]

Apparently heartbroken at Blanche's death, Will sold the house they shared, left his position at the Bennett Box Factory, and returned to his parents' home. His daughters, Madeline and Helen, went to live with their maternal grandparents, Willard and Helen Graves, while Jay and Catherine Woodin raised Will's son, Harold.[5]

Beginning in late 1905, Will worked as a clerk for the United States Post Office. That position accounts for his reference to letters he had seen addressed to Seattle in the Klondike and Alaska. On August 7, 1912, he married Miss Jean Renton. He began writing his memoir of his journey to the Klondike in 1910, probably while courting Miss Renton, and he finished it in 1914. It is obvious why he left out all references to his great homesickness for Blanche and how it hurt him when he received letters from her. While Will's children continued to live with their grandparents, he and Jean adopted a son, Jack, who was born in 1918. They lived around the corner and shared backyards with Jay and Catherine Woodin, who were raising Will's son, Harold. In 1939, Will retired from his job with the post office and became a real estate salesman.[6]

William Jay Woodin died in Seattle on June 15, 1949, at the age of seventy-five. In addition to his four children, he was survived by three grandchildren: Maurine Hein (1931-2012), Marjorie Hein (1934-1978), and Danny Lee Woodin (1945-2011), who was Jack's son.[7]

After working as a box maker for J. W. McDonnell Company for a year or two, Will's father Jay Abram Woodin opened his own business as a contractor and builder. By 1902, he and the entire family, which included all eight children and

Jay and Catherine Woodin's home at 4846 Morgan Street in Seattle, ca. 1910. This was the home where Will's son, Harold, grew up, and where his parents lived until they died. *Sandra Dunn Collection.*

two of their spouses, moved to a larger home a few blocks away from their original small home, suggesting he had recovered any losses he suffered by the Klondike expedition. In 1904, Jay took up carpentry work. In 1910, the family moved to a home around the corner from the one occupied by Will and his second wife, Jean, so that their grandson, Harold, could be near his father. Jay and Catherine would live at that address the rest of their lives. Will's mother, Catherine, died on May 9, 1936, and Jay Abram Woodin died on November 1, 1940, at the age of eighty-eight.[8] Grandson Harold lived in the home until after their deaths.

Jay's brother, Hiram Ulysses Woodin, stayed in Dawson four more years after Will and Jay left. In 1902, the real estate market declined in the Dawson area and the large mining companies bought out the small-time operators. Hiram returned to Seattle and went into business with Harry C. Davis to form Davis & Woodin, a company that sold real estate, invested in mines in the Yukon, and did mining promotion. The partners kept an office on Pike Street in downtown Seattle.[9]

Davis & Woodin did not last long. By 1903, Hiram became a speculator and promoter who worked on his own behalf out of an office in the Arcade Building

Jay and Catherine Woodin, 1935.
Sandra Dunn Collection.

on Second Avenue. Over the next few years, he promoted real estate and northern investments from an office at the Pioneer Building (now a National Historic Landmark), then as a partner of the real estate firm of M. B. Crane & Company, and later out of his home in the 1100 block of Seventh Avenue, located downtown.[10]

By 1910, Hiram secured a job as a county clerk for King County. He and his wife Caroline changed residences each year; they either rented homes, or bought, improved, and sold houses at a profit. Hiram won a free lot in a sales contest in May 1909, but he probably sold it rather than build on it. In 1910, Hiram and Caroline shared a household with a lumberman, John Hughes, and his wife, indicating that they supplemented their income by renting out rooms. No doubt Hiram still continued to sell real estate even after he took his position as a civil servant.[11]

Hiram probably obtained his position as county clerk through his political activities in the first decade of the twentieth century. As Will discussed in his unpublished "Autobiography," Hiram liked to dabble in politics. He was a judge in Saginaw, Michigan, at the age of twenty-seven; an experience that must have encouraged him to try for similar positions in Seattle. He lost his run for county treasurer in the Republican primary in February 1908, and he was an unsuccessful candidate for justice of the peace on the Progressive ticket in November 1912.[12]

No record of Hiram exists between 1912 and the 1920 census, when he was recorded living with carpenter John Houghton Watson and his wife, Annie Catherine, and their two small children. Anne was Hiram's niece, the oldest daughter of his sister Margaret Birdell "Birdie" Woodin and Alfred Lowe.[13] It is unknown where his wife, Caroline, was at the time.

Hiram and Caroline moved to Lansing, Michigan, by 1927. There, even though he was around seventy years old and of an age to retire, Hiram took a position as the foreman at a local motor car company. He died at age seventy-five, and was buried in the Constantine Township Cemetery, St. Joseph County, about one hundred miles to the southwest of Lansing. Caroline was buried next to him in 1936.[14]

It was not only Will who enjoyed telling stories about his Uncle Hiram; newspapers found him good copy as well. On November 6, 1891, the *Elkhart (IN) Review* repeated a story from the *Edwardsburg (MI) Argus* that Hiram had stepped into the line of fire of Ephraim Carpenter, an Elkhart druggist, who was shooting at a flock of birds on Hiram's property in Mason County "accidentally put three dozen fine shot into the head and neck of Mr. Woodin…Although painful, the wounds [were] not considered dangerous."[15] On April 27, 1908, the *Seattle Daily Times* reported that a street grader had stolen a watch from Hiram's vest where he had hung it on a post near his then current address of 823 North Fourth Street.

Hiram was the adventurer of the family, the one who could not stay long at the same house, office, or job title. Sometimes his ventures paid off; sometimes not. Of the men in Will's tale about the Klondike, Hiram took the most risks and was perhaps one of the most successful.

It was somewhat more difficult to discover what eventually happened to the rest of the Woodin party after they split up in Dawson. The men who joined Will and Jay on their journey to the Klondike all had very common names. In particular, no Bill, Will, or William Chamberlain (Chamberlin) could be found in the 1897–1900 Seattle City directories. The last time Will mentioned Chamberlain was on June 3, 1898, at Whitehorse Rapids.

Likewise, Will ceases to write about William L. "Ed" Green in his memoir after June 15 during the trek to the Pelly River. He was chosen to relay goods to the upper end of Little Salmon Lake. It is possible that Green, as a friend of George Milham's father, accompanied the young man back to Seattle after the drowning of George Sherwood. There he took up his previous occupation as an independent express man. He held that job until 1906, when he retired at the age of fifty-one. In 1909, he was interviewed by the *Seattle Daily Times* about his days as an express man, and he claimed to own real estate valued at $200,000. He attributed his fortune to his hard work as an express man, where he had started working for only $25.00 a month. He made no reference to having been in the Klondike. When asked why he had never married, he replied, "Sonny, I have yet to see the woman to whom I should desire to pay alimony after a few years."[16]

The *Seattle Daily Times* article expressed astonishment that an express man could accumulate a fortune of $200,000 (worth almost $5,000,000 in today's currency). Green may have inherited some money when his widowed mother, Mary G. Green, died in 1906. However, she was the widow of retired sea captain, an occupation not notorious for leaving fortunes. It seems more likely that Green had made a good portion of his wealth in the Klondike.

It is also possible that Green greatly exaggerated the extent of his wealth. By 1920, he came out of retirement to once again become an express driver. He died on March 11, 1924, at Fort Steilacoom, Pierce County, Washington—then the Western Washington Hospital for the Insane.[17] It was not possible to determine when or why he was committed.

The last Will and Jay saw of Jim Daugherty, aka "Malen," in mid-August 1898, he was on his way to Forty-Mile to work, as there was no position available for him in Dawson. He reappeared in Seattle by 1900, living in the Sixth Ward with a wife, Hattie, two stepsons, and a daughter, Clare. Once again a teamster, he was thirty-eight years old. He was still a teamster in Seattle in 1902, but no later mention was made of him in the directories. Because the names Hattie and James were common at the time, it is almost impossible to determine what happened to them.[18]

William H. Wells—"Mr. Wells" of Will's memoir—became widowed after he returned to Gratiot County, Michigan, from the Klondike. He moved in with his widowed daughter, Hattie Austin, and her three children, who lived near Seville, Michigan. He died of acute gastritis on May 30, 1911, at the age of sixty-eight, and was buried in French Seville Cemetery, Gratiot County, Michigan.[19]

Two other people who greatly affected the course of the Woodin party's fortunes in the Klondike were Abraham Kiger, who helped them locate claims on Lovatt Gulch, and Cal Johnston, who became Kiger's son-in-law. In his epilogue, Will stated that Abraham Kiger did well with the Lovatt Gulch claim. Records state, however, that Kiger went back to his job as an express man when he returned to Seattle. He apparently had enough gold to purchase a single-family dwelling for his family instead of returning to the apartment he had rented before the trip to the Yukon. In 1902 he stopped working and moved to the Fremont neighborhood near prestigious North Queen Anne Hill. Cal Johnston and his wife, Olive Ada (Ollie) Kiger, resided with her parents in Fremont. Johnston worked at the Rainier Grand Hotel, where another Kiger daughter, Myrtle, took a room.[20]

It was not until 1910 that Abraham Kiger felt it necessary to take up a job again, working as a laborer or a teamster until his death in 1923. The family, much reduced in size, moved south of the downtown area to a working-class neighborhood across the Green River from Boeing Airfield. It is possible Kiger still had some rental properties to supplement his income, but the fact that he returned to his working-class job indicates he did not make the fortune that Will supposed he did in the Klondike.[21]

Abraham W. Kiger died on May 16, 1923, at the age of seventy-eight. He was buried in Seattle's Lake View Cemetery next to his wife, Mary Anne, who was killed in an automobile accident four years earlier.[22]

Kiger's son-in-law, Cal Johnston, assisted the Woodin party perhaps more than any of the men they met in the Klondike and drew great praise from Will in several accounts. He had married Ollie Kiger in February 1898, before he went to the Klondike. She was seventeen years old at the time and a daughter was born to them very shortly afterwards. Once Cal returned from the Klondike, the couple moved into an apartment complex where Ollie's parents and siblings lived. The marriage did not last. On June 18, 1908, Cal started divorce proceedings against his wife, alleging desertion, and the divorce was finalized a year later in Olympia, Washington. He claimed she had left him in 1902, and he had not seen her since, nor could she be contacted.[23]

Cal's account seems unlikely. Ollie's sister, Clara May, who was only one year younger, married Cal's younger brother, Ruel Clyde Johnston, in 1907. Their father, Calvin A. Johnston Sr., was living with Ruel and Clara May in 1930.[24] It is difficult to understand how Cal's brother did not know where Ollie was, unless she no longer had any connection to her family.

One of the last records that could be found about Calvin A. Johnston was an obituary for his maternal uncle, Gary B. Peavey, on December 22, 1924. Cal was mentioned as a survivor, as well as his brothers, Ruel, Herbert, and Gary. Cal was then living in Yakima, Washington. He was listed in the 1929, 1932, and 1933 Seattle City directories as a machinist living in an industrial area across the Green River from Boeing Airfield.[25]

Another person who had made a lasting impression on Will was George Milham, the partner of George Sherwood, who drowned at the Big Salmon River on June 10, 1898. Milham apparently returned to Seattle shortly after the death of his friend. At the age of twenty-one, he became an apprentice at the Washington Iron Works, Iron Founds, Boiler Makers and Machinists in Seattle, and by 1902, he had become a full-fledged machinist. He continued to work for that company until about 1914. At that time, he was hired by the Locomobile Company of America, which touted him as an expert machinist. He was promoted to superintendent of the company and served in a managerial position until 1920, when he became an automobile salesman. In 1921, Milham went back to serving as a mechanic in Seattle. With the worsening economy in Seattle, he moved his family to Snohomish, Washington, where he went to work as a machinist for the Snohomish Iron Works. He weathered the Great Depression there by becoming a mechanic for the Russell Auto Company in 1932, and switching to Bickford Motors in 1937. He stayed with that company for more than a decade before going to work for the Snohomish Public School system in 1948, where he taught and then later became the custodian.[26]

Milham was single during his trip north. He married in Tacoma, Washington, in 1902, and the couple had three children. He divorced his first wife in 1909, and remarried in Victoria, British Columbia, two years later. As a tragic coda to the loss of his friend, George Sherwood, Milham's twenty-one-year-old son, Donald, drowned on a holiday outing to Vashon Island, Washington, on July 4, 1926. Milham retired from his job as a janitor in the Snohomish Public School system in the 1960s, and died March 4, 1976, at the age of ninety-three.[27]

It is ironic that Will ended his account by saying "Thus ended seven months of strife, hardships, sickness and disappointments in a fruitless search for gold." Will used the phrase "all for the greed of gold" twice as the culmination of reflections on the hardships others endured, including the death of a young man. Both during his journey and years later, as he remembered his trial, he did not necessarily believe the effort was worth what financial gains were realized. Perhaps his and his father's expectations had been rather high. After all, they made enough profit to pay all of their expenses and to support the family back home in Seattle. But upon later reflection, Will realized that the trip constituted an "adventure" rather than an enterprise or investment. And perhaps the leisure with which to afford an "adventure" is as much a characteristic of the middle class as its emerging ethos of moral restraint, hard work, and higher education.

Janet Floyd, who has studied the literature of mining, noted that the writings of people who went to the Klondike were almost entirely about the journey as a metaphor for life's obstacles.[28] While the hazards risked certainly did not justify the economic returns for most Klondikers, they did see it as a rite of passage. In a way, the lessons learned helped most of them adjust to their changing world as it entered the twentieth century. Sons and grandsons of farmers, these men moved from rural to urban settings. After returning from the Klondike, Will, Jay, and their companions invested in businesses and real estate, and acquired jobs that kept their families secure even during the Great Depression. In the process, these men, and others like them, redefined what it was to be a member of the middle class.

Appendix A

Biographies of People Encountered on the Trail, on the River, and in the Camps

These biographies have been included to illustrate how Will and Jay Woodin primarily associated along the trail with people of their same economic class. Demographically, the men were a mixed group of both young and older men; surprisingly, most of them were married with children. None of them were native to the Seattle area; most were born in the Midwest and had moved one or more times before going to the Pacific Northwest in the 1890s. The wives, mothers, and sisters who stayed in Seattle often had to work during these male expeditions to the North. While a few of these men stayed in Alaska after going to the Klondike, most of them returned to their former, working-class occupations on the West Coast.

Allen, John and James. These brothers were among the men with whom Will socialized at the Windy Arm camp in May. They had been clerks in Seattle: James at a clothing and millinery shop owned by John S. Graham, and John at the S. F. Shoe Company. Their sister, Amanda, also worked for Graham. By 1900 all of the siblings, along with John's wife and a second sister, shared a household in Seattle. John had gone back to selling shoes and James had taken up sign construction.[1] It is notable that the female relatives apparently grouped together in 1898, and that some worked outside the home while their husbands and brothers went to the Klondike.

Birnbaum, Alexander and Francine. On March 7, the Woodin party took beds at the Hotel Seattle in Skagway, which was owned by this couple, who Will stated were old friends of his father's. The hotel was located at 313 Fifth Avenue in November 1897, according to an advertisement in the *Skaguay News*. Birnbaum was an Austrian in his late thirties, had immigrated to the United States when he was eleven years old, and became naturalized in his mid-twenties. His wife, Francine, was ten years younger than he. Birnbaum was recorded in Bonanza, Alaska, in 1903 as a baker with Birnbaum and Hoffman, and as a druggist in Chena, Alaska, from 1909 to 1912. He was mayor of Chena in 1910. Francine died shortly after that time, and he returned to Seattle, where he remarried and went into the retail dry goods business.[2]

Clough, Myron E. This fifty-two-year-old was at the Windy Arm camp on May 14. His age explains why Will called him the more formal "Mr. Clough" (see May 14 diary entry). Born in Illinois, he had lived in the San Francisco area until 1892, when he and his wife and daughter moved to Seattle. Before he went to the Klondike in 1898, he was a machinist at the Puget Sound Machine Depot in Seattle. In Dawson, he became president of the Yukon Engineers' International Association. He left the Klondike after 1901, and returned to Oakland, California, where he again worked as a machinist.[3]

Eastman, George "Bert." At the Windy Arm camp on May 28, Will noted in his diary, "I have fallen in love" with this twenty-three-year-old carpenter from Omaha, Nebraska, who was traveling with his cousin, William Bruce Ives (see below). Eastman had lived in Ogden, Utah, before going to the Klondike. His skill in construction was highly marketable, and he was able to get a job before most of Will's fellow travelers did. In fact, Eastman offered to help Will obtain a position at Condahy Sky Company's Wholesale House in Dawson. Eastman stayed in Dawson through 1902, then moved to Juneau at least until 1905. By 1910 he had returned to his parents' home in Omaha, Nebraska. George was married to a woman who worked as a dressmaker while her husband was in the Klondike.[4]

Foster, John and Henry. Will encountered these brothers at Windy Arm. They were born to Abraham and Mary Foster: John in England in 1863 and Henry four years later in British Columbia. They had a younger sibling who was born in Oregon, suggesting that the family moved fairly often, and by 1880, they were in King County, Washington. The elder son, John, followed in his father's footsteps as a boilermaker, and Henry worked as an engineer for Western Mill, a logging company in Seattle. Henry, in particular, would have been a welcome addition to any group cutting lumber at Windy Arm in the vicinity of Giffert's Mill.[5]

Goodrich, Peter "Bert." Will encountered this old friend when the SS *Cleveland* stopped in Wrangell on March 5. He was probably Eberson Goodrich, one of Will's childhood friends who lived near the Woodin family in Gratiot County, Michigan. Will remembered Bert quite fondly in an unpublished autobiography of his childhood. About the time of the gold rush, Bert joined his brother, Francis (Frank) M. Goodrich, who went to Wrangell in 1896 and remained there until after 1930. Although Bert's occupation is not known, Frank worked at a sawmill, variously as a "planesman" or a fireman.[6]

Hering, Edward A. This twenty-three-year-old with whom Will socialized at Windy Arm was a salesman at the Puget Sound Machinery Depot. He also had been a wrapper in a clothing store in 1891 and a student in 1892. He was the son of German immigrant barber George Hering and his wife Jennie, who had moved from Michigan to Kansas, where Edward was born. From there, they went to Visalia, California, before moving to Seattle in 1888. Edward married Agnes, a young woman from Ireland, in 1896, and they had a son. When the Klondike rush started, Ed joined his neighbor, Zach Hickman (see below), who was ten years older, in going north. Hering was enumerated on Dominion Creek in 1901 with his parents, who joined him in the Yukon in 1899. He was working as a printer, probably for Hickman. He later followed his friend to Fairbanks, where he was a teamster in 1907, a wood dealer in 1909, and an express man in 1911. By 1918, he had become a postal clerk, a job he kept for the rest of his life. He was one of the few people mentioned by Will who stayed in Alaska until his death in 1927.[7]

Hickman, Zacharia F. This Seattle Metropolitan Printing and Binding Company secretary was among Will's group of friends at the Windy Arm camp, and was the partner of Ed Hering (see above). He had been a printer in Seattle since about 1888 and had spent some time in Guatemala, also as a printer. Born in Sabina, Ohio, to a minister, he was about thirty-three years old at the time of the gold rush. He was married and had two children, with a third on the way. He stayed in the North, at least during the summers, well into the 1910s. He did both mining and publishing in the Fairbanks area and worked as a compositor for the *Tanana Tribune* while maintaining a home in Seattle. After 1920, he moved his family first to Fargo, North Dakota, and later to Los Angeles, California. In both locations, he operated print shops.[8]

Hooper, Isaac Newton. Will encountered this forty-year-old barber at the Windy Arm camp. He studied medicine in his early twenties in Morenci, Michigan, but left for Kansas after marrying his first wife, Lydia Walker. They moved to Seattle in about 1888, where he became a barber. He left his wife and three children in Seattle when he went to the Klondike, but did not stay long. He was back in Seattle and tending to his barbershop by 1900. By 1910, he took advantage of his medical training and became a chiropractor, an occupation from which he retired before the Great Depression.[9]

Howie, Reverend William Maurice. The Woodin party first encountered this Presbyterian minister (who Will incorrectly referred to as "Howe") on board the SS *Cleveland* between Seattle and Skagway. Will mentioned him again in March near the summit of White Pass, as well as at Windy Arm in May. Howie was born in 1845 in Waukesha, Wisconsin, to a Scots farmer and obtained his divinity degree from Newberg Seminary, New York, in 1878. He married Mary E. Lackey, a minister's daughter, and they had two sons, both of whom also became ministers. He served as pastor to Presbyterian churches in Walton, New York, and Chicago before 1895, when he was called to Seattle. The Howies responded to a Presbyterian call for missions in Alaska and were one of fifty couples who went to the Klondike. Their sons, James and William, joined the couple in Dawson in 1899 and stayed through 1902, but there is no record of how much time Rev. and Mrs. Howie spent in the Klondike. After returning to Seattle, Howie served as minister in Garnett, Kansas, and after 1901 in Alliance, Nebraska. There, on March 31, 1904, William M. Howie contracted influenza, having suffered ill health ever since his trip to the Klondike, and died on April 10, 1904, at the age of fifty-eight.[10]

Ives, William Bruce. This twenty-three-year-old teamster was a partner of George Eastman (see above), and was also at Windy Arm. He was born in Independence, Kansas, to Rebecca Ruth Dean and Norman Henry Ives on August 29, 1875. He moved to Ogden, Utah, in 1889, where he first met George Eastman (see above). Ives worked as a teamster in Dawson, at least through 1902, when he moved to Valdez, Alaska, in 1904. There he married Ella M. Phillips Foulks, a cousin of George Eastman, through her father, Cyrus Eastman Phillips. Only three months after his wedding, Ives drowned at the age of thirty-one. A Juneau newspaper speculated that his death was actually suicide because he had taken out a bond on a mining claim and could not make it pay.[11]

Johnston [Johnson], Calvin A. This twenty-two-year-old machinist was a friend of William L. "Ed" Green and the son-in-law of Abraham Kiger (see below). Will first mentioned him in May at Windy Arm, in company with the Madison Street Car boys, and repeatedly referred to the young man in glowing terms throughout the rest of his memoir. In addition to piloting the Woodin party's boats through Miles Canyon and Whitehorse Rapids, Johnston later became an important decision-maker on the trek up the Little Salmon River. He was born in Bangor, Maine, in 1876 to Calvin A. Johnston Sr. and Ada L. Peavy, and he had three younger brothers. The family moved to Elk River, in Sherburne County, Minnesota, and then to Seattle in the late 1880s. By 1892 Cal was working as a machinist along with his father. A variety of manufacturing companies in the Seattle area employed Johnston between 1890 and the Great Depression, including, as Will wrote, the Puget Sound Machinery Depot.[12]

Jones, Oliver "Ollie." The young man from Seattle that Will encountered on the Skagway Trail on March 28, 1898, was twenty-three. He was single and worked variously as a carpenter, a lumberman, or a building contractor. Will states that Ollie was the brother-in-law of Lee Loomis (see below). Loomis's wife was Jennie Loomis, who had a younger brother named Joseph Jones. Oliver was either Joseph's middle name or Will was incorrect in describing the relationship between the two men.[13]

Kiger, Abraham. Kiger, who Will referred to as "Mr. Kiger" or "Keiger" in his memoir, was born in 1849 in Illinois to Ohio natives William and Rachal Kiger. He spoke better German than he spoke English, perhaps because he and his parents may have been raised in enclaves of German speakers. Kiger married Mary Ann Kerns on November 11, 1876, in Benton County, Oregon. By 1892, the couple had moved to Duwamish, Washington, and had eight children. Kiger then moved to Seattle, where he became a teamster. He was listed as an express man in 1898, the year he went to the Klondike. His oldest, George, is probably the boy who accompanied Abraham to the Klondike, as his other sons were only nine and seven years old at the time. Kiger and his son staked claims on Lovatt Gulch, located near the mouth of Bonanza Creek.[14]

Loomis, Lee. Will mentioned this young man as the brother-in-law of his friend, Ollie Jones (see above). He was a driver for Charles E. Downie, who owned a grain and feed store in Seattle. He was twenty-eight at the time of the gold rush. The Woodins may have known him because they used horses in their lumbering business.[15]

Lund, Charles. On April 23, Will lists this twenty-one-year-old conductor for the Madison Street Cable Railway Company among the Seattle friends at the Windy Arm camp. Lund also watched the camp at the Little Salmon River from June 12 to 21. He was born in either Denmark or Sweden, but his parents immigrated to the United States when he was still a child. His experience floating the Yukon River prepared him well for future jobs as a seaman, a carpenter at a shipbuilding company, and other boat-related occupations. Lund stayed in Dawson through 1905, where he called himself a miner. By 1907, he was in Skagway and worked for the White Pass and Yukon Route as a laborer.[16]

Lunn, Axel M. On April 23, while at the Windy Arm camp, Will identified the Lunn brothers as photographers. Axel Lunn emigrated from Sweden in 1887 at the age of twenty to join his paternal uncle, Andrew Lunn, who owned the Gold Bar

Hotel and Saloon in Seattle. He operated his uncle's saloon business until 1891, when he became a photographer with his own shop on Yesler Street. By 1897, he returned to his job as a bartender for his uncle. After the gold rush, he and his brother, John M. Lunn (see below) opened their own saloon on First Avenue. The Lunn brothers operated saloons until 1916, when the city enacted Prohibition laws. Axel Lunn turned to a job as a machinist by 1920, and by 1930, he and his wife had retired to the suburbs to open a poultry farm. He died in Bremerton, Washington, in 1947. Will probably did not mention the fact that the Lunn brothers were prominent saloon owners so as not to alarm the female family members who read his memoir.[17]

Lunn, John H. This saloon keeper (age twenty-six) was one of the Lunn brothers at Windy Arm. Though Will said both brothers were photographers, there is no evidence that John Lunn practiced the craft in a professional way. John followed his brother Axel to Seattle in 1889 at the age of 17. He married in 1899 after his return from the Klondike, and had four daughters and a son. By 1910, John became the manager of the Hotel DeAngleterre, a position he maintained until the Depression. He died in 1950 in Los Angeles.[18]

Lyman, Lewis and Lucinda. These old friends of Jay Woodin from Michigan operated the Rainier Hotel in Skagway, where Will and his father stayed before taking a ship to Seattle in late September. Will incorrectly recalled them as Mr. and Mrs. Lewis. Lewis was born in Jackson County, Michigan, in 1850; Lucinda in Pennsylvania in 1853. They married in Michigan in the early 1870s, and were still in Jackson County, Michigan, in 1880, where Lewis worked as a carpenter. Their daughter Cora preceded the family to Alaska, arriving in Juneau in 1895 at the age of twenty-four. There she secured a position as a stenographer. Her father followed with the surge of the rush in July 1897, and Lucinda brought their toddler, George, to Skagway in October 1898, only days before the Woodins returned from Dawson. The Lymans stayed in Skagway through the summer of 1900, when Lewis was working at his old occupation of carpentry. By 1910, the couple moved to the San Joaquin Valley of California where Lewis returned to farm work. Lewis died there in 1923 and Lucinda passed away in 1933.[19]

McKnight, James H. On April 13, 1898, Will stated that James McKnight, a thirty-eight-year-old man, was a friend of his father. On April 24, Will mentioned him as one of the group at Windy Arm. The McKnight brothers immigrated to Seattle by 1883, where James became a machinist. Two years later he worked for a lumber company, and in 1887, he was listed as a laborer. Over the next five years he would try a number of different jobs—a car oiler, a clerk at a hardware store, a porter at a hardware store. In 1893, he was a conductor for the Madison Street Car Company, where Will came to know him. In 1897, he obtained a position as a janitor with the Seattle Public School Department. At the time of the gold rush, he was married, had two sons, and supported his widowed mother-in-law.

McKnight, Samuel and Thomas. These brothers traveled to the Klondike in 1898 with their older brother, James (see above). Samuel apprenticed with the well-known Seattle photographer, D. R. Judkins, and by 1891 he had established his own gallery. He stayed in Dawson until at least 1901, and developed a mine on Bonanza Creek in connection with Sydney K. King, forming a company named the King, Williams & McKnight. The third brother, Thomas, was a good friend of Cal Johnston (see above).[20] It is possible that Will confused the Lunn brothers (see above), whom he identified as photographers, with Samuel McKnight and his brothers.

Simpson, Dr. James Kidd. This thirty-seven-year-old physician was one of two men who treated Will for typhoid fever on the Yukon River between Dawson and Whitehorse in the fall of 1898. He was born in Ontario, Canada, on September 19, 1861, to Joshua and Eliza Kidd Simpson. He obtained his medical degree at the College of Physicians and Surgeons of Minneapolis in 1886. Despite his illness on the river, he survived the trip to Skagway, went to Juneau, took up a medical practice, and started a hospital there. He died in Victoria, British Columbia, on September 2, 1915.[21] (It was not possible to determine the identity and background of Dr. Lindsey, who also treated Will.)

Smith, "Sport." Will and Jay encountered this flamboyant personality at Bennett Lake on their return trip to Skagway in late September. He later became a well-known dog musher in the north. He was said to be the partner of the famous Allan Alexander "Scotty" Allan, the musher who owned Balto, the dog immortalized as the hero of the Iditarod Trail during the serum run of February 1925. Thomas Rickard, a mining engineer who wrote one of the first scholarly manuals on the Yukon and Alaska, noted that Sport Smith was among the men who one should hire if he wanted a guide to the North Pole.[22] It was not possible to determine Smith's complete name.

Thompson, Franklin H. Will encountered this constable with the North-West Mounted Police (renamed the Royal Northwest Mounted Police in 1904) at the camp on the Little Salmon River. He was in the same position in Dawson between

1902 and 1908. After that time, he became a carpenter for the Mounties in Dawson.[23] (No information could be found about McKay, his fellow constable. It is possible that Will misremembered his name.)

Wells, William H. This Canadian-born farmer from Michigan was fifty-five years old to Jay Woodin's forty-six when they became reacquainted at Windy Arm. Wells's parents originally hailed from New York, lived in Canada a number of years, and moved on to Branch County, Michigan, in about 1844. In 1864, Wells volunteered with Company D of the 5th Michigan Cavalry and served for fourteen months in the Civil War. There he developed sciatica (rheumatism in the hips), and suffered from the affliction for the rest of his life.[24] Wells married Rachel E. Sherwood in Branch County, Michigan, after his discharge from the 5th Michigan Cavalry in 1866. They moved to Seville, Gratiot County, Michigan, where William took up farming, and where he met and became friends with Jay Woodin. By 1883, they had five children.[25] Rachel's brother, George Sherwood Sr., was the father of the George Jr., who drowned at Big Salmon on June 10, 1898.

Woodin, Hiram. Born on March 29, 1858, in Pine River Township, Gratiot County, Michigan, Hiram was six years younger than his brother Jay. (He was forty when Jay and Will joined him in Klondike City.) By 1870, an older brother, Wallace Woodin, had taken both Jay and Hiram into his household in the town of St. Louis, Michigan. There Hiram went to school while Jay apprenticed with Wallace as a carpenter. By the time he was twenty-two years old, Hiram worked as a laborer on Jay's farm in Michigan. In 1883, while a clerk for clothing merchant Levi Kallmeyer in Saginaw, Michigan, Hiram married Caroline Mathilda Scoville, "a dressmaker with aristocratic airs," according to Will's memoir of his childhood. The couple worked some farm land near Edwardsburg, Mason County, Michigan, until migrating to Seattle in 1890 with Jay Woodin and his family. As early as 1890, Hiram was listed as selling real estate in the Seattle city directory, but between 1892 and 1895, he earned most of his living as a conductor for the Seattle City Railway Company. By that time, Hiram wore several hats, including that of contractor, as well as conductor and real estate agent. When he went to the Klondike, he devoted himself to real estate, which became his life's work. Apparently, Caroline did not accompany Hiram to the Klondike.[26]

Appendix B

Supplies for the Klondike

Jay Woodin and his party probably consulted numerous sources as they drew up the list of equipment, supplies, tools, and personal possessions to take to the Klondike, both for their own use and for their potential customers. Such sources could have included a list published by the *Skaguay News* on December 31, 1897, and another list published by the *Seattle Post-Intelligencer (P-I)* on January 25, 1898. The two lists overlap to a certain extent, although the one offered in Seattle was more generous and contained more luxuries. The *Skaguay News* pointed out that when men grouped together in parties of three to five, they could share some of the equipment and tools. The following items were suggested by both sources to be shared by a party:

1 tent, 10 x 12 feet (*P-I* suggested an 8 x 10-foot tent for one man traveling alone)
1 Yukon stove
5 packstraps
2 coffee pots
6 cups (3 per man when traveling alone)
2 frying pans
6 knives and forks (3 per man when traveling alone)
3 knives, butcher
6 plates (3 per man when traveling alone)
6 spoons (*P-I* specified 3 teaspoons, 3 tablespoons, and 1 large spoon for a man when traveling alone)

1 medicine case
1 brace and bits
12 files, assorted (5 for one man traveling alone)
3 hammers
3 hatchets
1 knife, drawing
25 pounds nails, assorted (*P-I* specified types in smaller quantities)
15 pounds oakum (5 pounds per man when traveling alone)
8 pounds pitch (5 pounds per man when traveling alone)
1 plane
200 feet rope
1 whipsaw

Both the *Skaguay News* and the *Seattle Post-Intelligencer* suggested the following as necessary for each man in addition to the shared supplies:

30 yards mosquito netting (or 1 piece)

1–2 box candles

1 can matches 1/2 tin

2–3 pairs heavy blankets

2 pair boots, heavy rubber (the *P-I* suggested 1 pair high topped and 1 pair low topped)

1 coat each canvas, Mackinaw, and oiled or rubber

3–6 pairs mittens

4 pairs overalls

3–4 overshirts, heavy

1 pair snow goggles

24 bars soap, 1 box

12 pairs socks, heavy woolen

2 pairs German socks

2 sweaters

2–3 suits woolen underwear

2 suits light underwear

needles, thread, and repairing material

100–150 pounds bacon

10 pounds baking powder

75–100 pounds beans

10–25 pounds beef, dried

20–25 pounds coffee

50 pounds cornmeal

350 pounds flour (or 8 sacks)

100 pounds fruits, dried (the *P-I* recommended 20 pounds each of apples, apricots, peaches, prunes, and raisins)

2 bottles Jamaican ginger

5–10 pounds onions, evaporated

1 pound mustard

25–50 pounds pork, salt

25–50 pounds potatoes, evaporated

25–50 pounds rice

25–50 pounds salt

2 pounds soup, condensed (or 10 packages)

100 pounds sugar

10–15 pounds tea

1–2 pounds vinegar, evaporated

1 axe

1 gold pan

1 pick (the *P-I* specified 2 light picks)

1 pocket compass

1 shovel

The *Skaguay News* suggested the following additional requirements:

1 rifle

1 shotgun

calamine

quinine

2 pairs trousers, Mackinaw

whiskey, only if needed

rubber for mending gum boots

3 hacksaws per party

1 knife, stout clasp

The extra suggestions by the *Post-Intelligencer* were more numerous and many constituted true luxuries:

2 tarpaulins, 7 x 9
1 sled
5 pounds quicksilver
1 pair oars
2 camp kettles
3 drip pan
1 galvanized pail
3 pans, 1-quart
6 towels
blanket pins
buttons
1 cap
4 pairs gloves, 1 pair each buckskin
    and rubber, and 2 pairs wool
6 handkerchiefs, red
1 hat, Klondike
1 hood
2 pairs moccasins
2 overshirts, thin
safety pins
2 pairs shoes, not too heavy
6 pairs socks, cotton
2 pairs suspenders
1 ball yarn
beeswax
1 magnifying glass
2 pairs shoe pacs
1 ball shoe tread
1 cake shoe wax
sticking plaster
window glass
1 dozen beef, extract
1 pound cinnamon
25 pounds cracked wheat
6 packages eggs, evaporated

0.75 pounds ginger
1 sack graham flour
1 case milk
1 can nutmeg
1 pound pepper, black
0.75 pounds pepper, red
25 pounds rolled oats
2 pounds soda
10 pounds split peas
2 gallons syrup
1 dozen yeast, Magic
1 ax, extra handle for
1 ax, hunter
1 caulking iron
1 chisel, 1 1/2 inch
1 combination tool
door hinges
1 ball marlin
1 monkey wrench
1 pinchers
pins
1 box rivets, copper
1 rule, 2-foot
1 saw set
1 saw, one-man cross-cut
1 screwdriver bit
screws
1 shears
solder
1 package tacks
tape
1 tape line
1 whetstone
1 spool wire, copper
1 Yale lock

Finally, the *Seattle P-I* offered the following hints for luxuries that should be considered, according to taste: butter, canned beef, cheese, chocolate, cocoa, corn, peas, tomatoes, and tobacco.

It is curious that the Skagway newspaper suggested whiskey as an indulgence, whereas the Seattle newspaper thought a man might want tobacco. It seems likely that most men would have wanted both products. It is also interesting that the Skagway newspaper thought a party should have two kinds of firearms, but the Seattle newspaper made no mention of them.

APPENDIX C

The Woodin Party Costs and Profits

The *Skaguay News*, on December 31, 1897, printed an article entitled "When and How to Outfit," which offers insight on what it may have actually cost the Woodin party to go to the Klondike the following year. The article provided lists of supplies that the average party of four or five should take; it also outlined the types and quantities of food that would last a man one year, which amounted to just under 1,200 pounds (see Appendix B). Included was a list of clothing for both men and women, indicating that women needed more clothing than men. The newspaper noted that "an outfit such as the one outlined above can be purchased in Skaguay for from $150 to $500."[1] This basic outfit would cost between $4,000 and $14,000 in today's currency.

Sylvester Scovel, writing for the *New York World* on August 20, 1897, estimated the following costs: "For 2500 pounds of outfit, self and companion, from Chicago to Dawson City, railroad and steamer transportation from Chicago to Skaguay, $300; outfit of a year's groceries and clothing, purchased at Seattle and shipped to Skaguay, at least $750; cost of lightering and hauling outfit from beach to tents, $25; five horses (of no value afterward), $1,000; food for horses (two weeks at $2 a day, Skaguay prices), $140; good packer, two weeks at $8 per day, $112; assistant through to Dawson City to aid in boarding and porting [sic] goods, &c, $100; a boat at Lake Bennett, $125. Total, $2,562." Scovel's estimate would equal more than $70,000 in today's currency, and did not detail the duties collected by the North-West Mounted Police at each of their check points.[2]

In an unpublished letter to his mother, stampeder Kirke Johnson wrote from Skagway on March 17, 1898. "In regard to going into the Interior I think it would be foolish for a man to start from home with less than $600.00 as the Mounted Police won't let a man by with less than 1,100 lbs of grub. The duty on that and the rest of his outfit will be about $35.00. Add to that, the cost of it [the food], $100.00 for packing over or paying about $125.00 for a horse and run the risk of him getting killed first day and you won't have much money left." Johnson's $600 in 1898 translates to almost $16,000 in today's currency.

These accounts do not mention other costs incurred on the journey. Steamboat tickets ran an average of $45 apiece from Seattle to Skagway. Duties at the border cost the Woodin party $160 and a bribe of $5. Another bribe of $4 to $5 was required at the customs clearing point at Tagish post. Accident insurance, if you were wise enough to think about those you left at home, cost about $20 for a year. A pilot at Miles Canyon, which most men hired, ran from $25 to $40, depending on the size and weight of the boat. The Woodins paid $250 for their two horses in Seattle, but realized only $60 on their sale in late April. Most men bought some cut lumber from lumber mills for one reason or another. Will says that they paid $45 for three hundred board feet at Windy Arm in late May (although they worked for that amount and took a trade in labor).

Then there were lodging expenses. The Woodins paid $75 a month rental for a cabin in Klondike City. Robert Graham, another writer of the period, was luckier. He and his partner bought a cabin in Skagway in March 1898 for only $40, but had to finish it themselves. Lesser expenses could add up: $5 for a visit from a doctor, or $10 if a man needed him for an entire day; 25 cents to receive or mail a letter; 50 cents for a newspaper; 50 cents to cross the bridge between Dawson and Klondike City.[3] These additional expenses could run more than $1,000, or the equivalent of almost $28,000 in today's currency.

None of these estimates of the costs of the Klondike adventure allow for the support of family members left behind. It is obvious that no single individual, unless he was independently wealthy, could just quit his job and take off for the Klondike. Most people, upon encountering these often unexpected costs, would take on temporary jobs to supplement their grubstake or savings. The average laborer in the United States at the time earned about a dollar a day. Diarist Robert Graham observed men digging coal for a dollar an hour at Fort Hamilton, located twenty-five miles above the mouth of the Yukon, in July 1898. Labor on the White Pass and Yukon Route railroad was paid two dollars a day plus board. Letter-writer Kirke Johnson, a well-educated man, made $150 a month plus board as superintendent of construction on the telephone line along the Brackett Wagon Road in March 1898, but he had to quit the job when the company decreased his salary to $60 a month.[4]

The Woodin party earned about the same types of wages. They received $7 a day sawing lumber for Giffert's Mill at Windy Arm, and Jim Daugherty found a job working a claim for a mining company in the Forty Mile district for $15 plus room and board a day. Those wages were similar to what cooks earned in restaurants and hotels along the trails in August 1898. Robert Graham, who went into the north about the same time as the Woodins, earned $20 for hauling a man's gear up one hill on the White Pass Trail. Likewise, Will Woodin received $5 for helping a young man who was hurt get to a hotel where he could recover.[5] In today's dollars, it was possible to earn the equivalent of anywhere from $1,700 to $12,500 a month at a steady job, and anywhere from $140 to $550 at a time for a special task.

Costs could also be offset by selling items that were no longer needed, either upon reaching one's destination or upon deciding to leave the north. The Woodins sold their two horses for $60 in April, and their dog, Skookum, for $75 upon leaving Dawson in September. Robert Graham sold his dog for $50 in Circle City, as well as a large boat for $35, a stove for $7, and a sled and blanket for $5 each.[6] Accounting for inflation, these assets earned travelers from $140 for a blanket to over $2,000 for a good dog in today's money.

Of course, Jay Woodin's primary purpose for his trip to Dawson was to make a fortune selling the extra goods he had brought with him. As is obvious on reading Will's account of the time they spent in Dawson (Chapter 7), the Woodins only indulged in a perfunctory search for gold. They relied, instead, on the sales of their groceries, canned goods, and mining equipment to pay for their adventure. They bought cornmeal for 44 cents a bag in Seattle and sold it for $7.50, seventeen times what it cost them.

Will notes on August 19 that he and Jay sold their tobacco stock at $1.50 to $2.00 per pound. It was difficult to determine what they paid for it in Seattle, as it was usually sold as cigars, cigarettes, or plugs, not by the pound as detailed by Will. No advertisements could be found in Washington newspapers for tobacco by the pound. Midwest newspapers selling the product in that form noted prices varying from 15 to 75 cents, depending on the brand.[7] At worst, that was a profit of between four and ten times what they paid.

In fact, as shown in Table C-1, the Woodins realized profits from 143 percent for onions to over 2,000 percent for syrup, for an average of almost 800 percent. Will may have complained about the prices they got, but they still made a profit. Whether this profit was sufficient to cover the costs of the journey and to support the family left behind cannot be determined precisely, as Will never details the amount of goods they took to Dawson. However, if only a third of their expenses was devoted to the supplies they later sold, they would have made a very good living for themselves and the family in Seattle during the seven months they spent on the Klondike endeavor.

Table C-1. Prices paid for goods in Seattle, prices sold in the Klondike, and
           percent mark-up.[8] (Duplicate entries for some goods are from sales at
           different locations, i.e., along the trail, on the river, and at Dawson.)

product	cost	earned	percent mark-up
onions/pound	$0.35	$0.50	143
bacon/pound	$0.13	$0.25	200
evaporated potatoes/pound	$0.15	$0.50	333
beans/pound	$0.03	$0.10	333
butter/pound	$0.25	$1.00	400
ham/pound	$0.13	$0.60	480
bacon/pound	$0.13	$0.60	480
raisins/pound	$0.10	$0.50	500
ham/pound	$0.10	$0.68	675
cheese/pound	$0.12	$1.00	833
flour/sack	$0.85	$8.00	941
bacon/pound	$0.13	$1.50	1200
beans/pound	$0.03	$0.45	1500
cornmeal/sack	$0.44	$7.50	1705
syrup/gallon	$0.20	$4.00	2000
Average			782

NOTES

NOTES TO INTRODUCTION

1. The first Woodin of William Jay's line to come America was Timothy Woodin, one of four brothers who immigrated to Massachusetts from the Isle of Wight, England, in about 1722. His son, Amos (1753–1843), fought in the American Revolution in 1776. Amos's grandson, Abram (1809–1860), married Anna Bassett (1811–1902), who had an even more distinguished genealogy. One of her ancestors was William Bassett (1600–1667), who arrived in Plymouth Colony on the *Fortune* in 1621. Abram and Anna Woodin homesteaded in Michigan in 1854–55, where their son, Jay Abram Woodin (1852–1940), grew up and where William Jay Woodin was born in 1874. Kate Caffrey, "Passengers on the *Mayflower, Fortune, Anne,* and *Little James," The Ark Valley Crossroads* (Wichita, KS, Genealogical Society), Vol. 6:1 (January 1995), 25–27; Woodin Family Tree, trees.ancestry.com/tree/52694725/family; Woodins from Mt. Washington, MA, trees.ancestry.com/tree/1019360/person/-183915274/story/237720cd-22f7-46ee-802c-bd2deb4b4c59?src=search.

2. World War I Draft Registration Cards, 1917–1918; for an online transcription of Will's autobiography, see "Will Woodin," www.montanadawn.com/Will_Woodin.html, hereafter referred to as Woodin Autobiography.

3. Seattle City Directory, 1891–95, 1898.

4. Janet Floyd, *Claims and Speculations: Mining and Writing in the Gilded Age* (Albuquerque: University of New Mexico Press, 2012), 112; Pierre Berton, *Klondike: The Life and Death of the Great Gold Rush* (London: W. H. Allen, 1960), 434.

5. Edwin C. Bearss, *Proposed Klondike Gold Rush National Historical Park Historic Resource Study* (Washington, DC: U.S. Department of the Interior, Government Printing Office, 1970), 238.

6. Murray Morgan, photographs by E. A. Hegg, *One Man's Gold Rush: A Klondike Album* (Seattle: University of Washington Press, 1967).

NOTES TO CHAPTER ONE

1. Ancestry.com: Woodin Family Tree, trees.ancestry.com/tree/52694725/13394618132; Seattle City Directories, 1891–1895, 1898; Woodin Autobiography.

2. Seattle City Directory, 1897.

3. 1870 Census, Colorado Territory, Gilpin County, Central City, 282A; 1900 Census, Washington, King County, Seattle Ward 6, Enumeration District 108, 10A; British Columbia, Canada Marriage Index, 1872–1935.

4. 1860 Census, Wisconsin, Sauk County, Prairie du Sac, 749; 1880 Census, Wisconsin, Sauk County, Prairie du Sac, Enumeration District 258, 188A; 1887 Washington Territorial Census, Seattle Ward 4, Roll V228_5, line 30; 1892 Washington State Census, Seattle Ward 8, Roll V228_7, line 36; 1900 Census, Washington, King County, Seattle Ward 8, Enumeration District 113, 15A; findagrave.com, Mary Green, Memorial #29458653; Seattle City Directories, 1890–1907; Washington Deaths, 1883–1960, W. L. Green.

5. 1880 Census, Michigan, Isabella County, Union, Enumeration District 157, 532; 1900 Census, Washington, King County, Seattle Ward 7, Enumeration District 110, 6B; 1920 Census, Washington, King County, Seattle, Enumeration District 67, 13; 1885 Washington Territorial Census, line 31; Seattle City Directories, 1887–1917; *Seattle Daily Times*, August 1, 1911.

6. The cost of first class passage from Seattle to Skagway increased from $22 in the summer of 1897 to $50 in the spring of 1898; for second class, which Will and his party employed, it increased from $11 to $35. Shipment of freight increased proportionately. *Engineering and Mining Record*, "The Yukon Rush at Skagway," Vol. 65, No. 12 (March 19, 1898), 341.

7. Jay had been a partner in the firm since 1896. Seattle City Directories, 1896–1898.

8. Actually, the residence of Robert and Joan Dunsmuir was called Craigdarroch Castle. Dunsmuir was a railroad, mining, and shipping magnate from Victoria. He began building the castle in 1887; the family took up residence in 1890. "The Dunsmuir Story," thecastle.ca/about-the-castle/dunsmuir-family.

9. *Idaho Statesman* (Boise, ID), January 29, 1898; *Cleveland (OH) Plain Dealer*, January 30, 1898; *Oregonian* (Portland, OR), January 29, 1898; *Tacoma (WA) Daily News*, January 29, 1898.

10. A lighthouse was built on Lincoln Rock opposite Etoline Island in 1903. Pat Roppel, "Southeast History: Lincoln Rock Lighthouse from 1902," capitalcityweekly.com/stories/110712/out_1063358303.shtml.

11. Will left this date blank. Editor supplied the date.

12. This comment suggests that Will started writing his memoir before 1910.

13. Will appears to be describing Moore's Wharf, which was started in 1896. By the time the Woodin party arrived in Skagway in March 1898, there were three other wharves serving the steamships and freighters.

NOTES TO CHAPTER TWO

1. The conversion of 1898 dollars to modern (2014) currency was made with the assistance of "The Inflation Calculator" at www.westegg.com/inflation.

2. Bearss, *Proposed Klondike Gold Rush*, 238.

3. Julie Johnson, *A Wild, Discouraging Mess: The History of the White Pass Unit of the Klondike Gold Rush National Historical Park* (Anchorage: U. S. Department of the Interior, 2003).

4. "Seattle to Dawson—A Klondiker's Diary," *Frank Leslie's Popular Monthly*, Vol. 50, No. 1, (May 1900), 9.

5. Angelo Heilprin, *Alaska and the Klondike: A Journey to the New El Dorado with Hints to the Traveler* (New York: Appleton, 1899), 8.

6. Mary E. Hitchcock, *Two Women in the Klondike: The Story of a Journey to the Gold-Fields of Alaska* (New York: G. P. Putnam, 1899), 438–439.

7. Walter A. Starr, *My Adventures in the Klondike and Alaska, 1898–1900* (n.p.: Walter A. Starr, 1960), 5.

8. Letters of Kirke Johnson sent to his mother, manuscript, Klondike Gold Rush National Historical Park Stampeders File.

9. Starr, *My Adventures,* 5.

10. Frank W. Purdy diary, 1898–1900, Alaska and Polar Regions Collection, University of Alaska, Fairbanks.

11. Washington State Marriage Records, 1865–2004; *Seattle Daily Times,* August 29, 1905, 2.

12. Kathryn Winslow, *Big Pan-Out: The Klondike Story* (London: Phoenix House, 1952), 79.

13. Actually, the source of the Yukon is at the Llewellan Glacier above Lake Atlin. Some consider Lake Lindeman the source of the Yukon. Both lakes drain into Tagish Lake, as does Summit Lake. Therefore Summit Lake and the creek that runs out of it are tributaries to Tagish Lake. "Yukon River—Background Information and Map," www.yukoninfo.com/yukon-river.

14. Woodin no doubt refers to the infamous "Dead Horse Trail."

15. Will wrote this line sometime between 1910 and 1914. Log Cabin is now a rail stop on the White Pass railroad, but archaeological remains are the only evidence of the little community.

16. *Denver Post,* March 16, 1898; Helena, Montana, *Independent,* March 16, 1898, *Morning Oregonian,* March 16, 17, 1898; San Francisco *Examiner,* March 16, 1898 (reprinted in Howard Clifford, *Correspondence of a Crook,* Seattle: Sourdough Enterprises, 1997); Seattle *Post-Intelligencer,* February 27, March 16, 1898; *Tacoma Daily News,* March 16, 1898; Victoria *Daily Colonist,* March 16, 1898.

17. *Denver Post,* March 16, 1898; Seattle *Post-Intelligencer,* March 16, 1898; Victoria *Daily Colonist,* March 16, 1898; Catherine Holder Spude, *"That Fiend in Hell": The Legend of Soapy Smith* (Norman: University of Oklahoma Press, 2012), 35–46; *Saloons, Prostitutes, and Temperance in Alaska Territory* (Norman: University of Oklahoma Press, 2015), 46–47.

NOTES TO CHAPTER FOUR

1. 1901 Census of Canada, The Territories, Unorganized Territories, White Horse; Omaha City Directory, 1891; *Salt Lake Tribune,* October 28, 1904; Ancestry.com, Ives Family Tree, trees.ancestry.com/tree/55755628/person/46034338549.

2. Yukon Territory was not so designated until June 13, 1898. Before that time, it was part of the North West Territories of Canada.

3. *Denver Post,* April 11, 1909; New Orleans *Times Picayune,* April 25, 1909; Michael O'Donoghue, *Gems: Their Sources, Descriptions and Identifications* (Burlington, MA: Butterworth-Heinemann, 2006), 52, 395; Ann P. Sabina, *Rocks and Minerals for the Collector: The Alaska Highway, Dawson Creek, British Columbia to Yukon/Alaska Border* (Geological Survey of Canada, Miscellaneous Report, Vol. 50, 1992), 124.

4. Yukon and Alaska Directories, 1901–1910; *Tacoma Daily Times,* January 5, 1898.

5. 1870 Federal Census, Illinois, Warren County, Monmouth, 137B; 1901 Canadian Census, Unorganized Territories, Yukon, Upper Bonanza, 24; Fergusen directory of the Yukon and Alaska, 1901, online at www.familychronicle.com/klondike.htm; *The History of Washington County, Iowa, Des Moines* (Des Moines: Union Historical Company, 1880), 580, 585; Iowa Graves Survey, Works Progress Administration 1930's Graves Registration Survey, iowawpagraves.org; *Omaha World Herald,* March 8, 1938; Ancestry.com, Marion Howie, trees.ancestry.com/tree/54904405/person/26142215594; Kaufman Family Tree, trees.

ancestry.com/tree/52015135/person/13287645537?ssrc=pt_t54904405_p26022045682_kpidz0q3d26022045682z0q26pgz0q3d32768z0q26pgplz0q3dpid_m1&; Find A Grave Memorial #42055430.

6. Actually, William L. Green was not married. The boat may have been named for Green's mother, Mary G. Palletro Green (Washington Deaths, 1883–1960). This is another instance in which Will either misremembered details, or he changed his story slightly to protect the identity of the people in his memoir.

NOTES TO CHAPTER FIVE

1. 1850 Census, Ohio, Cuyahoga County, Royalton,156B; 1860 Census, Michigan, Calhoun County, Tekonsha, 707; Roots Web Death Records, userdb.rootsweb.ancestry.com/deaths; Ancestry.com, William Wells Family Tree, trees.ancestry.com/tree/70288446/person/42212641391.

2. Washington Territorial Census, 1885, Seattle Ward 3, line 32; 1887, Seattle Ward 4, line 26; Seattle City Business Directories, 1882–1910; Ancestry.com, Washington State Death Records, 1883–1960; *Seattle Daily Times,* April 4, 1909; April 7, 1911; August 27, 1938.

3. Robert F. Graham Diary, Stampeders Files, Klondike Gold Rush National Historical Park, Skagway, Alaska.

4. An interesting description of modern archaeological ruins at the headquarters of the Whitehorse Tramway Company is found in T. J. Hammer, "Canyon City," in Catherine Holder Spude, Robin O. Mills, Karl Gurcke, and Roderick Sprague, *Eldorado! The Archaeology of Gold Mining in the Far North* (Lincoln: University of Nebraska Press, 2011), 164–82.

5. The distance from the Big Salmon River to the Little Salmon River is actually sixty-two miles by following the Yukon River.

NOTES TO CHAPTER SIX

1. Will is in error about the cause of the color change in the salmon. While he, without a doubt, observed bruising on the fish, salmon turn a bright color during the season in which they spawn.

2. *Dallas Morning News,* March 30, 1898; *Evansville (IN) Courier and Press,* December 28, 1898; *Muskegan (MI) Chronicle,* May 4, 1898; *Rockford (IL) Morning Star,* January 14, 1898.

3. Will left the two dates in brackets blank; they were supplied by the editor.

4. The sediment in the White River actually comes from glaciers at its head.

5. Frederick Stephen Wombwell, "A Year in the Klondyke, 1898–1899," typed manuscript, Klondike Gold Rush National Historical Park Stampeder Files.

6. Advertisement reproduced in Norm Bolotin, *Klondike Lost: A Decade of Photographs by Kinsey & Kinsey* (Anchorage: Alaska Northwest, 1980), 10.

NOTES TO CHAPTER SEVEN

1. May 2014 gold prices calculated from Goldprice, goldprice.org.

2. Charles J. Roehr, *Klondike Gold Rush Letters* (New York: Vantage Press, 1976), 35, 38.

3. Will left the name of the mountain blank in his account. It has been supplied by the editor. Surely he would have recorded the name of this very obvious feature of the Dawson landscape when he first heard it. His inability to remember the name of this famous mountain is another indication that he did not have his diary when he wrote this section of his memoir.

4. Will did not fill in this blank, and it is impossible to determine at this point what claim he referred to.

5. James A. McRae Diary, Klondike Gold Rush National Historical Park Stampeder Files, August 15, September 2, 5, 1898.

6. The first battle of the Spanish-American War took place at Manila May 1, 1898. Woodin is probably, instead, referring to the Battle of Santiago, which occurred on July 3, 1898, and was decisive in winning the war with Cuba. That indicates it had taken the newspapers about three weeks to make their way from Seattle to Dawson.

7. The Seattle price for bacon at the time was 12.5 cents a pound. Bolotin, *Klondike Lost*, 10. The Woodins realized a 400 percent profit at these prices.

8. John F. A. Strong was governor of Alaska from May 21, 1913, to April 18, 1918.

9. North American Trading and Transportation Company, owned by John J. Healy. Will earlier referred to this firm as the Healy Company.

10. This Henderson was probably not Robert Henderson, who was credited with discovering the Klondike gold fields. The latter filed a discovery claim on Hunker Creek, but failed to work it. He spent most of his life wandering from creek to creek and making no great fortune. Berton, *Klondike*, 58, 406.

11. Will left the claim numbers blank in his draft. The editor supplied the numbers as taken from Berton, *Klondike*. Berton did not mention the Stanley claim.

12. The Seattle city council appointed William D. Wood (1858–1917) as mayor of Seattle to fill the unexpired term of Frank D. Black. In July 1897, Wood resigned to search for gold in the Klondike. "City Council appoints William D. Wood as Mayor of the City of Seattle on April 6, 1896," HistoryLink.org, www.historylink.org/index.cfm?DisplayPage=output. cfm&File_Id=2796.

Notes to Chapter Eight

1. Vincent J. Cirillo, *Bullets and Bacilli: The Spanish American War and Military Medicine* (New Brunswick, New Jersey: Rutgers University, 2004), 57–90.

2. Roy Minter, *The White Pass: Gateway to the Klondike* (Fairbanks: University of Alaska Press, 1987), 218–35.

Notes to Epilogues

1. Will is probably referring to the Northern Pacific, the Union Pacific, and the Great Northern railroads. HistoryLink.org, www.historylink.org/index.cfm?DisplayPage=output. cfm&file_id=1683.

2. By 1920, Seattle had 315,312 people; in 2010, the population had almost doubled again to 608,660. The numbers in brackets in the preceding paragraph are the actual population numbers for 1890, 1900, and 1910. "Population history of Seattle from 1890–1990,"

physics.bu.edu/~redner/projects/population/cities/seattle.html; "Seattle Population and Demographics," www.seattle.gov/dpd/Research/Population_Demographics/Overview.

3. Seattle City Directories, 1899, 1902.

4. 1900 Census, Washington, King County, Seattle Ward 7, Enumeration District 110, 6B; Seattle City Directories, 1897–99; *Seattle Daily Times,* August 29, 1905, 2; Ancestry.com, Woodin Family Tree, trees.ancestry.com/tree/52694725/family.

5. Besides Blanche's two daughters, the Graveses took in another Woodin "grandson" by the name of Clifford, born in 1911, six years after their daughter, Blanche, died. Clifford's parents were named John F. Woodin and Agnes Koyle. It has not been possible to determine how Clifford was related to the Graveses or Will Woodin. 1900 Census, Washington, King County, Seattle Ward 7, Enumeration District 110, 6B; 1910 Census, Washington, King County, Seattle Ward 12, Enumeration District 198, 1B; 1920 Census, Washington, King County, Seattle, Enumeration District 311, 5B; Seattle City Directories 1897–99; *Seattle Daily Times,* June 17, 1949, page 19.

6. 1940 Census, Washington, King County, Seattle, Enumeration District 40-314, 3A; Seattle City Directories 1906–35; *Seattle Daily Times,* July 2, 1906; August 7, 11, 1912.

7. *Seattle Daily Times,* June 17, 1949.

8. 1900 Census, Washington, King County, Seattle Ward 7, Enumeration District 112, 9A; 1910 Census, Washington, King County, Seattle Ward 12, Enumeration District 198, 1B; 1920 Census, Washington, King County, Seattle, Enumeration District 311, 5B; 1930 Census, Washington, King County, Seattle, Enumeration District 221, 56A; 1940 Census, Washington, King County, Seattle, Enumeration District 40-314, 61A; Seattle City Directories: 1899–1935; Washington Death Index, 1940–1996.

9. Family Chronicle's Alaska-Yukon Goldrush Participants, www.familychronicle.com/klondike.htm., last accessed February 2015; Polk and Company Alaska-Yukon Directory, 1901, 430; Seattle City Directory, 1902.

10. Seattle City Directories, 1902–1907; Pioneer Building, en.wikipedia.org/wiki/Pioneer_Building_(Seattle,_Washington).

11. 1910 Census, Seattle Ward 3, King County, Washington, Enumeration District 0087, 3A; Seattle City Directories, 1910–12; *Seattle Daily Times,* May 23, 1909, 39.

12. *Saginaw (MI) News,* August 31, 1885; *Seattle Daily Times,* February 6, 1908; August 30, October 26–November 1, 15, 1912; Woodin Autobiography.

13. 1880 Census, Washington, Walla Walla County, Walla Walla City, Enumeration District 47, 179A; 1900 Census, Washington, Walla Walla County, Walla Walla Ward 3, Enumeration District 89, 3B; 1920 Census, Washington, King County, Seattle, Enumeration District 312, 10B; *Seattle Daily Times,* June 17, 1949.

14. 1930 Census, Michigan, Ingham County, Lansing, Enumeration District 50, 59B; Lansing, Michigan city directories, 1927, 1930–1933; Find-A-Grave, Caroline Woodin, www.findagrave.com/cgi-bin/fg.cgi?page=gr&GSln=WOOD&GSfn=C&GSpartial=1&GSbyrel=all&GSst=24&GScntry=4&GSsr=441&GRid=81769428&, accessed February 2015.

15. Elkhart, Indiana, and Edwardsburg, Michigan, are about ten miles across the state line from one another.

16. *Seattle Daily Times*, April 4, 1909. The Green who accompanied the Woodin party should not be confused with William L. Green, a Skagway merchant who sold feed and hardware from September 1897 to at least 1901. The latter individual was from Ironwood, Michigan, not Seattle. The Ironwood newspapers regaled its readers with the stories of "their" Green, many of which place him in Skagway or Seattle at the same time that Will places his namesake on the trail and on the river. *Ironwood (MI) Times*, September 4, 11, October 9, November 11, 1897, March 5, October 10, 1898; *Ironwood News-Record*, May 7, November 5,1898; *Skaguay News*, October 15, 22, 29, November 19, December 10, 31, 1897; February 18, June 17, September 28, 1898.

17. 1920 Federal Census, Seattle, King County, Washington, Enumeration District 161, 12B; Washington, Pierce County, Steilacoom, Western Washington Hospital for the Insane; Seattle City Directories, 1921, 1922; Ancestry.com, Washington Deaths, 1883–1960; Findagrave.com, Lake View Cemetery, Steilacoom, Pierce County, Washington; Pacific Coast Architecture Database, digital.lib.washington.edu/architech/structures/13588.

18. 1900 Census, Washington, King County, Seattle Ward 6, Enumeration District 108, 10A; Canada Marriage Index, 1872–1935; Seattle City Directory, 1902, 445.

19. 1910 Census, Michigan, Gratiot County, Seville, Enumeration District 78, 10A; Michigan Deaths and Burials Index, 1867–1995; Michigan Find A Grave Index, 1805–2012; State of Michigan Certificate of Death, June 7, 1911.

20. Seattle City Directories, 1890–1905.

21. Seattle City Directories, 1910–22.

22. *Seattle Daily Times*, March 6, 18, 1919; May 20, 1923; September 4, 1940; Findagrave. com; Washington Deaths, 1883–1960.

23. 1900 Census, Washington, King County, Seattle Ward 7, Enumeration District 111, 13A; *Seattle Times*, February 5, 1898; *Morning Olympian* (Olympia, WA), June 18, 1908; *Olympia (WA) Daily Recorder*, February 2, June 26, 1909.

24. 1910 Census, Washington, King County, Seattle Ward 14, Enumeration District 219, 7B; 1920 Census, Washington, King County, Seattle, Enumeration District 218, 1A; 1930 Census, Washington, King County, Seattle, Enumeration District 217, 1A.

25. *Seattle Daily Times*, December 22, 1924.

26. 1910 Census, Washington, King County, Seattle Ward 3, Enumeration District 151, 5B; 1920 Census, Washington, King County, Seattle, Enumeration District 304, 9B; World War I Selective Service System Draft Registration Cards, 1917–1918, Washington State, King County, Draft Board 11; Seattle City Directories, 1900–1921; *Seattle Daily Times*, May 10, 1914; Everett, Washington City Directories, 1922–1939.

27. 1920 Census, Seattle, King County, Washington, Enumeration District 304, 9B; 1930 Census, Washington, Snohomish County, Snohomish, Enumeration District 121, 7B; Everette, Washington, City Directories, 1930–60; Records of the Selective Service System, Record Group 147, Fourth Registration Draft Cards (World War II), Washington State Headquarters, Seattle, Archive No. 563992, Box No. 137; *Seattle Daily Times*, October 17, 1909; July 13, 1926; Ancestry.com, Andersen Family Tree; Social Security Death Index; Findagrave.com, Grand Army of the Republic Cemetery, Snohomish County, Washington.

28. Floyd, *Claims and Speculations*, 112–13.

Notes to Appendix A: Biographies

1. 1900 Census, Washington, King County, Seattle Ward 4, Enumeration District 98, 4A; Seattle City Directory, 1898.

2. 1910 Census, Alaska Territory, Division 2, Fairbanks, 1A; 1920 Census, Washington, King County, Seattle, Enumeration District, 334, 17A; 1899 Skagway Business Directory; Seattle City directories, 1919–1925; Yukon and Alaska Business Directories, 1903, 1909, 1911; Alaska Governor's Report, *Reports of the Department of the Interior for the Fiscal Year ended June 30, 1910,* Administrative Reports, Vol. II, Territories, Serial Set Vol. No. 5976, H. Doc. 1006 (Washington, DC: Department of the Interior, 1911), 279; *Skaguay News,* November 5, 1897; *Seattle Daily Times,* July 9, 1912.

3. 1870 Census, California, San Francisco County, San Francisco Ward 4, 357A; 1880 Census, California, Alameda County, Oakland, Enumeration District 12, 234D; 1892 Washington State Census, King County, Seattle Ward 1, line 25; 1901 Census of Canada, The Territories, Unorganized Territories, District 206, Sub-District F-48; 1910 Census, California, Alameda County, Oakland Ward 7, Enumeration District 139, 3B; California State Library, California History Section, California Great Register, Collection Number 4-2A, 1867; Seattle City Directory, 1898; Yukon-Alaska Directories, 1901; California Death Index, Alameda County, December 8, 1915.

4. 1901 Census of Canada, The Territories, Unorganized Territories, White Horse; 1910 Census, Nebraska, Douglas County, Omaha Ward 8, Enumeration District 62, 5B; Omaha City Directory, 1891; Alaska-Yukon City Directories, 1901, 1902, 1905; *Salt Lake Tribune,* October 28, 1904.

5. 1880 Census, Washington, King County, Lake Union, Enumeration District 8, 272C; Seattle City Directory 1898.

6. 1870 Census, Michigan, Gratiot County, Pine River Township, 122B; 1880 Census, Michigan, Gratiot County, Pine River Township, Enumeration District 100, 589D; 1892 Washington State Census, Seattle, line 20; 1900 Census, Alaska, Southern Supervisor's District, Fort Wrangell, Enumeration District 4, 48B; 1910 Census, Fort Alaska, Division 1, Wrangell, Enumeration District 5, 34B; 1920 Census, Alaska Territory, First Judicial District, Wrangell, Enumeration District 21, 4B; 1930 Census, Alaska Territory, First Judicial District, Wrangell, Enumeration District 12, 7B.

7. 1880 Census, California, Tulare County, Visalia, Enumeration District 98, 44A; 1880 Washington Territorial Census, King County, Seattle Ward 2, line 34; 1892 Washington State Census, King County, Seattle Ward 3, line 22; 1900 Census, Washington, King County, Seattle Ward 6, Enumeration District 107, 2A; 1901 Census of Canada, The Territories, Unorganized Territories, Yukon, Dominion Creek, District 206, Sub-District F-49, 4; 1920 Census, Alaska, Fourth Judicial District, Fairbanks, Enumeration District 108, 11B; World War I Draft Registration Cards, Alaska, Fourth Judicial District; Seattle City Directories, 1891, 1893, 1898; Alaska-Yukon Directories, 1907, 1909, 1911; Find A Grave, Clay Street Cemetery, Fairbanks, Alaska.

8. Census, Ohio, Clinton County, Sabina, Enumeration District 61, 129A; 1892 Washington Territorial Census, King County, Seattle, line 29; 1900 Census, Washington, King County, Seattle Ward 8, Enumeration District 115, 4A; 1910 Census, Washington, King County, Seattle Ward 6, Enumeration District 121, 8A; 1920 Census, North Dakota, Cass County, Fargo Ward 7, Enumeration District 21, 7B; 1930 Census, California, Los Angeles County, Los Angeles, Enumeration District 506, 5A; Seattle City Directory, 1898;

Alaska-Yukon Directories, 1907, 1909, 1911; Emergency Passport Applications (Issued Abroad), 1877–1907, Volume 18.

9. 1889 Washington Territorial Census, King County, Seattle Ward 2, line 4; 1892 Washington State Census, King County, Seattle Ward 2, line 11; 1900 Census, Washington, King County, Seattle Ward 7, Enumeration District 109, 1A; Seattle City Directory, 1898; Ancestry.com, Hooper Family Tree, trees.ancestry.com/tree/22831205/person/1309632161.

10. 1860 census, Wisconsin, Waukesha County, Waukesha, 296; 1860 Census, Pennsylvania, Mercer County, Sugar Grove, 786; 1880 Census, New York, Delaware County, Walton, Enumeration District 83, 446B; 1880 Census, Pennsylvania, Crawford County, Fallowfield (East), Enumeration District 98, 140D; 1900 Census, Kansas, Anderson County, Garnett, Enumeration District 16; 1901 Canadian Census, Upper Bonanza, Yukon, Unorganized Territories, 24; Chicago City Directory, 1895; Fergusen directory of the Yukon and Alaska, 1901, online at www.familychronicle.com/klondike.htm; Yukon and Alaska Directories, 1901–10; Lawrence, Kansas City Directory, Chittenden Directory Co, 1902–3; Seattle City Directories, 1896–98; *Washington (DC) Evening Star,* May 31, 1887; *Chicago Daily Inter Ocean,* 1892–94; *Kansas City Star,* November 2, 1901; *Kansas Semi-Weekly Capital* (Topeka, KS), June 22, 1900; *Omaha World Herald,* March 8, 1938; *Philadelphia Inquirer,* May 28, 30, 31, June 1, 2, 1887; *Riverside (CA) Daily Press,* June 21, 1900; *Semi-Weekly Times,* Alliance, NB, April 12, 1904; *Tacoma Daily Times,* January 5, 1898; *Watertown (NY) Daily News,* September 30, 1891; Ancestry.com, Bell-Robertson-Young 3 Family Tree, trees.ancestry.com/tree/12491673/person/-248078654 accessed 4/10/2013.

11. 1901 Census of Canada, The Territories, Unorganized Territories, White Horse, 11; Omaha City Directory, 1891; Alaska-Yukon Directories, 1901, 1902; Ancestry.com, Ives Family Tree, trees.ancestry.com/tree/55755628/person/46034338549; *Daily Alaska Dispatch,* October 31, November 2, 1904; *Salt Lake Tribune,* October 28, 1904; *Seattle Daily Times,* November 8, 9, 16, 1904.

12. There is some confusion in the genealogical records about Calvin's middle initial. In the early records, he is recorded as Calvin A. Johnston, Jr. Some genealogists believe that he was actually Calvin Llewellen Johnston, but the connection is not convincing. The latter was born in May 1875, before Calvin A. and Ada Peavy were married. No record of death can be found for either Calvin A. Jr. or Calvin Lewellen. 1880 census, Minnesota, Sherburne County, Elk River, 162B; 1885 Minnesota Territorial and State Census Roll MNSC-44; 1892, Washington State Census, line 33; Seattle City Directories, 1890–1893, 1895, 1897; Marriage Index in the State of Maine; Roots Web, Mark Kulow, Joseph Peavey Descendants: freepages.genealogy.rootsweb.ancestry.com/~peaveysusa/PVNE/records/biographies/joseph_pv_desc_7.html; Ancestry.com, McCormack-Wikel Family Tree, Ada L. Peavy, trees.ancestry.com/tree/3441075/person/-1001608452.

13. 1880 Census, Iowa, Louisa County, Elm Grove, Enumeration District 129, 503D; 1900 Census, Washington, King County, Seattle Ward 8, Enumeration District 115, 4B; 1910 Census, Washington, King County, Seattle Ward 9, Enumeration District 167, 3B; Seattle City Directories, 1895, 1897, 1898, 1936, 1948.

14. 1850 Census, Illinois, Knox County, Township 11 N 3 E, 366A.

15. 1885 South Dakota Territorial Census, Edmunds, Enumeration District 9; 1910 Census, Washington, King County, Seattle Ward 9, Enumeration District 0167, 3B.

16. 1901 Census of Canada, Yukon Territory, Dawson City, District 206, Sub-District F-28, 6; Seattle City Directory, 1898; World War I Draft Registration Cards, Washington, King County, Draft Board 1.

17. 1889 Washington Territorial Census, Washington State Archives, Olympia, Washington; 1900 Census, Washington, King County, Seattle Ward 6, Enumeration District 0108, 3B; 1910 Census, Washington, King County, Seattle Ward 12, Enumeration District 0202, 1A; 1920 Census, Washington, King County, Seattle, Enumeration District 191, 10B; 1930 Census, Washington, King County, Springbrook, Enumeration District 369, 4A; 1940 Census, Washington, King County, Springbrook, Enumeration District 17-186, 9B; Seattle City Business Directories, 1889–1918; Ancestry.com. Swedish Emigration Records, 1887; Find A Grave, www.findagrave.com/cgi-bin/fg.cgi: accessed February 13, 2014; Washington State Death Records Index, 1947; Ancestry.com, Lunn Family Tree, trees.ancestry.com/tree/77174844/person/38355414935, last accessed February 7, 2014.

18. 1892 Washington Territorial Census, Olympia, Roll V228_8, line 21; 1900 Census, Washington King County, Seattle Ward 6, Enumeration District 107, 2A; 1910 Census, Washington, King County, Seattle Ward 7, Enumeration District 130, 6B; 1930 Census, Washington, King County, Maple Leaf, Enumeration District 320, 9A; Seattle City Business Directories, 1892–1932; Washington State Marriage Records, Washington State Archives, Olympia, Washington; Find A Grave, www.findagrave.com/cgi-bin/fg.cgi, accessed February 7, 2015.

19. Most of this information comes from editor C. H. Spude's original transcription of the 1900 Skagway, Alaska census on file at Klondike Gold Rush National Historical Park; 1860 Census, Michigan, Jackson County, Jackson Ward 3, 121; 1870 Census, Michigan, Jackson County, Jackson Ward 3, 228A; 1880 Census, Michigan, Jackson County, Blackman, Enumeration District 98, 14D; 1900 Census, Alaska, Southern Supervisors District, Skagway, Enumeration District 7, 37A; 1910 Census, California, San Joaquin County, Elkhorn, Enumeration District 118, 3A; 1920 Census, California, San Joaquin County, Elkhorn, Enumeration District 145, 14B; California Find A Grave Index, 1775–2012.

20. 1880 Census, Illinois, Randolph County, Sparta, Enumeration District 105, 561A; 1883 Washington Territorial Census, King County, Seattle, line 29; 1885, Seattle Ward 3, line 19; 1887, Seattle Ward 3, line 27; 1892, Seattle Ward 9, line 2; 1900 Census, Washington, King County, Seattle Ward 9, Enumeration District 117, 10A; 1910 Federal Census, Washington, King County, Seattle Ward 9, Enumeration District 173, 16B; Seattle City Directories, 1887, 1889, 1890, 1891, 1893, 1898, 1899–1906, 1911, 1915–18; Ferguson's Alaska-Yukon Business Directory, 1901; Polk and Co. Yukon and Alaska Gazetteer and Business Directories, 1901–1903; Ancestry.com, Washington Deaths, 1883–1960; *Seattle Daily Times,* February 5, 1898; April 28, 1906; June 5, August 21, 1908; October 25, 1917.

21. 1900 Census, Alaska, Southern Supervisors District, Juneau, Enumeration District 5, 59A; Alaska and Yukon Directories, 1901, 1902–10; Arthur Wayne Hafner, ed., *Directory of Deceased American Physicians, 1804–1929: A Genealogical Guide to over 149,000 Medical Practitioners Providing Brief Biographical Sketches Drawn from the American Medical Association's Deceased Physician's Masterfile* (Chicago: American Medical Association, 1993); Franklin Harper, ed., *Who's Who on the Pacific Coast* (Los Angeles, CA: Harper Publishing Co., 1913).

22. Jack Hines, *Minstrel of the Yukon: An Alaskan Adventure* (New York: Greenberg, 1948), 120; Thomas Arthur Rickard, *Through the Yukon and Alaska* (San Francisco: Mining and Scientific Press, 1909), 130.

23. Alaska-Yukon directories, 1902–1909.

24. 1860 Census, Michigan, Branch County, Sherwood, 771; National Archives; Special Schedules of the 1890 Census, Enumeration of Union Veterans and Widows of Union Veterans of the Civil War; Ancestry.com, Margaret Ella Shimp Tree, John B. Wells, Sr. Overview, trees.ancestry.com/tree/9631037/person/-569177473; William H. Wells Overview, trees.ancestry.com/tree/9631037/person/114788843.

25. 1870 Census, Michigan, Gratiot County, Seville, 133B; 1880 Census, Michigan, Gratiot County, Seville, 626D; 1900 Census, Michigan, Gratiot County, Seville, Enumeration District 0059, 6B; Ancestry.com, Michigan marriages, 1851–1875.

26. 1860 Census, Michigan, Gratiot County, Pine River, 165; 1870 Census, Michigan, Gratiot County, Saint Louis, 33B; 1880 Census, Michigan, Gratiot County, Pine River, 589D; Washington State Census, King County, Seattle, 1890–1892; Saginaw, Michigan City Directory, 1883; Seattle City Directories, 1890–95; *Elkhart (IN) Review*, June 5, 1878; Ancestry.com, Woodin Family Tree, trees.ancestry.com/tree/52694725/person/13394635346.

NOTES TO APPENDIX C: COSTS AND PROFITS

1. *Skaguay News*, December 31, 1897.

2. *New York World*, August 26, 1897.

3. Woodin Diary, March 29, April 28, May 9, 15, 25, June 3, July 17, 25, September, 1898; Kirke Johnson Letters, April 8, 24, 1898; Robert F. Graham Diary, Klondike Gold Rush National Historical Park Stampeder Files, June 2, July 7, 17, 21, 1898.

4. Graham Diary, April 20, July 12, 17, 1898; Johnson Letters, March 17, 27, June 6, 18, 1898.

5. Woodin Diary, March 20, May 25, July 25, 1898; Graham Diary, April 20, 1898; Johnson Letters, August 6, 10, 1898.

6. Woodin Diary, April 28, September 13, 1898; Graham Diary, June 28, July 3, 20, 21, 1898.

7. *Dallas Morning News*, March 30, 1898; *Muskegan (MI) Chronicle*, May 4, 1898; *Rockford (IL) Morning Star*, January 14, 1898.

8. The price the Woodins received for goods comes from Will's accounts of July 16, 26, and August 19, 1898. The prices they paid are estimated from the following sources: Bolotin, *Klondike Lost*, 10; various issues of the *Daily Tacoma News*, 1898; *New York World*, August 27, 1897.

BIBLIOGRAPHY

All federal, state, and Canadian censuses and city directories were accessed through Ancestry. com, with the exception of the Polk and Company Alaska-Yukon Gazetteer and Business Directories, which have not been digitized. The Ferguson directory of Yukon and Alaska, 1901, is online at www.familychronicle.com/klondike.htm. A number of family trees were also accessed through Ancestry.com, as specified in the endnotes.

Newspapers
Daily Alaska Dispatch (Juneau, AK)
Daily Colonist (Victoria, BC)
Daily Inter Ocean (Chicago, IL)
Dallas Morning News
Denver Post
Elkhart (IN) Review
Evansville (IN) Courier and Press
Evening Star (Washington, DC)
Idaho Statesman (Boise, ID)
Independent (Helena, MT)
Kansas City (MO) Star
Kansas Semi-Weekly Capital (Topeka, KS)
Morning Oregonian (Portland, Oregon)
Muskegan (MI) Chronicle
New York Times
New York World
Olympia (WA) Daily Recorder
Omaha (NE) World Herald
Oregonian (Portland, Oregon)
Philadelphia Inquirer
Cleveland (OH) Plain Dealer
Riverside (CA) Daily Press
Rockford (IL) Morning Star
Saginaw (MI) News
Salt Lake (UT) Tribune
San Francisco Examiner
Seattle Daily Times
Seattle Post-Intelligencer
Semi-Weekly Times (Alliance, Nebraska)
Skaguay (AK) News
Tacoma (WA) Daily News
Times Picayune (New Orleans, LA)
Victoria (BC) Record
Watertown (NY) Daily News

Archives and Manuscripts

Klondike Gold Rush National Historical Park Stampeders File

    Robert F. Graham Diary

    Kirke Johnson Letters

    James A. McRae Diary

    Frederick Stephen Wombwell. "A Year in the Klondyke, 1898-1899," typed manuscript

Sandra Dunn Collection

    Family photographs

    William J. Woodin Autobiography, manuscript

    William J. Woodin Memoir, manuscript

    William J. Woodin, "The Toll of the Yukon," manuscript

University of Alaska Fairbanks, Alaska and Polar Regions Collection, Frank W. Purdy diary, 1898-1900

Published Books and Articles

Alaska Governor's Report, *Reports of the Department of the Interior for the Fiscal Year ended June 30, 1910,* Administrative Reports, Vol. II, Territories, Serial Set Vol. No. 5976, House Document 1006. Washington, DC: Department of the Interior, 1911.

Bearss, Edwin C. *Proposed Klondike Gold Rush National Historical Park Historic Resource Study.* Washington, DC: U. S. Department of the Interior, Government Printing Office, 1970.

Berton, Pierre. *Klondike: The Life and Death of the Great Gold Rush.* London: W. H. Allen, 1960.

Bolotin, Norm. *Klondike Lost: A Decade of Photographs by Kinsey & Kinsey.* Anchorage: Alaska Northwest, 1980.

Caffrey, Kate. "Passengers on the *Mayflower, Fortune, Anne,* and *Little James,*" *The Ark Valley Crossroads.* Wichita, KS, Genealogical Society, Vol. 6:1 (January 1995).

Cirillo, Vincent J. *Bullets and Bacilli: The Spanish American War and Military Medicine.* New Brunswick, NJ: Rutgers University, 2004.

Clifford, Howard. *Correspondence of a Crook.* Seattle: Sourdough Enterprises, 1997.

Floyd, Janet. *Claims and Speculations: Mining and Writing in the Gilded Age.* Albuquerque: University of New Mexico Press, 2012.

Hafner, Arthur Wayne, ed. *Directory of Deceased American Physicians, 1804–1929: A Genealogical Guide to over 149,000 Medical Practitioners Providing Brief Biographical Sketches Drawn from the American Medical Associations Deceased Physician's Masterfile.* Chicago: American Medical Association, 1993.

Hammer, T. J. "Canyon City." In *Eldorado! The Archaeology of Gold Mining in the Far North,* edited by Catherine Holder Spude, Robin O. Mills, Karl Gurcke, and Roderick Sprague. Lincoln: University of Nebraska Press, 2011, 164–82.

Harper, Franklin, ed. *Who's Who on the Pacific Coast.* Los Angeles: Harper Publishing Co., 1913.

Haskell, William B. *Two Years in the Klondike and Alaskan Gold-Fields, 1896–1898.* Fairbanks: University of Alaska Press, 1998. First published 1898 by Hartford Publishing Company, Hartford, CT.

Heilprin, Angelo. *Alaska and the Klondike: A Journey to the New El Dorado with Hints to the Traveler.* New York: Appleton, 1899.

Hines, Jack. *Minstrel of the Yukon: An Alaskan Adventure.* New York: Greenberg, 1948.

The History of Washington County, Iowa, Des Moines. Union Historical Company, 1880.

Hitchcock, Mary E. *Two Women in the Klondike: The Story of a Journey to the Gold-Fields of Alaska.* New York: G. P. Putnam, 1899.

Johnson, Julie. *A Wild, Discouraging Mess: The History of the White Pass Unit of the Klondike Gold Rush National Historical Park.* Anchorage: U. S. Department of the Interior, 2003.

Minter, Roy. *The White Pass: Gateway to the Klondike.* Fairbanks: University of Alaska Press, 1987.

Morgan, Murray, with photographs by E. A. Hegg. *One Man's Gold Rush: A Klondike Album.* Seattle: University of Washington Press, 1967.

O'Donoghue, Michael. *Gems: Their Sources, Descriptions and Identifications.* Burlington, MA: Butterworth-Heinemann, 2006.

Rickard, Thomas Arthur. *Through the Yukon and Alaska.* San Francisco: Mining and Scientific Press, 1909.

Roehr, Charles J. *Klondike Gold Rush Letters.* New York: Vantage Press, 1976.

Sabina, Ann P. "Rocks and Minerals for the Collector: The Alaska Highway, Dawson Creek, British Columbia to Yukon/Alaska Border." *Geological Survey of Canada Miscellaneous Reports,* Vol. 50 (1992).

"Seattle to Dawson—A Klondiker's Diary," *Frank Leslie's Popular Monthly,* Vol. 50, No. 1 (May 1900).

Spude, Catherine Holder. *"That Fiend in Hell": The Legend of Soapy Smith.* Norman: University of Oklahoma Press, 2012.

————. *Saloons, Prostitutes, and Temperance in Alaska Territory.* Norman: University of Oklahoma Press, 2015.

Starr, Walter A. *My Adventures in the Klondike and Alaska, 1898–1900.* N.p.: Walter A. Starr, 1960.

Winslow, Kathryn. *Big Pan-Out: The Klondike Story.* London: Phoenix House, 1952.

"The Yukon Rush at Skagway," *Engineering and Mining Record,* Vol. 65, No. 12 (March 19, 1898), 341.

Internet Sites

Ancestry.com

British Columbia, Canada Marriage Index, 1872-1935.

California Death Index, Alameda County.

California Great Register, State Library, California History Section.

Canada Marriage Index, 1872-1935.

Emergency Passport Applications (Issued Abroad), 1877-1907.

Family Trees (as specified in end notes).

Iowa Cemetery Records, 1662-1999, Grave Records of Washington County, Iowa, *Works Progress Administration, Graves Registration Project,* Washington, DC.

Marriage Index in the State of Maine.

Michigan Deaths and Burials Index, 1867-1995.

Michigan Marriages, 1851-1875, Jordon Dodd, Liahona Research, compiler.

Records of the Selective Service System, Record Group 147, Fourth Registration Draft Cards (World War II), Washington State Headquarters, Seattle.

Social Security Death Index.

Special Schedules of the 1890 Census, Enumeration Union Veterans and Widows of Union Veterans of the Civil War, National Archives Microfilm Publication M123.

Swedish Emigration Records, 1783-1951, based on EMIGRANTEN POPULÄR 2006, coproduction between Emigrantregistret in Karlstad and Göteborgs-Emigranten in Göteborg.

Washington State Department of Health, Washington State Archives, Olympia, Washington, *Death Records Index,* 1883–1960.

Washington State Archives, Olympia, Washington, Marriage Records, 1865–2004.

World War I Draft Registration Cards, 1917–1918, National Archives and Records Administration, M1509.

The Dunsmuir Story, thecastle.ca/about-the-castle/dunsmuir-family, accessed February 2015.

Family Chronicle's Alaska-Yukon Goldrush Participants, www.familychronicle.com/klondike.htm, last accessed February 2015.

Find A Grave. www.findagrave.come (individual memorials given in end notes).

Goldprice, goldprice.org, accessed June 17, 2014.

HistoryLink.org: The Free Online Encyclopedia of Washington State History, www.historylink.org/index.cfm?DisplayPage=output.cfm&file_id=1683, accessed February 2015.

The Inflation Calculator; www.westegg.com/inflation, accessed February 2015.

Iowa Graves Survey, Works Progress Administration 1930's Graves Registration Survey, iowawpagraves.org, last accessed February 2015.

Pacific Coast Architecture Database, digital.lib.washington.edu/architect/structures/4626, accessed February 2015.

Population history of Seattle from 1890–1990, physics.bu.edu/~redner/projects/population/cities/seattle.html, accessed February 2015.

Roots Web

Death Records, userdb.rootsweb.ancestry.com/deaths, accessed February 2015.

Free Family History Pages, freepages.rootsweb.ancestry.com/directory/genealogy.html, (individual family trees cited in endnotes).

Roppel, Pat, "Southeast History: Lincoln Rock Lighthouse from 1902," capitalcityweekly. com/stories/110712/out_1063358303.shtml, accessed February 2015.

Seattle Population and Demographics, www.seattle.gov/dpd/Research/Population_ Demographics/Overview, accessed February 2015.

Will Woodin, Autobiography, www.montanadawn.com/Will_Woodin.html, accessed February 2015.

Yukon River, Background Information and Map, www.yukoninfo.com/yukon-river, accessed February 2015.

INDEX

Page numbers in *italic* indicate maps or illustrations.

Editor Catherine Holder Spude (right),
with Sandra Bixby Dunn, William J.
Woodin's great-niece and author of the
foreword to *All for the Greed of Gold*.

CATHERINE HOLDER SPUDE is a historian and archaeologist based in Santa Fe, New Mexico. She is the author of the books *Saloons, Prostitutes, and Temperance in Alaska Territory* and *"That Fiend in Hell": Soapy Smith in Legend*, which was a Western Writers of America Spur Award finalist. She is co-editor of *Eldorado! The Archaeology of Gold Mining in the Far North*. In addition, she has authored professional articles for history and archaeology journals and popular articles for history magazines and newspapers. More about her work can be found at www.bobcathistory.com.